Before the mid-1960's, Shamanism interested only a few anthropologists and historians. Now travel agents are booking "shamanic tours"... alternative healers advertise "shamanic counseling"... one ad offers "shamanic soul integration process weekend workshops." Meanwhile a walk through any large bookstore will produce scores of titles with shaman, shamanic, and shamanism in them. In fact, "how I became a shaman" is becoming a distinct literary category.

—Chas S. Clifton

What has given rise to the groundswell of interest in Shamanism? Is it, along with Witchcraft, "a passing fad to go the way of the pet rock?" (Karen Goeller). Or is it indicative of a deeper, more essential and universal need? *Witchcraft and Shamanism* attempts to shed some light on these and other issues surrounding the two spiritualities. Through the eyes and hearts of those on the front line of the movement, controversial subjects like drug use in spiritual practice, the mental health of a true Shaman, and challenges to white North Americans are handled with directness and sincerity.

Witchcraft and Shamanism provides a historical perspective with a specific examination of the different ways in which Shamanism has been practiced and the ways it is being appropriated today. Witchcraft and Shamanism are compared and contrasted in lucid detail, and parallels with Native American spirituality and other Earth religions are drawn for an illuminating educational experience. Explore the depths of the Shaman's journey as the authors alternately trip to the Otherworld, communicate with spirit guides and embark on a first-trance state.

Witchcraft and Shamanism is a highly-readable collection of Shamanistic and Wiccan accounts today. It is a groundbreaking examination of a movement whose popularity portends a future of growth among people all over the world.

About the Editor

Chas S. Clifton holds a master's degree in religious studies with an emphasis on the development of new religious movements. He lives in the Wet Mountains of Colorado where he writes about Western esoteric traditions.

To Write to the Editor

If you wish to contact the author or would like more information about this book, please write to the author in care of Llewellyn Worldwide and we will forward your request. Both the author and publisher appreciate hearing from you and learning of your enjoyment of this book and how it has helped you. Llewellyn Worldwide cannot guarantee that every letter written to the author can be answered, but all will be forwarded. Please write to:

Chas S. Clifton
c/o Llewellyn Worldwide
P.O. Box 64383-150, St. Paul, MN 55164-0383, U.S.A.

Please enclose a self-addressed, stamped envelope for reply, or $1.00 to cover costs. If outside U.S.A., enclose international postal reply coupon.

Free Catalog from Llewellyn

For more than 90 years Llewellyn has brought its readers knowledge in the fields of metaphysics and human potential. Learn about the newest books in spiritual guidance, natural healing, astrology, occult philosophy and more. Enjoy book reviews, new age articles, a calendar of events, plus current advertised products and services. To get your free copy of the New Times, send your name and address to:

The Llewellyn New Times
P.O. Box 64383-150, St. Paul, MN 55164-0383, U.S.A.

Witchcraft Today
Book Three

Shamanism and Witchcraft

EDITED BY

CHAS S. CLIFTON

1994
LLEWELLYN PUBLICATIONS
ST. PAUL, MINNESOTA 55164-0383, U.S.A.

Cover Photo: Malcolm Brenner

Library of Congress Cataloging-in-Publication Data

Witchcraft and shamanism / edited by Chas S. Clifton.
    p.   cm. -- (Witchcraft today : bk. 3)
    Includes bibliographical references.
    ISBN 1-56718-150-3   (softbound)
    1. Shamanism--Miscellanea. 2. Witchcraft.   I. Clifton, Chas.
II. Series.
BF1611.W78   1994
291.1'4--dc20   94-6181
                                                          CIP

Llewellyn Publications
A Division of Llewellyn Worldwide, Ltd.
P.O. Box 64383, St. Paul, MN 55164-0383

For Mary

Editor's Note

Witchcraft and Shamanism is the third anthology in Llewellyn Publications' ongoing *Witchcraft Today* series. The series is named partly in honor of Gerald B. Gardner, who helped create the modern magickal religion of Wicca or Neopagan Witchcraft in the mid-twentieth century. His own book *Witchcraft Today*, published in 1954, was the first to present Wicca in its modern form instead of as a superstitious practice of "primitive" peoples or of bygone centuries.

The first anthology in this series, *The Modern Craft Movement*, discusses a wide range of topics from the sacramental use of sexuality to Wicca as an Earth religion to the legal and political problems faced by present-day Pagans. It was followed by *Modern Rites of Passage*, which is devoted to creating a living Pagan culture, exemplified by the basic stages of life: birth, puberty, partnership, and so forth.

In this book, which covers both historical and modern witchcraft and shamanism, I have capitalized Witchcraft and Witch when they refer to the modern magickal religion of Wicca and its followers. When not capitalized, the reference is to historical witchcraft, principally during the witch-trial period that lasted from the late Middle Ages into the eighteenth century, and to "witch" in the unfortunate anthropological sense of "evil magic-worker." Many contemporary Pagan writers also use the spelling "magick" to distinguish "the art of effecting changes in consciousness at will" from stage magic or other misconceptions created by outsiders.

Finally, while it is impossible to discuss historical shamanism seriously without addressing the topic of psychoactive plants, some of the plants discussed in this book are toxic and/or illegal in various jurisdictions. Neither the contributors nor the publisher advocate their use, and any readers who do so act at their own risk.

—Chas S. Clifton

It is impossible to fight the new with its own weapons. But to go back, back to the dimly understood truths that lie dormant in dead faiths and living bloodstreams—that is the secret of seers and dictators, of power and success. For mechanical progress, being change, is evanescent. What endures is only the enduring.

—Frank Waters, *People of the Valley*

Try!

—Pascal Beverly Randolph
American magician, 1825-1875

Table of Contents

Principles of
Wiccan Belief

In 1974 one group of American Witches meeting in Minneapolis adopted the following group of principles. Since then several versions of these principles with minor differences in wording have been circulated. These principles are not required of anyone, but they do reflect the thinking of many modern Pagan Witches whether in the United States or elsewhere.

The Council of American Witches finds it necessary to define modern Witchcraft in terms of the American experience and needs.

We are not bound by traditions from other times and other cultures, and owe no allegiance to any person or power greater than the Divinity manifest through our own being.

As American Witches we welcome and respect all teachings and traditions and seek to learn from all and to contribute our learning to all who may seek it.

It is in this spirit of welcome and cooperation that we adopt these few principles of Wiccan belief. In seeking to be inclusive, we do not wish to open ourselves to the destruction of our group by those on self-serving power trips, or to philosophies and practices contradictory to those principles. In seeking to exclude those whose ways are contradictory to ours, we do not want to deny participation with us to any who are sincerely interested in our knowledge and beliefs.

We therefore ask only that those who seek to identify with us accept those few basic principles.

1. We practice rites to attune ourselves with the natural rhythm of life forces marked by the full of the Moon and seasonal quarters and cross-quarters.

2. We recognize that our intelligence gives us a unique responsibility toward our environment. We seek to live in harmony with Nature, in ecological balance offering fulfillment to life and consciousness within an evolutionary concept.

3. We acknowledge a depth of power far greater than that apparent to the average person. Because it is far greater than ordinary, it is sometimes called "supernatural," but we see it as lying within that which is naturally potential to all.

4. We conceive of the Creative Power in the Universe as manifesting through polarity—as masculine and feminine—and that this same Creative Power lives in all people, and functions through the masculine and feminine. We value neither above the other.

5. We value sex as pleasure, as the symbol and embodiment of life, and as the interaction source of energies used in magical practice and religious worship.

6. We recognize both an outer world and an inner, or psychological world—sometimes known as the Spiritual World, the Collective Unconscious, Inner Planes, etc.—and we see in the interaction of these two dimensions the basis for paranormal phenomena and magical exercises. We neglect neither dimension for the other, seeing both as necessary for our fulfillment.

7. We do not recognize any authoritarian hierarchy, but do honor those who teach, respect those who share their greater knowledge and wisdom, and acknowledge those who courageously given of themselves in leadership.

8. We see religion, magic, and wisdom in living as being united in the way one views the world and lives within it—a world view and philosophy of life which we identify as Witchcraft, the Wiccan Way.

9. Calling oneself "Witch" does not make a Witch—but neither does heredity itself nor the collecting of titles, degrees, and initiations. A Witch seeks to control the forces within her/himself that make life possible in order to live wisely and well without harm to others and in harmony with Nature.

10. We believe in the affirmation and fulfillment of life in a continuation of evolution and development of consciousness giving meaning to the Universe we know and our personal role within it.

11. Our only animosity towards Christianity, or towards any other religion or philosophy of life, is to the extent that its institutions have claimed to be "the only way" and have sought to deny freedom to others and to suppress other ways of religious practice and belief.

12. As American Witches we are not threatened by debates on the history of the Craft, the origins of various terms, the legitimacy of various aspects of different traditions. We are concerned with our present and our future.

13. We do not accept the concept of absolute evil nor do we worship any entity known as "Satan" or "the Devil" as defined by the Christian tradition. We do not seek power through the suffering of others nor accept that personal benefit can be derived only by denial to another.

14. We believe that we should seek within Nature that which is contributory to our health and wellbeing.

© Zelda Gordon

Shamanism and Neoshamanism

by Chas S. Clifton

Before the mid-1960s, shamanism interested only a few anthropologists and historians. Now travel agents are booking
"shamanic tours" to sites such as the ruined Inca city of
Machu Picchu while alternative healers advertise "shamanic counseling" next to acupuncture, channeling, and body-
work. One ad in a Santa Fe, New Mexico, newspaper offers
"shamanic soul integration process weekend workshops"
led by a man calling himself a "Toltec nagual" and also ad-
vertising his master's degree in international management.
Another healer advises the opportunity to: "Find your total-
ity through a guided journey to totem animals who balance
body and spirit." Meanwhile, a walk through any large
bookstore will produce scores of titles with shaman,
shamanic, and shamanism in them. In fact, "how I became a
shaman" is becoming a distinct literary category.

Clearly, the rebirth of shamanism—or, as it might better
be called, "neoshamanism"—is one of the prime spiritual
and religious events of the late twentieth century. It was unexpected. Before the 1970s, religious innovation seemed

more likely to come from Asia in the form of yoga, Zen Buddhism, and other traditions. Like Wicca, neoshamanism leaps into a nonhistorical realm—which is not at all the same as prehistoric, but is a realm of cosmic significance—and into a worldview that permits the archaic to mingle with the scientific. Like all changes, this one was prefigured, but too often the conventional explanation for shamanism's renewal focuses on the "psychedelic era" of the 1960s, which means mistaking the symptom for the cause.[1] But in an era when artists create "shamanic art" and anyone with a computer and a modem can claim to be a "techno-shaman," what is shamanism really?

One of the bedrock definitions was laid down by the late Mircea Eliade, an esteemed historian of religion who taught at the Sorbonne in Paris and later at the University of Chicago. In his book *Shamanism: Archaic Techniques of Ecstasy*, first published in France in 1951 and revised in the 1960s, Eliade compared the work of shamans in Asia, the Americas, ancient Europe, and the Pacific islands.[2] When he began his research during the 1940s, he said, "shamanism had a rather limited interest even for specialists"; at that time only two works on Siberian and Central Asian shamanism existed.[3]

Eliade used "ecstasy" in its original Greek sense: to be driven out of one's senses, one's body, one's "normal" consciousness. And he concentrated his analysis of shamanism particularly on the peoples of northern Asia: the word "shaman" itself comes from a Russian transliteration of a word used by the Tungus people of eastern Siberia. The Tungus word *šaman* has in turn been traced back to the Sanskrit *śramaṇás*, meaning an ascetic, someone who leads a life of religious self-discipline, similar to a yogi. In this chain of meaning, Eliade notes, lies the history of Indian religious influence, particularly through Buddhism, on much of central and northern Asia.

But the group of practices we call "shamanism" is or was universal, discovered at some point in virtually all cultures. The ecstatic experience, he concludes, is a "primary phenomenon fundamental in the human condition and hence known to the whole of archaic humanity."[4] Whether or not everyone has the capacity to be a shaman, all peoples have experienced shamanism, whether they do still or not and whether they call it by that name or some other.

Surveying many past and present cultures, Eliade assembled a definition of shamanism that is still appropriate. First of all, it is not a religion but a technique. Shamans are not the same as priests; they may coexist with priests or even fulfill priestly functions as well as shamanic ones. A shaman is more a mystic than a priest or minister.*

Nor are shamans strictly medicine men/women, magicians, or healers. A shaman is not "possessed" and is not a medium or trance-channeler; shamans control the spirit-beings with whom they work, or at least they do not surrender to them. Like a medium or channeler, a shaman may appear unconscious when working, but upon returning, the shaman can tell where he or she has gone. The shaman is not the instrument of the spirits. Traditional shamans cure people through their trances, accompany the souls of the dead to the Otherworld, and communicate with the gods. "This small mystical elite not only directs the community's religious life but, as it were, guards its 'soul.'"[5]

Nor are traditional shamans simply to be dismissed as mentally ill, epileptic, or otherwise unwell. The tribal peoples among whom shamanism flourished knew the difference. Even if epileptic seizures were interpreted as meetings with the gods, as in parts of Siberia, the significant difference is that the shaman can control his or her "seizure" and even bring it on at will. Although the shaman's calling is often signaled by a life-threatening illness or a serious accident or injury at puberty and sometimes later in adulthood, once trained, the traditional shaman is a functioning, energetic, respected member of the community. Having studied scores of fieldworkers' reports, Eliade wrote, "I recorded no case of a shaman whose professional hysteria deteriorated into serious mental disorders."⁶

Through dancing, singing, drumming, and ingestion of hallucinogenic plants, traditional shamans "went somewhere." In Arctic regions the shaman's performance more frequently ended in a cataleptic trance: the practitioner's body lay rigid and unconscious while the soul went elsewhere. Or the shaman would act out the journey—climbing a ladder to the Upper World, for example. The use of plant agents produced different sorts of trances, but, again, the shaman was expected to report back on the journey and to show results, even as mystics in other religious traditions produced books based on their visions. ⁷

It can be argued that Western culture retained shamanic elements, but not shamanism itself. (See "What Happened to Western Shamanism.") Therefore, I prefer to call the current revival neoshamanism. Not only is it partly reconstructed and partly imported from other cultures, it differs in important ways from the traditional shamanism described by Eliade and other scholars. Perhaps the largest difference is the way neoshamanism has been presented as a new self-help movement, particularly by therapists trained in other methods who then discovered it. But although it is "neo" that does not mean neoshamanism must be lesser. We can only do what we are historically capable of doing at this particular time and place. Therefore, neoshamanism could be described as the type of shamanism that is possible and practical here and now. If at times it has been developed from books rather than from a person-to-person tradition of teaching, we can only say: Books are our grandparents!⁷

A watershed event in the rise of neoshamanism was the 1968 publication of Carlos Castaneda's *The Teachings of Don Juan: A Yaqui Way of Knowledge*. Offered as his master's thesis in anthropology at the University of California-Los Angeles, it became a bestseller for the University of California Press and in turn started a small industry of Castaneda-explaining, Castaneda-debunking, and Castaneda-plagiarizing. Mircea Eliade himself referred to the sudden growth of the "para-shamanistic underground movement" that began in the 1970s. Daniel Noel, a contributor to this anthology, edited a 1976 collection, *Seeing Castaneda*, in which he described *The Teachings of Don Juan* and its first three successors, *A Separate Reality, Journey to Ixtlan*, and *Tales of Power*, as works of "profound and lasting significance."[8] One contributor to *Seeing Castaneda*, Joseph Chilton Pearce, said that the mysterious Yaqui sorcerer Don Juan presented "the most important paradigm since Jesus."[9]

As paradigm, model, exemplar, whatever, Don Juan seized a portion of the American imagination. I well remember one of my freshman classmates at Reed College galloping down the dormitory stairs from his room with a paperback copy of *The Teachings of Don Juan* in his hand. I would really get into it, he promised, and I should just ignore the dry "Structural Analysis" that made up the book's second portion. Later that year Castaneda himself came to give a talk on campus—a practice he soon abandoned, perhaps under the directive to "erase personal history." Of course, given subsequent stories of Castaneda's many tricks on would-be interviewers, I have sometimes wondered if the soft-spoken, round-faced man with the South American accent, who sat in the Faculty Office Building lounge and told the stories that would soon see print as *A Separate Reality*, in fact was Carlos Castaneda. My friends had joked about expecting a beaded and feathered shaman who would walk without leaving footprints; for now, I will assume that the short-haired man in the conservative suit, who looked a lot like one of my junior-high Spanish teachers, was indeed Castaneda.

Castaneda debunkers included Richard de Mille, whose collection *The Don Juan Papers*[10] pointed out possible published sources of almost everything Don Juan said. He and his contributors attacked the Don Juan material on grounds ranging from alleged anthropological inaccuracy to suggesting that Castaneda's descriptions of the Sonoran desert were ecologically impossible. But valid or not, authentic or not, the impetus provided by Castaneda's books set the neoshamanism wheel to rolling fast.

Another marker in neoshamanism's progress was the 1980 publication of Michael Harner's *The Way of the Shaman: A Guide to Power and Healing.* Wiccans joined the rush to the bookstore and gave each other copies with the message, "Read this book!" Harner, an anthropologist who had edited a valuable anthology called *Hallucinogens and Shamanism,* had stepped across the line from academic study into practice, set up his own Foundation for Shamanic Studies,[11] and began to offer a distilled version of different cultures' shamanic practice which he called "core shamanism."

But whether taught by Harner or, as was too often the case, by a recent graduate of a weekend workshop, one clear sign of neoshamanism's "neo" character was the loss of any sense of community. No longer was the shaman seen as a religious expert who used alternative psychic states, nor did Castaneda's shamans ever help a sick or suffering person beyond their small circle of disciples. The same is true of the alternative view of Don Juan and the others offered by another UCLA anthropology graduate student, Florinda Donner.[12]

Even if they would be healers, neoshamans face a major change in their would-be patients' models of disease. Traditional shamans, while often knowledgeable about herbal remedies, massage, and other treatments, see most illnesses as having spiritual causes.[13] But even the modern Pagan community is ambivalent toward this idea as demonstrated by our actions when sick: whether with herbs or antibiotics, we primarily treat symptoms. The acceptance of a purely mechanistic model of disease by most modern people (who are mostly non-Pagan), is a major barrier to any large-scale rebirth of shamanism. That is not to say that people today do not recognize a mind-body link. Virtually everyone admits the part that stress plays in illness; among my teaching colleagues, for example, the end-of-term cold or flu is commonplace. And some esotericists can assign a mental or spiritual cause to any bodily ill: back problems reflect a lack of emotional support, tuberculosis reflects selfishness or possessiveness, while birth defects are karmic, chosen by the individual while between lives.[14] But the majority of modern people do not currently accept "soul loss" as causing "dis-ease," let alone the intrusion into the body of a magickal "object" sent by an angry sorcerer or by the spirits. As a culture, we are still groping from many different starting points toward a model of curing that incorporates spiritual as well as physical factors.

Blocked from its primary task of curing and freed from a tribal or traditional community, shamanism has been reinterpreted as therapy, as self-improvement, as art, as a justification for the use of psychedelic drugs, and as a religious practice of its own. Even with those limitations, neoshamanism is powerful and still offers "techniques of ecstasy." As one British participant in a recent workshop sponsored by Michael Harner's Foundation for Shamanic Studies put it, "But once I got over being too 'scientific' and let it all happen, it was great! Some of the experiences were profoundly emotional and moving. The Power Animal retrieval bit was unbelievable!"

For followers of Wicca, who drew power from and yet could feel uncomfortable with the sometimes negative connotations of the word witch, shamanism offered the lure of redefinition. The claim "witchcraft is European shamanism" was frequently made in the 1970s and on into the present. First, this claim reinforced Wicca's alleged link with pre-Christian Europe, a tribal landscape with its own mysterious "wise ones" of whom the legendary Merlin was but the first among many. The modern Pagan revival owes much to novelists' visions. Robert Heinlein's *Stranger in a Strange Land* and Dion Fortune's *The Sea Priestess* are merely two well-known examples. Likewise, the protoneoshaman Wulf and his apprentice Wat Brand in Brian Bates's *The Way of Wyrd: Tales of an Ango-Saxon Sorcerer*[15] replicate

Don Juan and Castaneda in a story flavored with the few scraps of Anglo-Saxon magical practice that survived Christianity.

Although the best-known form of the Craft, Gardnerian Wicca, had emphasized ritual and spellcraft over trance journeying (which is not to say that trance-journeying had no part in it), the new identification of Wicca with shamanism gave Wicca a touch of "primitive chic" and opened an important door for Neopagan Witches. In fact, the rise of neoshamanism has benefited the Craft immensely. Particularly in the United States, where issues of religious freedom and church/state conflict are never out of the news (witness President Clinton's signing in 1993 of the Religious Freedom Act, written to further codify religious freedom after several key court decisions had favored government over individuals), many Wiccan groups and organizations have put immense effort into solidifying their legal status and fitting the statutory definition of a church, as determined by state and federal tax codes. These actions reinforced the religious freedom of modern Witches, who have at times suffered various forms of religious discrimination from police forces, courts, landlords, schools, and so forth, not to mention the more subtle discrimination of not being considered truly spiritual or a "real" religion.

But if we build boxes (organizations), we must put something into them. The neoshamanic revival confronted the reinvented religion of Witchcraft with important questions: What is your relationship with the Otherworld and its powers? What are your "techniques of ecstasy," archaic or otherwise?

This book offers a spectrum of answers to those questions. And its contributors also offer answers to some other pressing questions; for example, how does a person start in shamanism? How do shamanic practices of solo trance fit in with traditional Wiccan rituals, which more often emphasize sacred sexuality, fertility (if only metaphorically) and development of a group mind?

Like Michael Harner, Felicitas Goodman emerged into the world of practicing shamanism from the world of teaching anthropology. Unlike him, she grew up in Hungary, which has its own indigenous shamanic tradition. Because of her background and language knowledge, she has been able to teach widely in Europe as well as North America. Her contribution summarizes her and her students' explorations with the effects of body posture on trance, a subject further examined in her book *Where the Spirits Ride the Wind*.

One convincing argument for the existence of some sort of indigenous European shamanism in early modern times (the sixteenth and seventeenth centuries) has been witch trial accounts of the use of potent plant-based drugs by the accused witches, records too numerous and detailed to be fabricated. Michael Howard, editor of one of the longest-running British Wiccan publications, *The Cauldron*, offers his own thoughts on this survival and how it possibly tied in with traditions of the Wild Hunt and modern ideas of Earth mysteries in "The *Unguenti Sabbati* in Traditional Witchcraft."

In her analysis of common elements in Witchcraft and shamanism, Karen Goeller notes that, whatever the situation long ago, in historic times shaman and traditional Witch differed in their social roles and prestige. Nowadays, however, both practices are converging, for they offer similar kinds of healing to a materialistic, technological society.

The "core shamanism" taught by Michael Harner does not require the use of any psychoactive plants or drugs. Today's Witches may see it as lying closer to the pathworking techniques used by a variety of Western esoteric traditions. In "Seeing the Sun at Midnight" Kisma Stepanich offers ideas about attaining this type of inner vision.

Neoshamans have been accused of stealing their practices outright, along with New Agers who burn sage while offering English translations of traditional tribal prayers, hold vision quests, and smoke traditional-style sacred pipes. Such cultural appropriation represents "the final phase of genocide," said the director of the Center for Support and Protection of Indian Religions and Indigenous Traditions, John LaVelle. "First whites took the land and all that was physical. Now they're going after what is intangible."[16] A poet named Chrystos published a poem called "Shame On" (say it aloud) in the activist anthropological journal *Cultural Survival* with the lines:

> *fastest growing business in america*
> *is shame men shame women*
> *you could have a sweat same as you took manhattan*
> *you could initiate people same as into the elks*
> *with a bit of light around your head*
> *and some 'Indian' jewelry from hong kong*
> > *why you're all set*[17]

Modern Wiccans are sensitive to this issue. Whether in the Americas, Australia, or elsewhere, we have seen effects of the relatively recent (and, in some cases, ongoing) collision between indigenous cultures and newer arrivals. Rather than appropriating other traditions, we are in the process of introducing, rediscovering, and developing our own that we believe will harmonize with others. But, like the poet and bioregionalist Gary Snyder, we can claim that the "native myth-mind" of wherever we live "is perennially within us, dormant as a hard-shelled seed, awaiting the fire or flood that awakes it again."[18]

In this collection, Maggie Mountain Lion (pen name of a Canadian writer of British descent who lives and works in close contact with First Nations people in British Columbia) discusses seeing their culture from a Pagan rather than a missionary Christian or bureaucratic viewpoint, a task made more complicated by missionaries' and anthropologists' use of the word "witch" to mean only "evil magic-worker." On a related topic, George Dew speaks of problems that arise when a shamanic outlook and practice is imposed on a Western worldview.

Shamanism's focus has always been on the journey to the Otherworld, and here Angela Barker, an experienced

English occultist, offers one such imagined journey, while Evan John Jones describes how his coven uses masks as an aid to trance work inside the sacred circle. To make a mask, one might wish to encounter a power animal. G. A. Hawk, coauthor of *Shamanism and the Esoteric Tradition*, offers a core shamanic approach to finding that special creature. Oz, an Albuquerque Witch whose work also appeared in the first two volumes of this series, here has written on one of the most crucial of the traditional shaman's abilities: communication with spirit guides.

In some cases, however, we are fortunate enough to take outer journeys that can parallel inner journeys. Ashleen O'Gaea, author of *The Family Wicca Book*, is an experienced caver—and how better to enact a journey to the Underworld than a journey on one's own into a deep and tortuous cavern? (The element of risk helps make it real.) Her chapter, "The Second Gate," describes how modern Pagans make that transition from the daylight world.

Of all Western psychologies, the school of analytic psychology begun by Carl Jung has been most open to ecstatic and mystical experience, treating it as real and useful instead of a delusion or a psychopathology. Jung developed his own form of inner journey and dialog with those powers he called archetypes. Daniel Noel brings a strong background in Jungian psychology plus a long-standing interest in shamanism to his chapter on the interaction of psychology, Neopaganism and neoshamanism, "Nobody in Here Now But Us Neos."

I spoke above of the problems neoshamanism faces in determining which community it serves. As the writer of a recent magazine article about package tours to "power places" combined with short but intensive shamanic training sessions, observes, "a sacred vacation is just a vacation—with a return ticket to Cleveland at the end of it. Even after experiencing the seven hells and thirteen heavens of Quetzalcoatl [sic], one must still come home to make peace with the culture of *Beverly Hills 90210*."[19] In other words, the dominant culture is still alien to shamanic journeys, packaged or otherwise, and too often the line between student and customer is blurred. The Pagan community, growing and young in traditions as it is, can offer an alternative, a place to come home to where these experiences can, we hope, be integrated in a world that does include computers, television dramas, fashion magazines, and freeways. Our mission, as always, remains creating such a community, one that will deserve shamans to serve it.

Notes

1. A few of the works that either prefigure or help explain this era: Aldous Huxley, *The Doors of Perception* (New York: Harper and Row, 1954); William Burroughs, *The Yage Letters* (San Francisco: City Lights, 1963); R. Gordon Wasson and V.P. Wasson, *Mushrooms, Russia and History* (New York: Pantheon, 1957); Gordon Wasson, *Soma: Divine Mushroom of Immortality* (New York: Harcourt Brace Jovanovich, 1971) and other works; Martin Lee, *Acid Dreams: the CIA, LSD and the Sixties Rebellion* (New York: Grove Press, 1985).

2. Mircea Eliade, trans. Willard R. Trask, *Shamanism: Archaic Techniques of Ecstasy* (Princeton: Princeton University Press, 1964).

3. David Carrasco and Jane M. Swanberg, eds., *Waiting for the Dawn: Mircea Eliade in Perspective* (Boulder, Colorado: Westview Press, 1985). 15

4. Eliade, 504

5. Eliade, 8.

6. Eliade, 31. Hysteria is not meant in a negative sense here but merely as a synonym for ecstasy.

7. Gary Snyder, *The Practice of the Wild* (San Francisco: North Point Press, 1990), 61.

8. Daniel Noel, *Seeing Castaneda: Reactions to the "Don Juan" Writings of Carlos Castaneda* (New York: G. P. Putnam's Sons, 19760. 13-14.

9. Pearce wrote *The Crack in the Cosmic Egg* (New York: Julian Press, 1971) about Castaneda's effect on his own life.

10. Richard de Mille, *The Don Juan Papers* (Santa Barbara: Ross-Erikson, 1980).

11. The Foundation for Shamanic Studies. P. O. Box 670, Norwalk. Connecticut 06852. Telephone 203-454-2825.

12. Florinda Donner's works include *The Witch's Dream* (New York Pocket Books, 1985) and *Being-in-Dreaming: An Initiation into the Sorcerer's World* (San Francisco: Harper San Francisco, 1991).

13. Eliade, 327.

14. Louise L. Hay, *Heal Your Body: Metaphysical Causations of Physical Illnesses* (Los Angeles: Louise L. Hay, 1976).

15. Brian Bates, *The Way of Wyrd: Tales of an Anglo-Saxon Sorcerer* (San Francisco: Harper and Row. 1984).

16. David Johnston. "Sacred rites exploited, Indians say," *The Denver Post*, 27 December 1983, pp. 1A, 12A. (Originally published in the *New York Times*.)

17. Chrystos, "Shame On," *Cultural Survival Quarterly*, Fall 1992, p. 71.

18. Snyder, 13.

19. Judith Hooper, "The Transcendental Tourist," *Mirabella*, January 1994. pp. 70-73.

About the Author

Chas S. Clifton lives in the southern Colorado foothills, where in recent years he has worked as a newspaper reporter, counted owls in nearby mountains for the Bureau of Land Management, and taught university writing classes. In addition to editing *Llewellyn's Witchcraft Today* series, he is the author of *The Encyclopedia of Heresies and Heretics* (ABC-Clio, 1992). He is a contributing editor of *Gnosis*, and his column, "Letters from Hardscrabble Creek," is carried in several Pagan magazines.

© Malcolm Brenner / Eyes Open

Shamans, Witches, and the Rediscovery of Trance Postures

by Felicitas D. Goodman

At first glance, shamans and historic witches seem vastly different. References to shamans conjure up the context of an array of non-Western societies, of men or women in ornate robes holding a drum, dancing and singing, and sacrificing a reindeer. Modern Wicca notwithstanding, we are linguistically seduced to think of the witches' sabbath and the Inquisition, of the late Middle Ages and Renaissance, a world far removed from the tundras of Siberia, the home of classical shamanism. On the face of it, they seem to have nothing in common. However, if we look beyond the numerous and confusing present-day notions about shamans and witches, which lead to the promiscuous use of both terms and muddy the picture, intriguing commonalities emerge. To point these up should sharpen our perception and might enable us to sort out what is trustworthy in modern popular culture, and what is sham.

A convenient starting point for such an undertaking is to get some guidance from experts such as Mircea Eliade,[1] the doyen of shamanic studies. As to the witches, let us

compare this enduring figure as she is positioned at the
time of the waning of the Middle Ages and as she emerges
from the research of such modern writers as the German
ethnographer Hans Peter Duerr[2] and the Italian historian
Carlo Ginzburg.[3]

Eliade, as the subtitle of his work indicates, thinks of the
shamans as the masters of archaic techniques of ecstasy. Although covering a huge area of distribution from northern
Asia to the Western hemisphere, he is able to show that
shamans have a great deal in common. Generally, they play
a pivotal role in producing the contact between their community and the spirit world by journeying between the two
realms; they are healers, diviners, counselors, in possession
of the traditional lore of their tribes. Witches, both men and
women, on the other hand, were characterized at the time of
the Inquisition, as Ginzburg points out, by the fact that:

> they used to assemble at night, usually at an out-of-the-way
> place, on fields or mountains. After having anointed their
> bodies with salves, they sometimes arrived there flying on
> a stick or a broom, or on the backs of animals, occasionally
> turning into an animal themselves. When they went to such
> an assembly for the first time, they would have to renounce
> their Christian faith, desecrate the sacraments and pay
> homage to the Devil, present in human or more frequently
> in animal or semi-animal form. There followed a festive
> meal, dances, sexual orgies. Before the witches returned
> home, they were awarded magic ointments prepared from
> the body fat of children and of other ingredients.[4]

While it contains glaring inaccuracies, this conventional picture seems to support the notion that shamans and
witches are very different indeed. But let us look at the
above sketchy descriptions a bit more closely. True, the
shaman produces a connection between humans and the
kindly spirit world, while by contrast the historical witch of
the late medieval to early modern period encountered the
Devil at her dance court. Different in content, yes, but neither the spirit world nor the Devil can be located in ordi-

nary reality. Instead, they both belong to a world apart, to the "separate" or "alternate" reality, as it has come to be termed—in other words, the realm of religion. This statement immediately brings up the thorny question about what exactly is "religion"? Many different definitions for religion have been suggested in the literature, centering on a belief system and on whatever additional topic the respective author wants to pursue. That might for instance be philosophy, sociology, anthropology, psychology, or theology. For the present discussion, however, let us introduce a different approach, one which is neglected by the authors on comparative religion, but which neither shaman nor witch would have a quarrel with: Let us propose that first and foremost religion should be viewed not as a matter of faith, of belief, but rather as of experience not of matters of the ordinary reality, but that of the alternate, the sacred one. And so our definition will simply read that religion is a human behavior that deals with experiences of the alternate reality. And since it is with this world that the activities of the shaman and the witch are principally concerned, both of them have to be classed as religious specialists, as practitioners of religion.

The next logical question then is: How do these religious practitioners go about accomplishing their extraordinary task of contacting, or entering into the alternate, the sacred reality? As mentioned above, Eliade classes the shaman as the master of certain ecstatic techniques, which involve fasting, dancing, drumming, as well as possibly the ingestion of hallucinogenic drugs. At least in the latter respect, the witch does something similar, namely anointing her body with a particular salve, having "special ingredients." From the research of the German ethnographer Hans Peter Duerr it emerges that indeed, those salves contained hallucinogenic substances.[5] In other words, both practitioners do something to their bodies, which strategy then so changes their bodily functions that they become capable of entering the alternate reality, or, of having a religious experience. Put differently, these physical changes are their doorway to the religious experience.

As to the shamans, Eliade gathered his material in the library, so he has little to say on the physical manifestations of shamanic activity other than voicing the prejudice of his era, namely that psychopathology may in some way be involved. But when the description given by an author is based on actual observation, we learn a great deal about such behavioral changes. The Russian ethnographer Arkadiy F. Anisimow vividly describes the physical changes which he observed in an Evenki shaman of northern Siberia, as the latter carried out a lengthy healing ritual, involving the presence of his helping spirits.[6] He speaks of the stiffness of the shaman's muscles, his salivation, the reddening of his face, his trembling hands.

As to the witches, we have only sketchy remarks in the protocols of the Inquisition. Yet, as we learn from quotations from a number of contemporary sources assembled by Duerr, witches lay stiff and immobile in their homes while their souls went to the "Witches' Sabbath." This stiffness, a catatonia-like condition, is also a striking physical change. For the longest time, however, the presence of physical changes during a religious experience escaped the observers, and it was not until a generation ago that research on this aspect of religious behavior became a topic of serious concern. Today, it is part of a burgeoning branch of psychological research into the subject of the altered states of consciousness.

This field of inquiry first started fascinating me when in the late 1960s I was a graduate student at Ohio State University. At the time, I was researching the speech behavior called glossolalia, the "speaking in tongues" of Pentecostal communities. I presented a paper at the annual meeting of the American Anthropological Association about my discovery that linguistically speaking, glossolalia utterances had some curious features of accent and intonation that were identical cross-culturally, no matter what the native tongue of the speaker was. For this reason, I argued, we had to assume that they were not rooted in language, but rather were generated by the physical, the bodily changes that the speaker underwent when he or she had a religious experience. I had observed many of those changes during fieldwork with various Pentecostal congregations in the United States and elsewhere when people reported "opening up" their bodies and allowing the Holy Spirit to enter in and "move" their tongues.

After my presentation, I was challenged from the floor. Being possessed by the Holy Spirit, the challenger said, had absolutely nothing to do with the body; it was purely something perceived by the soul. In rebuttal, I argued that when humans experienced anything, it always had both a physiological as well as a psychological dimension. After all, we did not float as disembodied spirits in a vacuum. The interchange illustrates why research on the important physiological changes during a religious trance, an ecstasy, was so slow in coming: That religious experience had nothing to do with the body was a deeply ingrained conviction at the time. My field, psychological anthropology, by contrast holds that humans are biopsychological systems, and consequently a religious experience had to have also a concurrent physical manifestation. We are missing a very important aspect of what shamans and witches are about if we do not understand this point.

In subsequent years, my and my group's laboratory research has clarified some of the dramatic processes occurring in the body during a religious experience.[7] Alternating-current EEGs reveal that the electric activity of the brain is modified, with slow, high-amplitude theta waves replacing the beta waves of ordinary consciousness. Examined with a direct-current EEG, the negative potential of the brain, which amounts to only about 60 microvolts during rest or at most to 250 microvolts during learning, increases up to a dramatic 2000 microvolts during a religious trance. Simultaneously, the pulse increases while blood pressure drops. Chemical analysis of the blood serum registers the appearance of beta endorphin, an opiate generated in the brain, which accounts for the euphoria and intense joy associated with a religious experience.

These findings also throw a light on the difference between imagery seen during visualization and the content of a religious vision. Visualization takes place as a result of intense concentration, a beta-wave brain activity. So, what is seen during visualization is created within ourselves, the result of our own effort. What is perceived during a religious experience or "vision" is accompanied by a very different, complex neurophysiological process, and is perceived as being "out there" in the sacred realms of alternate reality.

The question is how is the religious altered state of consciousness, the religious "trance" induced? The use of hallucinogenic drugs is apparently quite old. The role of the fly agaric mushroom in Siberia is attested to by archeological finds as early as the Paleolithic, 20,000 years ago and more. South American shamans, for instance of the Yanomamo people and many others, use various kinds of hallucinogens extensively.[8] The components of the famous "witches' salves" were reported by noted "natural philosophers" of the Renaissance. (See "Flying Witches: The *Unguenti Sabbati* in Traditional Witchcraft") It should be emphasized here, however, that hallucinogens cause no physical harm and addiction only if applied as part of a strictly structured and controlled religious ritual. This fact, no doubt, was also known to the witches, for there are no reports of witches "overdosing" or becoming addicted in the modern sense.

Rhythmic stimulation is another way to induce the physical changes of the religious trance, and this strategy, drumming, clapping, singing, and dancing, is known worldwide. The method is used extensively by shamans everywhere, but is hardly reported of the historical witches.

The physical changes produced by these various induction strategies alone are not synonymous with a religious experience, however. What needs to be added is the religious ritual, which facilitates the entry into the alternate reality. The shamans have many beautiful prayers and songs used in conjunction with their induction strategy. Rituals the historical witches might have used are unclear (we will return to this point later). The ritual also determines the specific nature of the religious experience. As to the latter, shamans and witches share principally two types of experience, changing shape or metamorphosis, that is turning into animals, and the spirit journey. Both are attested in the literature, but very few details emerge about the details of the visions, and even less about their tenor, their emotional content.

One well-known replication of the spirit journey was initiated by Michael Harner, who in his early work simply guided his participants into the Lower World.[9] A more manifold religious trance experience was made possible by my unearthing of an ancient system of ritual body postures, which I describe in my book *Where Spirits Ride the Wind.*

My initial discovery came in 1977 when, almost by accident, I stumbled upon some body postures represented in non-Western art, which acted the same way as do other kinds of ritual: They structured; they gave specific form to the religious trance experience. In combination with rhythmic stimulation from a gourd rattle, lasting only fifteen minutes, one posture would mediate an encounter with the Bear Spirit and its healing energy, another might provide answers to a question or lead into divining, and still others replicated the two most important experiences that shamans and witches share, namely the turning into animals and the spirit journey. As a result of this discovery, we modern city dwellers, who of course still possess the same nervous system as do the shamans, are able to recreate the adventure, the thrill, the ecstasy of what amounts to a sojourn in the alternate reality such as the shamans know so intimately and which was once the treasured experience for the witches as well.

Let us first consider the experience of metamorphosis. There are a number of different body postures capable of mediating such a change. At Cuyamungue, our research institute in New Mexico, we recently (1991) explored such a posture (FIGURE 1). It should be noted here that the participants are never told beforehand what experience to expect, and in the case of newly encountered postures, no one knows, of course. The posture in question was included in a publication about the art of Ecuador.[10] This ceramic figure of the Machalilla culture was created between 1500 and 1200 B.C.E. It represents a naked man wearing only a hat. He sits with his legs raised and with his soles flat on the ground. His hands are placed on his knees, with his right hand slightly higher than his left hand. His eyes are closed. One of our participants reported the following experience after coming out of the trance:

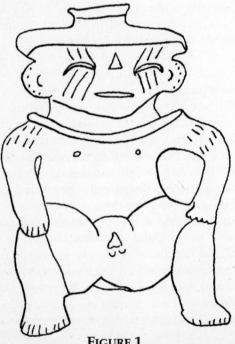

FIGURE 1

Wendy: What I saw at first was simply a jumble of the elements of ordinary life. I told myself that I should let go of that, and when I did that, I turned into rain, and I felt how the wind was swirling me around. There was a buffalo on the meadow and when I looked at him, he winked, and in that instant, I turned into a buffalo myself. I objected, I did not really want to be a buffalo, but there was nothing I could do about it. So I accepted it and was a buffalo. I started eating the grass, it tasted very sweet, and I could feel my enormous weight. I was not alone, there was a whole herd of buffaloes, and that gave me great pleasure. I lay down and started rolling over in the soft grass, and at that moment, I felt my skin becoming scaly and I became a horned toad. I was moving eggs around, carrying them in my mouth, I knew they had to be relocated. I was not even done with that task when suddenly I turned into a fish, swimming around in the water. A bear came and ate me, and I changed into the bear myself. I gave birth to cubs. After that I, that is, the bear, started digging a hole and buried the skeleton of the fish in that. Then I defecated on the spot, stomped on it, and started frolicking around, rolling on the ground and feeling connected to the earth. There was a tree growing nearby, and there was a chipmunk in it that kept watching what I was doing.

There is a lot that is noteworthy about this report, and I have many similar ones on file. We note the effortlessness with which Wendy not only accomplishes the first metamorphosis, into a buffalo, but also the seeming ease with which she slips from one shape into another. No wonder that Eskimo shamans, for instance, call the human body merely a robe. She remains who she is in human form in ordinary reality, a critical, thoughtful woman with a healthy sense of humor. Yet as a buffalo, she in addition has the attributes and experiences of "buffaloness," feeling her tremendous weight and tasting the sweetness of the grass. One additional fact stands out: to maintain over time the shape achieved in metamorphosis apparently takes a lot of energy. Suddenly Wendy's strength runs out, she is unable to stay a buffalo, and becomes a horned toad, then a fish. Only when her energy level recovers can she revert to a more permanent form. She turns into a bear and remains a bear for the rest of the session.

This sequence of events is a striking example of how important it is to recognize the interplay between physiological processes, in this case the fluctuations of the energy level, and its experiential and mythological consequences. Shamans are reported as riding first on a dog and then on a horse or as becoming in succession a goat, a bullock, or a horse. When a Hungarian shaman, the famed *táltos*, engages another *táltos* in an alternate-reality struggle, both of them may turn into bulls, stallions, goats, pigs, or birds, as well as into colored fireballs.[11]

The most frequently reported shamanic experience is that of the spirit journey. As we saw in the quote from Ginzburg, this is a pivotal activity of witches too. In the course of a single complex healing ritual Anisimov hears the Evenki shaman tell of his spirit-journey adventures to the Lower World, where the Bear Spirit guards the souls of the unborn; to the Middle World with its spirit fences; and up to the Upper World, the abode of the reigning gods, the recipients of the reindeer sacrifice. And for the witches the spirit flight to the dance court is clearly an important undertaking.

In the course of our research concerning ritual trance postures, we succeeded in discovering postures for each one of these realms. In the following, I should like to give some examples of the attendant experiences.

Let us first consider a trip to the Lower World. The posture we like to use for that was recorded by a German traveler in the seventeenth century during a trip he took to the Saami (Lapp) reindeer herders (FIGURE 2).[12] It involves lying prone on the ground, with arms stretched forward, so that the right one is somewhat further extended than the left. The face is turned toward the right and the legs are crossed at the ankles, with the right one over the left one. Here is one example of an experience in this posture:

Elsa: I felt a swirling in my chest, it spread through my body, and then I jackknifed into the earth and landed on my feet. There were colorful flowers all around, they had a beautiful design which I tried to remember. I sat down on a bench and noticed that I was wearing a bright, white, iridescent cloak. A wolf approached, it glowed like a spotlight. He put his head on my shoulder, then licked my heart. I got up and started walking through that garden, I walked and stopped to look around, I did that many times. Suddenly I rose up and started to fly, then landed with my feet down, but I could not tell what I was. The wolf and I continued walking, past some rocks, then we got to a river. We both put our faces down into the water and drank, the light of the wolf illuminated everything.

Typically, the direction of the journey is downward. Elsa "jackknifed" into the ground. The sojourn in the Lower World frequently resembles a sight-seeing trip, Elsa sees flowers, rocks, a river. She encounters a "glowing" wolf, the famed animal helping spirit of shamanic literature. By the way, he continued being her companion whenever she subsequently entered the Lower World.

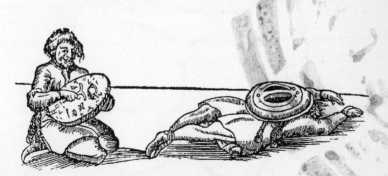

FIGURE 2

For a trip across the Middle World, we found only one posture, that of the priestess of Malta (FIGURE 3). It was discovered on the lowest level of the Hypogaeum, a temple on the island of Malta in association with numerous skeletons and may be 5,000 or more years old. It is an upright posture with the legs slightly apart. The knees are not locked; the right arm hangs down loosely at the side of the body; the left arm is bent at the elbow and is placed on the body's midriff. The following is the example of the experience of a Hungarian woman, who had come to Cuyamungue for a trance workshop.

Ildikó: At first everything I saw was in black and white. Then the horizon became very wide, it became like a circle as it appears on our Hungarian plain. There were clouds in the sky; hills appeared, then gray mountains. Then a yellow bird flew by: its body was yellow, its head was yellow, also

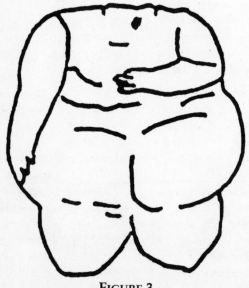

FIGURE 3

its wings. It flew away, and suddenly I realized that the yellow color was coming from me, I looked around and wondered whether I was a bird too. From a distance, I saw the entrance to a tunnel through the mountain, so I flew there and wanted to get through the tunnel, but I had to fold my wings very tightly around my body, and then I was able to fly through it. I flew through it, straight like an arrow. When I got to the other side, the scene was covered as if by a violet-colored curtain, and when that parted, to my great joy, there was the land and the village where I was born. There were people moving about; I saw a bird's nest on the ground, but everything floated by very fast.

In contrast to the trip to the Lower World, this journey takes place in a horizontal direction: The tunnel Ildikó sees does not lead down; it takes her merely to the other side of the mountain. She flies over the landscape, and we should recall here that the witches' flight is equally one over the Middle World. It is a happy journey, very much like that of the witches, who after all flew to a celebration. The fact that when Ildikó arrives at the other side of the mountain, she sees her home village, recalls certain shamanic traditions from Inner Asia. According to these traditions, it was the task of the shaman not only to guide the soul of the recently deceased to the entrance of the Realm of the Dead, but also to take it on a farewell flight first, so it could see once more how beautiful its homeland was. Judging from the fact that the priestess of Malta is represented in this particular posture seems to indicate that this tradition was known on Malta too at the time. It may account for the presence of all those skeletons in association with the figurines of priestesses in the Hypogaeum. In a most intriguing way, traditions associated with the witch and with the shaman are intertwined in this journey over the Middle World.

The third direction for the spirit journey to take is that to the Upper World. One of the oldest postures that we have explored mediates this kind of experience. It is the posture of the well-known stick man of Lascaux cave in southern France (Figure 4), drawn about 12,000 to 16,000 years ago. The man lies supine on a kind of hillock, and in relation to the horizontal, his body is inclined at 37 degrees. His right arm is placed at some distance from his body in a leisurely fashion, so that his thumb is up. His left hand is stiffly extended, the palm of the hand is turned away from the body, and there is an obvious effort exerted so that the left thumb points down. The man has an erect penis—it is the only representation of a posture in our archive that exhibits this feature. The following is an example of a spirit journey to the Upper World:

Tom: As soon as the rattle started, I was surrounded by rose and lime-colored lightning against a dark background. It kept coming toward me. Then everything changed, I could see a mountain range below me. Suddenly there were only

FIGURE 4

clouds that were tinged with light. They kept coming toward me, then turned into purple spirit beings, which dissipated, then appeared again. They came on from the left and had ruby eyes. I was given to understand that it was difficult for them to take on a more distinct shape because of disturbances caused by human activity. So I apologized, and then I could see the blue sky, and from the right, that lime-colored lightning appeared again. I was amazed at the fast rate of travel and that I did not lose my breath. I seemed far removed from the present.

There is no doubt about the direction of this spirit journey either. Tom passes through lightning and then through clouds until he arrives at the realm of the spirit beings. These beings, however, have difficulties taking shape due to human activity. Tom apologizes, and apparently that is why he had been taken to the spirit realm in the first place. Here we touch on one of the most ancient shamanic traditions: Human activity disturbs the cosmic order, and it is the task of the shaman to repair the damage. After having accomplished the restoration, Tom is allowed to return, taking the road back through the clouds and lime-colored light, as he had come.

If we now compare the shamanic spirit journeys and that reported of the witches, we see both an agreement and also a narrowing. Witches and shamans both take a spirit journey, but the spectrum of the witches is reduced: Their trips take them only over the Middle World.

Of the many questions that remain to be answered about the historic witches' culture while carrying out this comparison, I should like restrict myself to commenting on only two. One concerns the topic, alluded to above, namely ritual. We know a vast amount of detail about shamanic rituals, but after having induced the physical changes by the use of the salves, what ritual did the witches use to give shape to the amorphous process? They must have had them, but how come they remained invisible? I think that the answer is hidden in the little-known fact that the telling of magic stories is as powerful an induction strategy as is drumming or dancing. What may have made this particular strategy "invisible" may indeed be its unassuming character. But there is a hint in the literature quoted by Ginzburg.[13] He mentions that in the writings of Procopius, a Byzantine historian of the sixth century, there is a passage about a mysterious island called Brittia. The inhabitants of the coastal fishing villages facing Brittia have the task of ferrying the souls of the dead to this island across the narrows. When they leave, in the middle of the night, their boats are heavy with their invisible cargo; upon their return, they are light.

In our context, two features stand out. One is the fact that Procopius excuses his including this section in his account of the war against the Goths by saying that, "To be sure, this relation seems to me to be completely unbelievable, but it was reported to me by numerous people who asserted that they experienced it themselves and heard about it with their own ears." And the second observation is one by Ginzburg, who says that at this point Procopius switches into solemn, stately oratory, quite different in style from his chronicling of the famous war. It seems credible that at this point, Procopius, perhaps quite unconsciously, switches into the myth-telling mode, which he had heard from so many people. It may have been this mode, and the structure of the magic tale itself that acted as the induction strategy for those who "in the middle of the night suddenly heard the doors slamming, and the voice of an invisible one summoning them to their task."

Secondly, how did the witches of central Europe know anything about changing into animals and especially about the alternate-reality trip in the first place? Eliade gives what seems an oversimplified answer: "The sacred does not cease to manifest itself, and with each new manifestation it resumes its original tendency to reveal itself wholly." The first part of this opinion is of course correct. Despite intense secularization in connection with the spreading of urban life styles and secularization, religion in its many forms simply refuses to go away. In view of what was discussed above, however, it is clear that the original tendency does not reveal itself "wholly."[14] The shamans are specialists in the service of their community, the witches are isolated individuals. The shamans traverse the cosmos in all three directions, but by the time the witches come along, the trip is reduced to it horizontal direction only.

The bigger problem with the above statement is the idea of the original tendency "revealing itself." How exactly does that happen? In pursuing that sort of question, Ginzburg, as a historian, came up with some fascinating findings. It seems that the knowledge about the spirit journey, be that to the apocryphal "Sabbath," or to the fields to protect the crops, in association with the spirits of the dead or even in the retinue of a goddess, persisted in the Celtic settlement areas of Europe only. The Celts, apparently, were the conduits of the Asiatic shamanic tradition. If we then add the observation of anthropologists that, cross-culturally, women tend to hang on to inherited religious traditions longer than men, we understand the predominantly female culture of the witches. It was the women who were mainly targeted by the Inquisition and its Protestant counterparts, which burnt at the stake not only the articulate city women but vast numbers of villagers, whose names were not even recorded. So it is understandable that with the vanishing of the human substrate, the entire complex of European witchcraft eventually more or less collapsed.

32   *Witchcraft Today*

Notes

1. Mircea Eliade, *Shamanism: Archaic Techniques of Ecstasy*, Bollingen Series LXXVI, trans. W.R. Trask (Princeton: Princeton University Press, 1964 [French original 1951]).

2. Hans Peter Duerr, *Dreamtime: Concerning the Boundary between Wilderness and Civilization* (Oxford: Basil Blackwell 1985 [German original 1978]).

3. Carlo Ginzburg, *Ecstasies: Deciphering the Witches' Sabbath* (New York: Viking Penguin, 1991 [Italian original 1989, German 1990]).

4. Ibid, 7. (Page numbers are from the German edition; translation by Felicitas Goodman.)

5. Duerr, 2-3, 76.

6. Arkadiy Federovich Anisimov, *The Shaman's Tent of the Evenks and the Origin of the Shamanic Rite*, translated from Trudy Instituta etnografii Akademii nauk SSSR, 1952, vol. 18, pp. 199-238. In Henry N. Michael, ed., *Studies in Siberian Shamanism* (Toronto: University of Toronto Press, 1963) 84-123.

7. Felicitas D. Goodman, *Where the Spirits Ride the Wind: Spirit Journeys and Other Ecstatic Experiences* (Bloomington: Indiana University Press, 1990).

8. Napoleon A. Chagnon, *Yanomamo: The Fierce People* (New York: Holt, Rinehard, and Winston, 1968).

9. Michael Harner, *The Way of the Shaman: A Guide to Power and Healing* (San Francisco: Harper and Row, 1980).

10. Goodman, plate 9.

11. Mihaly Hoppal, *Shamanism in Eurasia* (Göttingen: Herodot, 1984), 408-409. *Ecuador: Gold und Terrakotten*, (Vienna: Museum für Voelkerkunde, 1990).

12. Michael Oppitz, *Schamanen im Blinden Land: Filmbach* (Frankfurt A.M.: Syndikat, 1981).

13. Ginzburg, 110.

14. Eliade, xix.

About the Author

Felicitas D. Goodman was born in Hungary of German parents and attended school in the Hungarian part of Rumania. She received her undergraduate training at the University of Heidelburg in German and graduated in 1936 with a master's degree as a translator. She emigrated to America with her family in 1947, taught German and English as a foreign language at Ohio Wesleyan University and Ohio State University, and worked as a scientific translator for Battelle Memorial Institute and *Chemical Abstracts* (American Chemical Society). In 1965 she enrolled in graduate school at Ohio State University and received her M.A. in linguistics in 1968 and her Ph.D. in psychological anthropology in 1971. From 1968 until her retirement in 1979 she taught linguistics and anthropology at Denison University.

Since graduate school days, her principal research interest has been the religious altered state of consciousness, first as it manifests itself in glossolalia, "speaking in tongues" in Christian contexts, and later on a broader base as it is used cross-culturally in religious rituals. Her most important discovery came in 1977, when she unearthed an apparently ancient complex of knowledge, namely that of ritual body postures. In 1979 she founded Cuyamungue Institute in New Mexico, a nonprofit educational research institute.

Felicitas Goodman has written over forty articles as well as a number of books, most recently *Ecstasy, Ritual and the Alternate Reality: Religion in a Pluralistic World* and *Where the Spirits Ride the Wind: Trance Journeys and Other Ecstatic Experiences*.

© Malcolm Brenner / Eyes Open

Flying Witches:

The *Unguenti Sabbati* in Traditional Witchcraft

by Michael Howard

One of the most persistent folk legends associated with witches in many cultures is their alleged ability to fly through the air. This belief is found in the medieval witch trials, in popular folk tradition, and is mentioned in accounts of witchcraft from both the Old and New Worlds. In fact the witch flying on a broomstick has become a stereotyped image in the public mind.

The earliest reference to witch flying is the famous tenth-century *Canon Episcopi* which also, interestingly, associates witches with the Goddess and with the folk tradition of the Wild Hunt. It describes how witches "ride on certain beasts with Diana, goddess of the pagans, and a great multitude of women...over great distances in the silence of the deep night." One of the earliest illustrations of witches flying on a forked stick dates only from 1489. However, a written reference from the thirteenth century, credited to Stephen of Bourbon, relates that the "good women" (an early medieval name for witches before the Inquisition blackened their reputation!) who attended the mythical

Dame Abundania (the witch goddess) rode on sticks to the witches' sabbat. By the time of the Persecution it was generally assumed that witches could physically fly through the air and that they used this method of transportation to attend their meetings.

If it is conceded that witches were physically incapable of actually flying through the air, what exactly does this widespread and popular belief represent? One answer is given by the British traditional Witch Nigel Aldcroft Jackson. He claims that "the witch riding the broomstick in magical flight recalls *Yggdrasil*, the steed of *Yggr*, through whose Nine Worlds the Masked One (Odin) travels." Flight, in the shamanistic sense, does not refer to flying as it is ordinarily understood but rather denotes a state of shamanistic ecstasy that the Witch experiences, a flight both through states of perception and also through various Otherworlds."[1] It is this "shamanic ecstasy," how it is achieved in traditional Witchcraft, and its relationship to shamanism that is the focus of this essay.

As we shall see, at least some medieval witches used natural psychedelic drugs, usually in the form of a "flying ointment," the so-called *unguenti sabbati*, to achieve magical flight to the Otherworld. The witch experienced a sensation of flying in both a psychic and physical sense, an altered state of consciousness familiar to shamans in other cultures worldwide. The astral body of the witch "traveled" along the leys or spirit-lines across the countryside and entered the Otherworld. This astral experience, as far as it could be understood by the witch-hunters from their Christian viewpoint, was interpreted by them as the witch dreaming of flying to the witches' sabbat while under the influence of a narcotic agent. On a popular level, it seems that people actually believed that witches were capable of physically flying through the air on broomsticks.

The use of natural hallucinogens by witches, past and present, represents a legitimate and established form of Western shamanism. Unfortunately this important aspect of historical witchcraft and its links with shamanism in other countries, has been sadly neglected by most historians and anthropologists and also by many modern Crafters. The shamanic elements relating to the use of hallucinogenic plants within the medieval witch cult and present-day traditional witchcraft, suggests a survival of beliefs and practices over an extended time. That these beliefs and practices have survived into modern forms of Witchcraft is a test of their durability and importance This fact is, of course, not palatable to those historians who would prefer to regard medieval witchcraft as a Christian delusion and modern Witchcraft as a recent invention.

Obviously, the use of such natural drugs today—many of which are poisonous or illegal—raises both moral and medical issues, especially as few modern practitioners are sufficiently trained or experienced in their use. The employment of natural drugs represents not only a chemically induced experience but also an act of spiritual transformation and realization. This culminates in communion with other levels of reality—the spirit world of shamanic experience—and their inhabitants. To use a modern Craft term, the participant has to be "properly prepared" for this experience. These factors need to be taken into account and firmly addressed by anyone contemplating following this particular path.

Although the broomstick seems to be the preferred vehicle for magical flight, various other implements are also mentioned in the old accounts of witchcraft. These include pitchforks, stangs (walking sticks or staves), hurdles, distaffs, animals such as goats, and even the stalks of the fennel plant. As with so much of the material dating from the Persecution, at first glance these methods of transport seem to be very fanciful until we examine the symbolism they conceal. The broomstick is, of course, the traditional travel mode, and it is one that is rich in magical symbolism. The traditional Witch's besom is made of three woods: ash, birch and willow. These represent the three elements of earth, air, and water. Ash is used for the stake or handle and birch for the twigs of the brush, which are bound with willow ties. Because of the esoteric nature of these woods and the elemental forces they represent, the broom is usually regarded as "feminine." However, it can also be used as a working tool symbolizing both the male and female energies, represented by the stake and the brush.

The besom is traditionally used in ritual for sweeping the circle or the meeting ground. This purification cleanses the circle of negative influences, but it also creates "the sacred place between the worlds." The broomstick, at its most archetypal level, is the magical vehicle of transportation between the physical plane and the spirit world.This ritual of sweeping used in the Craft has also filtered into English folklore. For instance, in Morris dancing and mummer's plays the man-woman "Betty" often carries a besom and may use it to sweep the path before the dancers or players. In Lincolnshire folklore it is recorded that in 1820 the local witch was paid two shillings and sixpence (about 50 cents today) for sweeping the church out.[2] However, the broomstick's association with the Otherworld was also noted in such folk customs, for in the Scunthorpe Plough Monday play the "Betty" character warns the audience, "If you don't give me money. I'll sweep you out...I'll sweep you all out to your graves."[3] There are also recorded instances of witches being accused of 'sweeping the luck' away from their neighbor door.

Alternatively, the broomstick is an obvious fertility symbol and for this reason it has become associated with phallic symbolism. On the Isle of Man in 1617 a woman and her son were burnt at the stake for allegedly riding a broomstick in the fields to encourage a good harvest.[4] The former Museum of Magic and Witchcraft at Castletown, Isle of Man, exhibited a broomstick used as a riding pole. The end of the handle was carved in the shape of a phallus. It has also been hinted but never proved that in some traditions the broomstick was used by the Man in Black as a dildo in initiation rites.

The pitchfork is a blatant symbol of the Horned God and is therefore an obvious alternative to the besom as a Witch's vehicle. Likewise the stang or staff, the primary working tool of the traditional Witch, is another representation of the Horned God and a masculine version of the besom. Hurdles and the distaff are strange methods of transport until we examine their symbolism in more depth. A hurdle is another example or an artificial version of a hedge or boundary. In medieval accounts the witch was sometimes called in Old German and Old English a *hagazussa* or *haegtessa*, the "hedge rider" or "person who sat on the fence."[5] The fence or hedge in the old days was the symbolic boundary between the village and the wilderness outside, the heath or forest where the "heathens" or the witches still live. On another level, the hedge symbolized the boundary between this world and the next. This idea of specific physical boundaries dividing Middle Earth from the Otherworld is essentially a Celtic one but is also found in Germanic and Norse tradition. While the emphasis today in the Craft is on the Celtic origins of many of its beliefs, we should also be looking at other Northern European sources.

The "hedge witch" has the magical ability to cross from one world to another through the mist-gates in the landscape. This closely parallels the role of the shaman in ancient and indigenous societies as the middle-person or intermediary between this level of reality and the spirit world. The shifting of boundaries, or the opening and closing of the mist-gates (the points or gateways where one world meets the other or, in Craft terms, "the sacred space between the worlds") is important in terms of understanding how natural hallucinogens can be used to create the conditions for contact with the spirit world and its inhabitants.

The distaff is significant due to its symbolism as both a feminine tool and a symbol of the Goddess. A distaff is a cleft stick which holds wool or flax, employed in spinning and weaving. It also refers to the female branch of the family, "the distaff side," indicating matrilineal descent. Because of its association with spinning and weaving the distaff symbolizes the Dark Goddess of death, destiny, sexuality, spiritual transformation, and the Underworld who is the true Witch goddess. Finally, the plant fennel is a magical herb associated with strength, virile power, fertility, and psychic protection.

Having established the type of magical vehicle preferred by witches, we will now examine the various types of *unguenti sabbati* or flying ointment used by practitioners of the Craft to facilitate the journey. One of the earliest records of this special ingredient is to be found in the celebrated trial of the Irish noblewoman Lady Alice Kyteler in 1324. When her house was searched, "in rifling the closet of the ladie, they found a pipe of oyntment, wherewith she greased a staff, upon which she ambled and galloped through thick and thin, when and in what manner she lists."[6] In most cases, it seems this ointment was presented to new initiates by the "Devil" or Man in Black, together with the staff or besom, at their induction into the Craft, and this is how Lady Alice seems to have received it.

In the 1664 trial of the Somersetshire witches, one of the defendants, Elizabeth Styles, confessed that "Before they (the witches) are carried to their meetings they anoint their foreheads and hand-wrists [sic] with an oil the Spirit [coven leader] brings them, which smells raw, and then they are carried in a very short time, using these words as they pass 'Thout, tout a tout, throughout and about.' And when they go off from their meetings they say 'Rentum Tormentum.' All are carried to their own homes in a short time." Another of the accused, Alice Duke, confirmed this information and added that the oil or ointment was of a greenish color. A third defendant, Ann Bishop, who was described as "the officer of the coven," told the court that "her forehead being first anointed with a feather dipped in oil she hath been carried to the place of the meeting. After all was ended, the Man in Black vanished. The rest were of a sudden conveighed to their homes."[7]

Several recipes for the actual flying ointment have survived. Its contents are a mixture of psychoactive herbs and other, more sensational, ingredients added either for reasons of sympathetic magic or by the witch hunters to add to the horror of their allegations against the witches. A typical example is the following description by Sir Francis Bacon written in 1676. He claims that "The oyntment that witches use is reported to be made from the fat of children dragged from their graves, of the juyces of Smallage [wild celery], Wolfbane [aconite], Cinquefoil mingled with the meal of fine wheat. But I suppose that the soponferous medicines are likest to do it; which are Henbane, Hemlock, Mandrake, Moonshade, Tobacco, Opium, Saffron and Poplar Leaves."

The 16th century writer on witchcraft Reginald Scot said that the traditional flying ointment was made by seething baby fat in water in a brass vessel. The resulting liquid was kept until required and mixed with aconite, *Eleoselinum* (belladonna or deadly nightshade), *Frondes populeas* (poplar leaves), and soot. A second recipe acquired by Scot during his investigations into witchcraft was composed of *Sium* (smallage), *Acarum vulgare* (sweet flag), *Pentapyllon* (cinquefoil), *Solanum somniferum* (belladonna), and *oleum* (oil) mixed with the blood of a flitter-mouse (bat).[8] According to archaeologist Margaret Murray, a typical medieval flying ointment contained a mixture of parsley, poplar leaves, deadly nightshade, and cinquefoil. Mandrake was also another popular ingredient.[9]

Ignoring the alleged use of children's fat, which has no doubt been added for its sensational value, we are left with a selection of highly poisonous, psychoactive plants renowned for their hypnotic or narcotic properties and others known to have significant occult properties. Aconite depresses the cardiovascular system, producing irregularities in the heart beat, and also acts on the central nervous system causing sensory paralysis. Atropine, a principal ingredient in belladonna, can cause extreme excitability, delirium, and eventual unconsciousness. According to Professor A. J. Clark, the irregular action of the heart in a person falling asleep produces the sensation of falling through space, and its combination with Atropine might produce the sensation of flying through the air.[10] Some of these plants would also cause a numbing sensation if rubbed on the skin.

On the magical level, aconite is sacred to the Greek goddess of the underworld, Hecate. It is said to have originated from the saliva of Cerebus, the three-headed hound that guarded the gates of Hades. Cinquefoil was known to medieval herbalists and magicians as a plant that could increase communication, induce dreams, and attract the perfect partner. Parsley was sacred to the classical underworld goddess Persephone and was used for scrying. Henbane was popularly regarded as a plant of death and was used in incenses to evoke spirits and astral entities. Mandrake, of course, is surrounded with magical lore and is used to increase psychic powers and sexual energy. Hemlock, another plant with underworld associations, is aligned with the planetary energy of Saturn in magical correspondences. *The Greater Key of Solomon* recommended that the athame, or ritual black-handled knife of the magus, should be dipped in hemlock juice as part of its consecration. It is probable that soot and bat's blood were added for reasons both pragmatic and magical. Soot disguises the body at night while bats are renowned for their night-flying and ability to see in the dark.

There were several methods of applying the ointment to the body. Scot says, "They (the witches) rubbe all parts of their bodie exceedinglie, until they looke red and be verie hot, so that the pores may be opened and their flesh soluble and loose."[11] According to the French writer Grillot de Givry writing in 1929, medieval witches used a small wooden wand to smear their palms with the ointment and then "placed the wand between their legs."[12] Another method was to smear the broomstick with the ointment and then "ride" it. Modern traditional witches say that this broomstick riding's purpose was to rub the anointed handle against the perineum. This sensitive area of the body between the anus and the sexual organs is the site of one of the most important psychic centers and stimulating it can activate the "serpent power" at the base of the spine. A combination of small doses of hallucinogenic plants with this psychic exercise would have startling effects.

What evidence do we have, apart from the testimony of witches, that the flying ointment actually worked? Several researchers have tried it, both in medieval and modern times with interesting results. The famous fifteenth-century magician Abramelin the Mage met a young witch in Austria who demonstrated the *unguenti sabbati* to him. She gave him a salve to rub on his hands, and he immediately fell into a trance and experienced sensations of flying. On another occasion, the witch used the ointment to astrally project and observe the actions of a friend of the magician. In 1545, the pope's personal physician tested a sample of flying ointment that had been confiscated from a witch. He applied it to a woman volunteer who fell into a deep sleep for thirty-six hours and when she awoke described strange dreams.[13] A Swedish couple who ate pieces of bread smeared with a witches' ointment in 1793 also fell into a deep sleep and later reported vivid dreams about flying.[14] In 1555, a flying ointment was tested on the wife of the public hangman; she was anointed with it from head to foot. After hours in an unconscious state, she awoke and informed her husband, "Knavish lout, know that I have made you a cuckold and with a lover younger and better then you."[15]

Scot admits that he was skeptical about the alleged powers of the flying ointment but persuaded a witch he knew to demonstrate it to him and his companions. She ordered them to leave the room, undressed, and smeared her naked body with "certiane oyntments" (Scot and his friends apparently observed this by spying through a hole in the door!). The witch then fell down into a heavy sleep, and although the men banged loudly on the door, she did not stir. After several hours she awoke and in Scot's words,

"began to speake manie vaine and doting words" claiming
to have passed over mountains and seas in her travels
while she was asleep.

In more recent times Gustav Schenk has described his
personal experience of ingesting henbane. He reported that
his teeth clenched; he felt a dizzy rage and felt that his feet
had become lighter then the rest of his body and were breaking loose. His head also felt lighter and seemed to be coming
away from his shoulders. He also experienced a sensation of
flying and traveling over a surrealistic landscape containing
herbs of animals, slowly falling leaves, and molten flowing
rivers.[16] Probably the most famous experiment with flying
ointments in modem times was carried out by Dr. Erich Will
Peuckert, a German university professor, in the early 1960s.
He used a recipe contained in Johannes Baptisa Porta's book
Magia Naturalis, written in 1568. Its ingredients include thor-
napple, wild celery, parsley, and those old favorites, henbane and belladonna. Instead of children's fat Dr. Peuckert
wisely used ordinary lard from the local supermarket.

The doctor decided to test the salve on himself and
chose a friend of his who was a lawyer to be a witness and
coparticipant. This friend was unaware of the nature of the
experiment and the alleged effects of the ointment. At six
o'clock one evening the two men applied the ointment to
their foreheads and armpits. Within a short time they had
both fallen into a deep sleep. This state lasted for nearly
twenty-four hours. When they awoke, they were suffering
from sore throats, dry mouths, and severe headaches. Without consulting each other, the two men sat down and wrote
detailed reports about their experience. When these were
compared later, they were almost identical. They described
sensations of flying through the air and landing on a mountain top, dancing with naked women and rituals involving a
Devil-like creature. Incidentally, Dr. Peuckert believes
knowledge of flying ointments was imported into Europe
by the gypsies. He claims its knowledge was then disseminated by groups of women whose female secret societies

represented the survival of an ancient matriarchal culture rooted in southern France.[17]

Despite his belief in the use of flying ointment as part of a non-Christian tradition, Peuckert also suggests that the narcotic present in the ointment creates chemical reactions in the brains of the user and caused the hallucinations reported. He assumes that the medieval witches could not distinguish between their experiences in trance state caused by the effects of the ointment and everyday reality. He likens this process to small children who sometimes cannot separate dreams from real incidents experienced when they are awake. This may be the case in some examples but it does not explain how similar, if not identical, experiences are recorded by those who have experimented with the ointment, whether they are nonwitches or actual Crafters.

This naturally leads us to the question of how "real" are the experiences of flying recorded by witches and others while under the obviously narcotic effect of the *unguenti sabbati*. Do these experiences correspond in fact to the concept of witches "flying" to the spirit world as outlined at the beginning of this essay? Recent research carried out into the effects of cannabis by scientists at the University of Aberdeen, Scotland, has revealed that the plant contains psychotropic substances known as *cannabinoids*. These are capable of changing human sensory perception creating brighter colors, more vivid music, and the illusion of the slower passage of time. However, independent research at the National Institute of Mental Health in Maryland has also found that cannabis, like many other narcotic plants, works by mimicking a chemical that occurs naturally in the human brain. This chemical has now been isolated and is called anandamide. The suggestion is that the brain has been engineered by evolution to produce a receptor that is capable of interacting with natural hallucinogens.[18] There is also evidence that certain psychoactive plants act on the pineal gland—the physical location of the so-called "Third Eye"—and can trigger out-of-the-body travel and other psychic experiences. In her book *Where Science and Magic Meet,* Serena Roney-Dougal describes this process and the use of natural hallucinogens by South American shamans. She links this knowledge of psychotropic plants with the European witches' flying ointment.[19] Roney-Dougal's book is recommended reading for all Crafters wishing to understand in scientific terms the way in which natural drugs interact with the brain to promote psychic powers and experiences.

Many natural hallucinogens have been used in religious practices for thousands of years, and in many cases similar experiences are reported. A classic example of this are the spirits or messengers who are associated by different cultures with the use of natural drugs, especially the so-called "magic mushrooms," psilocybin and *Amanita muscaria* or fly agaric. Siberian reindeer-hunters, for instance, describe the so-called "mushroom men" who appear to guide them into the spirit world and who are regarded as the actual spirit of the fungi. A similar experience is described by "Gracie," a Western user of psychedelic drugs for religious purposes. In her experiences she encounters "elves" who act as her guides and, it seems, guardians while she is under drug influence.[20] In the same reference, an LSD user describes her regular trip to a place she calls the Hall of Colors. This is inhabited by shape-shifting elf-like beings, usually associated with mushrooms, and these entities offer the subject a range of (shamanic) experiences which include flying all over the universe or becoming part of the Earth. Incidents such as these indicate that the use of psychedelic drugs, far from creating chemically induced hallucinations in the human brain, in fact opens the way for the participant to explore altered states of consciousness, experience out-of-the-body journeys, and visit other levels of reality.

Recently new research into Earth Mysteries (EM)—and specifically ley lines or landscape alignments—has revealed new information and insights into the cults of night-flying witches. The pioneer in this research is Paul Deveraux, who is editor of the British magazine *The Ley Hunter* and the author of two recently published books on the new theories about leys.[21] Deveraux believes that leys—the straight line alignment across open countryside linking ancient sites—were originally associated with actual roads or trackways, the marking out of boundaries and the cult of sacred kingship. He points out that in shamanic belief spirits were believed to travel in straight lines. In ancient times shrines were deliberately sited on these alignments to propitiate these spirits and other wayside deities, such as Hermes, Hecate, and Odin.

Deveraux, and other EM researchers have found references in British folk traditions to death roads and ghost paths. These always lead in a straight line and originate or end in cemeteries or other burial grounds. In medieval times corpses were carried along these special routes, even when they did not coincide with contemporary roads offering a quicker and safer passage. Such ghost roads have been associated in popular mythology and folklore with fairies, vampires, and, more significantly in terms of this essay, night-flying witches and the Wild Hunt led by gods and goddesses of the underworld. One EM researcher, Bob Dickinson, has found references in Lincolnshire folklore to "hedge-riding" witches who traveled specific "witch ways" or "hex ways" (landscape alignments) across the countryside either in human form or shape-shifted into hares. Esoteric information on this practice is contained in "The Witches' Death Song," whose twenty verses were sung by an old Lincolnshire wise woman on her death bed. One verse refers to "the Lord" taking the witches "over dykes and fields, straight away to Heaven." Dickinson believes this is a reference to the use of spirit paths by witches.[22]

Writing in *The Ley Hunter* magazine, Nigel Aldcroft Jackson has pointed out that the Wild Hunt is often associated with specific routes across the countryside. He quotes a nineteenth-century source who says, "There are often places where Woden [the Germanic version of Odin] is accustomed to feed his horse or let it graze, and in those places the wind is always blowing. He has a preference for certain tracks over which he hunts again and again at fixed seasons, from which circumstance districts and villages in the old Saxon land received the name of Woden's Way."[23] The same writer reported that on Dartmoor in Devon the "Hell Hounds" are said to hunt the souls of the dead only along the ancient Abbot's Way, a track way dating back to prehistoric times. Aldcroft Jackson adds that in early medieval times the Wild Hunt was often led by Dame Holda, a Germanic version of the old Norse goddess of the underworld, Hel, who gave her name to the Christian concept of Hell. She was traditionally the witch-goddess and spiritual leader of the *haegtessa* or night-flying, hedge-riding witches.[24]

Paul Deveraux believes that the spirit lines followed by witches date as a concept back to Neolithic times and he associates them with shamanic beliefs in which they were an important feature in communication between the worlds. There are many references in folk traditions and mythology all over the world to using webs or threads for spirit traveling. Such references may be linked to leys and also to the Witch-goddess with her connection to weaving and spinning the web of Wyrd or Destiny.

The shaman contacted the spirit world through an ecstatic trance state in which his or her astral body was liberated. Techniques included ritual drumming, breathing exercises, and natural hallucinogens. This shamanic "soul flight" was translated into terms of an actual journey along the landscape's spirit lines. Eventually, especially in the post-Christian era, these alignments became identified with physical routes and landmarks such as ancient trackways, the "death roads" or so-called "royal roads," and sacred sites such as standing stones, burial mounds, and stone circles. In Deveraux's opinion, spirit lines are connected with altered states of consciousness, gateways to other levels of reality, giving rise to a series of well-known stories: witches riding on broomsticks, humans visits to Faeryland, Santa

Claus (in other words, Odin) riding on his sleigh through the midwinter sky, and even encounters with unidentified flying objects and "aliens."

Both contemporary accounts from past centuries and folk tradition attest that the old-time village wise woman and "cunning man" had an extensive knowledge of herbs, healing remedies, love potions, and poisons. This ethnobotanical tradition survives today among among practitioners of traditional witchcraft and elements can be detected in revivalist Wicca. Gerald Gardner makes several references to the use of drugs in the modern Craft. He refers to the use of an anointing oil to "cause a shifting of the centers of consciousness" and a special incense called Kat "to release the inner eye" and stimulate astral projection.[25] The Gardnerian *Book of Shadows* specifies that one of the Eightfold Paths is drugs, specifically hemp or cannabis. It has been suggested that this reference resulted from Gardner's career in the Far East. However, my *Book of Shadows* (which is three times removed from Gardner) also refers to the use of mushrooms as one of the Eightfold Paths, and it is known that the New Forest coven into which Gerald Gardner was initiated in 1939 used fly agaric.[26] There is also a recipe for flying ointment in the *Book of Shadows* that I received at my initiation in 1969 containing two of the traditional ingredients but substituting vegetable fat for unbaptized children! Doreen Valiente has also described a contemporary recipe for flying ointment. This consists of aconites, poppy juice, foxglove, poplar leaves, and cinquefoil in a base of beeswax, lanolin, and almond oil. This recipe probably originates from a traditional rather than Wiccan source.[27]

It is also a fact that the New Forest coven had a witches' ointment. However, this largely consisted of bear's grease (one wonders where they obtained this) and was similar to the preparation worn by long-distance swimmers crossing the English Channel. It protected the naked body from the cold at outdoor meetings where the participants went skyclad.[28]

Other traditional witches use goose grease in the flying
ointment, and the goose or gander was an archetypal symbol of spirit flight in shamanism. Nigel Aldcroft Jackson describes the popular English nursery rhyme *Old Mother
Goose* as a coded reference to Dame Holda (Hel) and her
night-flying witches. In 1596 the German witch Agnes Ger-
hardt confessed that she and her companions shape-shifted
into geese to fly to the sabbat.[29] Similarly, Cecil Williamson,
owner of the Witches' House museum in Cornwall, claims
rural "wayside women" or witches rub themselves with
goose grease because the geese follow migratory paths each
year and have become symbolically associated with the
spirit lines.[30]

Aldcroft Jackson notes that toad grease was used by
Hungarian witches because it contains the chemical bu-
fotenin, which can create the sensation of flying. The sweat
of frogs and toads is known to excrete various chemicals
capable of producing enhanced mental states and super
physical strength. The role of toads in European witchcraft
is paralleled by the exploitation of rain forest frogs by
shamans of South American tribes. The skin glands of am-
phibians also secrete magonins, chemicals that can cure
bacterial and fungal infections including tuberculosis. In
Herefordshire and Shropshire the old wise women recommended strapping frogs and toads on to the body as living
bandages to treat warts, wounds, and cuts. This rather
cruel superstition therefore seems to have some basis in
fact. The extraordinary side-effects of toad sweat would
also explain why these creatures were often the chosen familiars of witches.

The present-day use of natural hallucinogens in the
Craft has been limited by a lack of knowledge of these substances and the obvious dangers their use by the inexperienced can create. The explosion of interest in mind-
expanding drugs during the psychedelic revolution of the
1960s brought in its wake a whole range of serious social
problems. While some people were genuinely interested in

psychedelic drugs for spiritual exploration, many others abused them for pleasure or curiosity. In shamanic cultures natural hallucinogens are only used under strict controlled conditions and within a spiritual context divorced from casual social use which could lead to inexperienced experimentation or addiction. They are used to achieve specific religious goals and not merely for recreational purposes.

The serious dangers involved in the misuse or abuse of natural hallucinogens are very real, and even the most skilled practitioner can be guilty. For instance, Doreen Valiente refers to one traditional witch she worked with who, in her words, allegedly "became obsessed with the ritual use of herbal psychedelic drugs." She claims that a young couple who were members of his group wanted to have a handfasting and the witch agreed to perform the ceremony. At the climax of the ritual the couple were allegedly given a brew made from deadly nightshade to drink "to see if the Gods would accept or reject them." Luckily, Valiente claims, the dose was so large that they became violently sick and this saved their lives.[31]

Such incidents as the one described above are clear indications of the physical dangers inherent in the use of drugs. There is also the question of legality and at present (under British law) many of the traditional hallucinogens known to the old-time witches are classified as illegal. These include cannabis, the psilocybin mushroom, and opium. Considering modern-day Wiccans' and Neopagans' craving for middle-class respectability, the use of such drugs is naturally frowned upon and not recommended. However, natural psychedelics are only one route to the spirit world and are generally regarded by most serious practitioners as short cuts. Alternative methods of attaining altered states of consciousness and astral projection exist in the witch's repertoire and these can be used without damaging our public image. This does not, of course, invalidate the historical tradition of using natural hallucinogens in the Craft. Morally individuals must make their own choices in such matters and be aware of the dangers inherent in such a choice. Unless those involved have a high degree of knowledge relating to poisonous plants, it would be best to seek alternative methods.

Today, too many historians and too many Neopagans regard the accounts of medieval witchcraft as merely fantasies invented by the Church. There is some truth in this idea. At face value, Christian propaganda and confessions extracted under torture are not the most reliable sources of information about the practices and beliefs of medieval witches. However, in recent years new research by historians such as Carlo Ginzburg[32] and Hans Peter Duerr has placed historical witchcraft in a new context. They have proved that beneath the populist veneer of Christian propaganda, rural superstition, and folklore associated with witchcraft in the Middle Ages there exists evidence of the survival of pre-Christian, Pagan practices whose roots lie in the prehistoric Northern European shamanism. It should be understood that we are not talking here about an unbroken, hereditary tradition surviving from the Stone Age, which is a product of modern fantasy, but of the continuity of certain beliefs and practices in a cultural and historical sense.

Ultimately, behind the stereotyped image of the witch flying on a broomstick lies one of the great mysteries of the Craft. "The witches' sabbat is a convocation of powers in the Otherworld and also a state of inner communion with deathless root wisdom. The celebrants of this nocturnal mystery gather in spirit 'between the times' on the meadows of Hel to honor the Black Goat and Our lady of Elfland and to attain the magical numen of the ghost-world. From this realm the discarnate spirit returns to Middle Earth, enriched with the lore of the ancestors and divine inspirational gifts."[33] This is the true meaning of the symbolism of the flying witches and their magical flights to the spirit world.

Notes

1. Personal correspondence, 1991.

2. Bob Dickenson, coeditor of the British Earth Mysteries magazine *Markstone* 1993, personal correspondence, 1993, quoting Ethel Rudkin's *Lincolnshire Folklore*.

3. Dickenson, 1993.

4. Gerald Gardner, *Witchcraft Today* (London: Arrow, 1970 [1954]), 38.

5. Hans Peter Duerr, *Dreamtime* (London: Blackwell, 1985), 46.

6. Raphael Holinshead, *The Chronicles of England, Scotland and Ireland* (London: G. Bishop, 1977 [1808]).

7. Joseph Glanvil, *Saddicus Triumphatus* (1681), quoted in Margaret Murray, *The Witchcult in Western Europe* (London: Oxford University Press, 1921) 101-102.

8. Reginald Scot, *The Discoverie of Witchcraft* (1584), quoted in Murray, 100.

9. Margaret Murray, *The Witchcult in Western Europe* (London: Oxford University Press, 1921).

10. Murray, 280.

11. Scot, *Discoverie*, quoted in Murray, 100.

12. Thomas Rogers Forbes, *The Midwife and the Witch* (New Haven: Yale University Press, 1966).

13. Forbes.

14. Forbes.

15. George Andrews, ed. *Drugs and Magic* (London: Panther Books, 1975) 276.

16. Andrews, 276.

17. Jack Dunning, "I Attended a Witches' Sabbath," *Fate*, 1963, 51-54.

18. "At Last, the Secret of Internal Bliss is Revealed," *The Independent* (London), 15 February 1993.

19. Serena Roney-Dougal, *Where Science and Magic Meet*, (Shaftesbury, Dorset: Element, 1991), 87.

20. Gracie and Zarkov, "Gracie's Visible Language," *Gnosis* 26 (Winter 1993) 60-63.

21. Paul Deveraux, *Symbolic Landscapes* (Glastonbury, Somerset: Gothic Image, 1992) and *Shamanism and the Mystery Lines* (London: Quantum, 1992).

22. Bob Dickerson, "Lincolnshire Spirit Lines," *Markstone* 8 (Spring 1993), 6-15.

23. Charles Hardwick, *Traditional Superstitions and Folklore*, 1872.

24. Nigel Aldcroft Jackson, "Trance Ecstacy and The Furious Host," *The Ley Hunter* 117:8.

25. Gardner, 60, 178.

26. Francis King, *Ritual Magic in England* (London: Neville Spearman, 1970), 141.

27. Doreen Valiente, *ABC of Witchcraft* (London: Robert Hale, 1973), 147.

28. King, 141.

29. Paul Deveraux "Witch Ways," *The Ley Hunter* 117 (1993), 17, 30.

30. Deveraux, 33.

31. Doreen Valiente, *Rebirth of Witchcraft* (London: Robert Hale, 1989), 133.

32. Carlo Ginzburg, *The Night Battles: Witchcraft and Agrarian Cults in the Sixteenth and Seventeenth Centuries* (London: Routledge and Kegan Paul, 1983) and *Ecstasies: Deciphering the Witches Sabbath* (New York: Pantheon, 1991).

33. Nigel Aldcroft Jackson, "Hag Way and Sabbat Stone," *The Cauldron* 67 (1993), 9.

About the Author

Michael Howard first began studying Witchcraft, folklore, mythology, Earth Mysteries, and the magical tradition in 1964 and was one of the early members of the Witchcraft Research Association. He spent several years training with the astrologer, Tarot reader, and magus Madeline Montalban in her Order of the Morning Star and was initiated into Gardnerian Wicca in 1969. Today he follows a more traditional path. He has written twelve books on the Anglo-Saxon runes, Earth Mysteries, ritual magic, Celtic spirituality, traditional folk remedies, and occult parapolitics. Since 1976 he has edited and published *The Cauldron*, a Pagan journal of the Old Religion, Wicca, and Earth Mysteries.

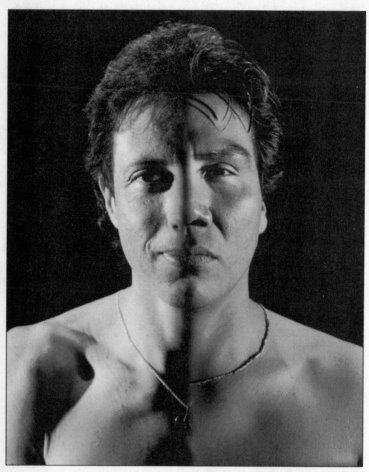

© Malcolm Brenner / Eyes Open

Common Yearnings:

What Witchcraft and Shamanism Share

by Karen E. Goeller

Interest in European-style Witchcraft has been swelling since the 1940s in Europe, North America, and elsewhere. Whether called Wicca, Paganism (or Neopaganism), Druidism, or any of a thousand other names, witchcraft traditions have given birth in recent years to innumerable groups, newsletters, and organizations. Simultaneously, some would say from common ground, there has been a surge of mainstream interest in shamanistic traditions, particularly Native American. Since the publication of *Bury My Heart at Wounded Knee*,[1] the first bestseller sympathetic to the Native American way of life, two generations of Americans have adopted Southwestern art, turquoise jewelry, bleached cattle skulls, and "genuine" Native American spiritual traditions. Likewise, books, including this one, have sprung up in ever-increasing numbers.

What has propelled and supported these twin cultural movements? Are these merely fads, to be replaced by the "pet rocks" and pet causes of the next generation? Or are they indicators of something deeper in our society—a communal yearning for things that are missing from our high-tech, high-stress lives? And, are these really the same movement? Or are they vastly different, with different aims and ideals?

In this chapter, we'll look at all of these issues. First, by looking at the past and present realities of Witchcraft and shamanistic traditions, we will begin to separate fact from fiction. Then, we'll take a closer look at today's American and European societies to see the depth and breadth of these movements. And finally, with a little crystal scrying, we'll take a look at some future possibilities.

Some Definitions

Before we can discuss Witchcraft or shamanism in a meaningful way, we must define the terms clearly—to really separate fact from fiction. Most people probably have a "mind's eye" view of both Witchcraft and shamanism: one they find difficult to put into words but that contains many vivid images. Even now, most encyclopedic definitions of Witchcraft link the Craft to selling one's soul to the Devil; shamanism is, likewise, depicted as mere "primitive" superstition. Neither of these definitions even remotely approach reality, but both reinforce stereotypes and misunderstandings. Here's a fairly generic picture of reality based on ample anthropological evidence and the first-hand experiences of many people.

Witchcraft, in the traditional European sense, is a celebratory religion that has several common elements wherever it is found. Above all, it is animistic and personal. By this, I mean that a core belief is in the spark of divinity that exists in all of Nature's creations. By learning to see the spark of divinity in all people and things, Witches learn to respect and love Nature in all of its aspects. The Craft is also intensely personal; Witches learn early on that each person's judgment is trusted equally; that the solitary practitioner is no less powerful or respected; that leadership in a group is temporary and is in reality a true position of service to the group (not a power position); and that the personal definition of spirituality is the only true definition. Through meditation, ritual, divination, and other "magical" workings, celebrants attempt to influence the forces within themselves and within nature to achieve balance, accomplish tasks, or fulfill desires: things that could be described as prayers in more traditional religions. Anthropologically speaking, the Craft is a nature-based spirituality, totally nonhierarchical in nature.

Shamanism is found throughout the world in remarkably consistent forms, from Siberia (where the term "shaman" originated) to Japan, Australia, throughout Europe, and to the Americas. Wherever it is found, the practitioner (or shaman) holds a tremendous position of power and respect within his or her culture. The shaman is simultaneously respected, trusted, and feared, for it is he or she who personally maintains the spiritual and physical health of the tribe. Shamanism is not, in itself, a religion, although it is, like Witchcraft, intricately linked with spirituality and religion. Shamanism is, rather, a set of practices and techniques that maintain the essential balances in the universe—light and dark, heat and cold, good and evil, etc. The traditional shaman is, almost without exception, chosen by the spirit world. The form of the choosing may be survival of a near-death experience, mental illness, physical handicap, or some other trial beyond the scope of ordinary humans. In the few cultures where the shamanistic position is either hereditary or a chosen voluntarily path, the training and initiation invariably contains an induced trial: a vision quest, poisoning, or other near-death experience. Shamanistic techniques range from drumming to ingestion of hallucinogenic drugs, physical exhaustion, meditation, ritual, and "magic."

Does Witchcraft Equal Shamanism?

I used to believe that what little we know about the historic European witches shows the remnants of a shamanistic tradition. I now believe that we can never know enough about traditional European witchcraft to determine this. While the modern techniques of ritual, meditation, and ecstatic experience in the Craft owe a great deal to our knowledge of shamanistic techniques, few would claim that these rituals have been passed intact through the centuries. Rather, the "midwives" of the modern Craft movement have melded what they view as the best or most useful techniques from traditions all over the world to create what we think of as the Craft today.

There are some essential differences between Witchcraft (both historical and modern) and shamanism. In pointing out these differences, I place no value judgement on either path—both are equally valid for their followers; rather, it is important for us not to confuse the paths, lest we lose the value of each!

In historical terms, one of the greatest differences between the witch and the shaman concerns societal position. While few written records survive concerning the European witches, this very absence tells us a great deal about their social position. Nowhere are there records of witches counseling kings, outside of *Macbeth* and occasional later Arthurian tales. Serious mention of witches is almost nonexistent, and those few that do exist paint an almost universal picture of the witch as female, a village-dweller, usually a midwife or herbcrafter, occasionally a woman seen as too beautiful (the temptress) or too powerful (she must be consorting with demons). Keeping in mind the status as virtual nonentities that women held in this society, it is not surprising that the Craft, a woman-affirming spirituality, was never associated with secular power. Not so in shamanistic societies. Almost without exception, the shaman holds great secular power within his/her tribe. The duties of a shaman include wise

counseling of kings and chiefs, escorting the spirits of the
dead, healing the sick, and safeguarding the welfare of the
tribe against evil spirits. In many cultures, the shaman is
also held responsible for the proper turning of the seasons,
the fertility of the fields, etc. His or her position is highly respected and his or her physical welfare (food, clothing, etc.)
is provided for by the rest of the tribe.

Joseph Campbell has said, and many others have con-
curred, that "the social function of the shaman was to serve
as interpreter and intermediary between man and the powers behind the veil of nature." The witch, on the other hand,
has no official social function. Moreover, there is a belief inherent in today's Witchcraft movement that no intermediary
is necessary between the individual and the deity(ies). The
historical witch might have been the midwife, herbcrafter,
village baker, or "housewife." Today's Witch may be a
banker, cook, teacher, technical writer, computer program-
mer, or midwife. Her "witchiness," like that of her historical
counterpart, lies in her worldview and her personal spirituality. For the shaman, his or her "shamanism" is not only inborn, but also inextricably woven into the fabric of the tribal
culture. This is true both historically and in contemporary
shamanistic societies.

Another essential difference between the Craft and shamanism, at least in modern times, deals with the nature of
the spiritual experience. Craft rituals are true celebratory
rites, ripe with laughter, joy, positive feelings, and positive
energy. Most work done by Witches in recent years, ritually
speaking, has been on the positive side in an attempt to balance the perceived negatives pouring in from the rest of society. Shamanism takes a somewhat narrower and darker
view. Much of shamanism deals with death, and the experience thus takes on a heavier, darker tone. The work being attempted is serious and often frightening, even to the
shaman. Because of the level at which the shaman is working, most of his or her energy is spent at the micro level or,
at most, at the tribal level.

There is a danger in this narrow focus, in that both shamanism and the Craft have a tendency to fall too much into one pattern or the other. The Craft is prone to becoming, as Doreen Valiente has described it, "airy-fairy." Shamanism, likewise, can become too serious, bogging itself in its weighty attempts to deal with the darker side of the universe. In both traditions, it is essential that we maintain balance, perspective, and focus. Otherwise, all of our work is lessened in potency, and our ability to accomplish real things diminishes.

Where Have We Come From?

In trying to grasp the whole picture of either Witchcraft or shamanism today, it is important to acknowledge the historical factors shaping their development. Shamanism throughout the world has a virtually uninterrupted heritage dating back centuries, well-documented and preserved through written or oral traditions within indigenous cultures. Except for the relatively few shamans persecuted in Europe during the Inquisition and its Protestant equivalents during the thirteenth through seventeenth centuries, little has been done in an organized fashion to endanger the preservation of shamanistic techniques globally. The same is not true of witchcraft.

Witchcraft seems to have existed primarily in the Western European and Mediterranean regions, from the beginnings of recorded history (and earlier) through modern time. In early Greece, records exist of female-oriented religions that fit the basic definition of the Craft. Italy has been the site of several long-lasting Craft traditions—including one that may be the only true surviving pre-Inquisition tradition. France, Germany, the United Kingdom, and the Scandinavian states have likewise been home to well-developed Witchcraft traditions. However, these were also the areas principally targeted by the Roman Catholic, Lutheran, and Calvinist churches as hotbeds of "heresy" during those centuries. As a result, thousands of women, men, and children, were tortured, burned, mutilated, and intimidated, in a well-organized attempt to cleanse the land of non-Christian beliefs. Especially targeted were any remnants of pre-Christian religions or spiritual traditions. The brutal efficiency of the Inquisition rang the death-knell for most Pagan spirituality in these regions. Those practicing their spirituality openly were tortured and killed; others were driven underground, where it became next to impossible to pass on their knowledge and traditions, leading to their rapid and permanent loss. In any case, it is a virtual certainty that witchcraft as described by the Inquisition was simply a distorted view of a pre-Christian fertility and nature-based religion bearing little or no resemblance to today's Craft practices.

Where Are We Today?

In the early to middle twentieth century, primarily in the United Kingdom, people started once again openly discussing nature-oriented spirituality. "Family-tradition" (sometimes called "fam-trad") Witches began to teach others outside their families. Rituals were a little safer to practice semi-openly, and networking began among the various vocal practitioners. As this networking increased, the true scope of the lost information became apparent. Simultaneously, people stepped forward to help rewrite the lost mythology and recreate the lost techniques. Ranging from Dion Fortune through Aleister Crowley, Gerald Gardner, and Raymond Buckland, those with vision and insight took up their pens and began to create. Their works have been regarded as anything from revealed truth to pleasant fiction, and whether you agree with their writings or not ultimately doesn't matter: Their main purpose was served. The channels of non-Christian thought and worldview were opened. Z Budapest, Starhawk, Doreen Valiente, Scott Cunningham, and many others took up the challenge and began creating the new guidebooks—hands-on, how-to techniques for creating ritual, defining spirituality, and shaping your personal Craft (no matter what you call it).

Shamanism has, likewise, undergone a fairly dramatic change in the last century. Prior to that time, it was, as Mircea Eliade describes: "...considered to be either a psychopathic phenomenon or a primitive healing practice and archaic type of black magic, but contemporary scholarship has convincingly demonstrated the complexity, the rigor, and the rich spiritual meaning of shamanistic initiation and practices."[2] As scholarship began to treat shamanism with respect, so did popular tradition, leading to what I refer to as "pop shamanism" or the "weekend-warrior" mentality. As this occurred, a major divergence—the traditional shaman versus the urban shaman—began to occur within shamanism today.

Native shamanistic cultures that have persisted to this day have largely done so by ferociously guarding their traditions and ways of life. Constant threats by those who wish to acculturate them, exterminate them, or "help" them have taught indigenous peoples that the best way to survive is to withdraw as much as possible from contact with the outside world. As a result, traditional shamanism has remained alive within these cultures; it has also remained the sole purview of these cultures. With the increased sympathetic interest in indigenous peoples, more information has become commonly available about all aspects of their lives, including shamanism in all its forms. While most tribal cultures have continued to guard their sacred traditions against outside view, a few have opened their hearts and teachings to outsiders. From these teachings, others have branched out to provide access to the medicine paths for virtually all who seek it (and who can pay for it). Other indigenous cultures, seeing their ways threatened, and seeing the often commercial distortion of their teachings, have retreated into even greater silence and have refused all spiritual access to nontribal seekers.

Thus, two main paths have emerged within shamanic practice. The traditional path has become more closed to outsiders over the last couple of generations. These practitioners have, by and large, retreated into the "true" practice of their medicine and have chosen to maintain its purity. In other cases, the traditional practice is represented by those whose contact with the outside world has been extremely limited by geographical or cultural necessity. Examples of these forms abound throughout the world—in Siberia, Alaska, South America, India, North America, and Korea. Several areas of commonality exist with these practitioners: they rarely accept money for their work although they are usually supported by their tribe; they rarely teach nontribal members about their craft; they undergo arduous physical training and initiation; they do not choose their path, but are chosen by the gods.

The urban shaman's path has grown rapidly and visibly over the last several years. Made up of practitioners from all cultures and all walks of life, this is a freely chosen path that can be followed by anyone. Within this path, information is disseminated to all through books, workshops, retreats, and discussion groups. Some can be quite costly while others are priced just to defray costs for the presenter. Physical training is often tame, symbolic, or nonexistent. Participants are rarely required to hunt and kill a bear armed only with a short knife and their wits. (Imagine the liability insurance!) The emphasis in this path is mostly on the symbolism and harmonic balance of this type of worldview. Even the healing techniques that may be taught are relatively "civilized" when compared with true shamanic healing in indigenous settings.

None of this, however, is to detract from "urban shamanism's" efficacy. It can be a positive and potent way to manifest your spirituality and find expression and balance with your world. It has become increasingly difficult within our modern urban culture to find and maintain a connection with the forces of nature. It is in this that urban shamanism excels and makes its most positive contribution to the world today. In this, as in the modern Witchcraft movement, however, it is essential that a differentiation be made between true practitioners and opportunists. Pricing is the easiest way to tell the difference. An exorbitantly priced "weekend warrior" workshop is likely to be organized by someone whose prime motivation is the monetary factor in the New Age marketplace. Likewise, an overpriced Tarot reading by a "renowned psychic and Witch" is likely to be a ripoff. True practitioners of either craft, while they may need to be able to support themselves and their families, are not likely to be driving high-priced cars and living in palatial homes, things that are basically at odds with the worldview they are espousing. It is up to you, the consumer, to differentiate and to choose the approach that best fits your personal worldview and needs.

Another marker I use to monitor the motivation of the teacher is their approach to the balance of light and dark. Both the Craft and Shamanism deal with balances of all the forces in Nature—not just those of light. A shaman's workshop that purports to teach all about "love, money, and peace" and that fails to mention the dark side is very likely a powerless sham. Think for a moment about voodoo (or Voudoun or Santería, or any of the similar Caribbean/South American traditions). This is a powerful, fascinating, mysterious cultural tradition. And yet, there are no classes springing up at your local New Age hangout on voodoo practices. I believe this is because voodoo, unlike most other shamanistic religions, has never hidden the darker aspects of its practice. Perhaps the knowledge of sacrifice, possession, and frightening darkness keeps the casual practitioner away. If so, this may be a good thing.

Neither shamanism or the Craft should be dabbled in or taken lightly. The forces involved, whether psychic, physical, or supernatural, are powerful and can do harm as well as good. In times and cultures where these paths were taken seriously and seen as lifetime commitments, very few (if any) toyed with the profession—you were either chosen or not chosen. No appeal, no regrets. You take the dark with the light, and strive to be true to the ultimate nature of your role—to serve and protect your people and community; to maintain the balance between dark and light in the universe. And you don't expect to get rich doing it.

Where Are We Going?

The Neopagan movement has been growing rapidly since the 1960s, and as it grows it gains speed and momentum. In some ways, it has taken a course parallel with the Civil Rights movement in the United States, as people with alternate spiritualities begin to use the constitutionally guaranteed right to freedom of religion to dissuade persecution and discrimination against their practice of nonmainstream spirituality. As local statutes, such as a recent attempt in Florida to prevent a Santerían church from practicing animal sacrifice during ritual, are struck down on a federal level, more people can feel safe in practicing their chosen spirituality. When this happens, the movement becomes more visible, and many who feel drawn to this type of spiritual path find outlets to ask questions, get information, and receive support for their choices. It is in the area of education and positive service that I see the greatest potential in the future of both shamanism and Witchcraft.

To understand this, I believe it is vital that we understand what draws people to these spiritual paths, for even if the paths themselves are different, there is an identical central attraction: personal empowerment. Our modern, technologically advanced world deindividualizes us in many ways every day. Each time we use an automatic teller machine and enter our personal identification numbers, identify ourselves through our Social Security Number, use our numbered credit cards, or flash our company identification badge, we are subconsciously reduced to a set of numerical identifiers—one of a thousand, million, or billion. It is easy to buy into this feeling and attempt to conform rather than to truly celebrate the power of individuality and uniqueness. Corporate culture reinforces and rewards conformity and safety. And yet, it is often the truly eccentric, mold-breaking people who become geniuses in the business world. What has this to do with Witchcraft and shamanism? Everything.

When our worlds attempt to reduce us to an impersonal set of numbers, and our workplace rejects all parts of us that don't fit the corporate mold, the strong, instinctive, and intuitive sides of our natures are repressed. Those sides remain repressed and build up steam until they must seek expression and empowerment. Some take refuge in risky sports, like skydiving or race car driving, looking for that elusive thrill that imbues them with a sense of being "on top of the world." Others immerse themselves in traditional spiritualities, looking for the answers in religious texts, sermons, and philosophy. Still others turn to artistic hobbies to nurture their intuitive natures. And some turn to the empowerment of nontraditional spirituality, seeking harmony with Nature, personal communion with the Deity (or Deities), and a sense of oneness with and control over their universe. For people who seek the *personal* meanings and responsibility, with the immediacy of communion that occurs when no intermediary or priest comes between the Deity and the person, both Neopaganism and shamanism can provide that outlet.

As the world becomes increasingly complex, shamanism, Witchcraft, and similar spiritualities provide a way for people of like minds to focus their energies together to make our world better. Support for environmentalism, social responsibility, health care reform, pacifism, and many other positive movements is very high within the Neopagan and shamanistic communities. As these people begin to work together to achieve their goals, personal power is magnified and focused and the goals soon become realities.

In researching this chapter, I interviewed many people who consider themselves Pagans or shamans. The common thread in the interviews was the need these people expressed to serve their communities or their world. This need guided some into their chosen career paths. Others have found ways within "corporate" careers to serve by using their unique spirituality. One of my favorite stories involves Janet, a Witch in Silicon Valley, who helped her employer, a small software company, through some difficult financial circumstances with a well-placed (and obviously well-executed) prosperity spell. The spell was placed with the knowledge and agreement of the top officers in the company. Necessary sources of capital were found just in time to pull the company out of dire straits.

Others I interviewed spoke of their political or environmental activism as being intrinsically tied to their spirituality. Several mentioned volunteering with inner-city youth, the homeless, or people with AIDS. Still others spoke of their hobbies in spiritual terms, from several "adopt-a-highway" programs to flute playing. These movements and choices can be summed up in the words of Jim, a Wiccan from San Francisco:

> The common thread…is healing/helping others, which I see as the guiding fundamental myth of my life. I believe that I give back because that is what needs to be done, that is what I can do, and that is what I seem to be skilled at doing. I also find a…restoration of personal hope when I enter the dimensions of caring that are necessary for true healing to occur.

Whether on the micro level, teaching others in their family or local community how to use herbs for healing or recycle, or on the macro level as environmental activists or political watchdogs, shamans and Witches feel a sense of responsibility to serve their communities. And within this responsibility the lines of definition between varieties of Witches and/or shamans become less important on any but the personal level.

So what does all of this portend for the future? Are these movements just passing fads? Or will they contain deep relevance for the future of our society and our world? When we look at the effects of the environmental movement in recent years, we see a tangible result of largely grass roots efforts. It is not at all unlikely that the zeal of the pioneering environmentalists is closely related to the reverence Witches and shamans feel for the Earth Mother. Continuing and expanding efforts along these lines, obtaining the "buy in" of large segments of mainstream society, and maintaining the enthusiasm for the movement relies on maintaining this zealous attitude. Witches and shamans, alongside their more mainstream counterparts, will play a large role in this.

As our society reacts to the mechanization of our lives, a return to small-town community and nature-oriented lifestyles becomes more attractive. Within these movements, those who are called to service in the community grow in stature and respectability. Traditional medicine is changing, with the recognition that so-called alternative healing methods have gained tremendous popularity. And with this comes the realization that many of the alternative healing methods cited in recent studies are, in reality, the earliest traditional healings—midwifery, herbalism, chiropractic, etc. Many practitioners of alternative healing have nontraditional ways of thinking, including their spiritualities. In this avenue, as in so many others, there is ample room for growth for Witches and shamans.

And most importantly, the intrinsic willingness to reach out and help other human beings, giving love, healing, help, and support, is the greatest gift that the Witches and shamans of the future have to give to the world. No matter what the differences in ideology, practice, or secular power between the two movements, the end results are the same: empowerment of the individual, respect and love for our world, and a recognition that both light and dark have a place in the world.

Notes

1. Dee Brown, *Bury My Heart at Wounded Knee* (New York: Holt, Rinehart, and Winston, 1970).
2. Mircea Eliade, *Shamanism: Archaic Techniques of Ecstacy* (Princeton: Princeton University Press, 1964).

About the Author

Karen Goeller has been a professional writer since the mid-1980s. She works for Bellcore, the research and development arm of the regional telephone companies, where her primary responsibility is the design of information flows in the software development process. Karen's regular column, "Read Anything Good Lately" appears in the women's spirituality quarterly *Of A Like Mind*. She is also writing a book, *Spiritual Pregnancy*, which contains meditations/visualizations and natural stress-relief techniques for use during pregnancy and the transition to new parenthood.

Karen is married, the mother of two beautiful daughters, and lives with her family in Mechanicsville, Pennsylvania.

© Zelda Gordon

What Happened to Western Shamanism?

by Chas S. Clifton

Cinderella was a shaman—or at least she started out as one. That may come as surprise to anyone who has heard only the more recent versions of her story. In those, she appears only as a passive girl, a mannequin who never complains, gets a makeover from her fairy godmother, and wins the handsome prince without actually doing much. Yet her story conceals a more interesting past, and it says much about shamanism's course in the Western world. Like a river meeting the sea and splitting into numerous branches, it divided and changed. Some parts kept flowing, but now they were different than they had been. And others slowed and spread out into wide wetlands where the wild ducks flocked and swam, and only a faint, slow current persisted to suggest the former river's flow.

A single shoe floated in that slow-moving water. It may have been a glass slipper, or a fur slipper, or a simple sandal, or an Asian horseman's boot.

To follow some portions of this river, we might start in ancient Greece. Although some modern Pagans work with

the Greek or Roman pantheon, Wicca claims mainly Western European roots. I myself long resisted studying ancient
Greek religion for ideas to bring forward into my present
practice. I placed too much emphasis on my Anglo-Irish
family heritage and not enough on the Greek spiritual and
intellectual heritage that screams out every time we use a
word like "pantheon."[1] Eventually I ended up reading Plato
for a new perspective on shamanism, an approach not often
found in introductory philosophy courses.

Tracing one stream of Western shamanism through
chiefly Greek materials has several advantages. If we include its archaic forms, written Greek is more than three
thousand years old. Scanty as they are, "very few texts, a
few inscriptions, a few mutilated monuments, and some vo-
tive objects,"[2] we can still read large amounts of ancient
Greek Pagan material unfiltered by a Christian or other
worldview. And compare the advantage of the enormous
amount of literary material (even though epics like the *Iliad*
were written down after having been told orally for generations) that was then quoted and commented on by generations of literate persons seeking ancient roots for their own
"modern" understanding of divinity, the soul, the afterlife.[3]
(The so-called Dark Ages, the decline in urban life and formal learning that marked western Europe, never happened
in the Eastern Roman Empire.) That continuity was lost with
works like the Old English *Beowulf* or the Old Welsh *Mabino-
gion* that only reach us having been copied—and who
knows how censored—by monastic scribes of the Middle
Ages. Many Irish tales were not even collected until the
nineteenth century, for example. Only with some of the
Celtic tales, Norse sagas, and a few Old English magical
fragments can we see bits of the Western European Pagan
past unedited; and folklore, while fascinating, is not as pure
a conserving force as people often believe.

Thanks to the time-binding effects of ancient Greek literature we can see some familiar patterns emerge. A diffuse
polytheism of many local cults and local forms of the gods is

countered by a growing skepticism and an attempt to spec-
ulate rationally on the physical world—is it made up of tiny
bits called atoms, asked the philosopher Democritus (C. 460-
362 B.C.E.). Is it ultimately composed of air, fire, or something
else? Where do souls go after death, and how much of reality is an illusion? This is not to say that the Greeks and only
the Greeks asked such questions. No doubt they have been
asked around the world. The Chinese and the Indians, for
instance, asked similar questions and likewise wrote them
down, the difference being that their thought entered Western civilization much more recently and has only had a significant impact since the nineteenth century.[4]

Because ancient Greek religion had many centers, many
stories, and its cults and initiations were not necessarily in
conflict with one another, modern Pagans can feel an affini-
ty with it that we cannot feel with the exclusive, judgmental,
and dogmatic scriptural traditions. Often, reading the classical thinkers does not give the same sensation one gets
nowadays of a divorce between the intellectual life, the life
of feeling, and the mystical life.[5] The same persons who
coolly discussed philosophy might well also have drunk the
mind-altering potion some researchers believe was passed
out at the climax of the Eleusinian Mysteries—and they kept
the secrets required of initiates.[6] Even in Plato, whose
writings (which include the ideas of his teacher, So-
crates) seem so rational, some scholars discern a cross-
fertilization of "Greek rationalism with magico-religious
ideas whose remoter ideas belong to the northern
shamanistic culture."[7]

The phrase "northern shamanistic culture" refers to two
shadowy cultures, those of ancient Thrace and particularly
ancient Scythia—shadowy because all we can do is speak of
them by geographical region, so many changes have tran-
spired there since those times. "Thrace" refers to an area
now divided between Greece, Bulgaria, and European
Turkey; it was at various times part of the kingdom of Mace-
donia, the Roman Empire, and the Byzantine Empire before

coming under Turkish control after the fall of Constantinople in 1453. Scythia was a catch-all term for the land north of the Black Sea, and "Scythian" likewise was applied to various horse-riding pastoral nomads ranging from Hungary to Turkestan, including some of the peoples referred to as Huns.[8] Greek and later Roman writers sometimes referred to Scythia as Hyperborea, the land "behind the North Wind," which could be understood simply as "way up north." The names of two famous shamanistic Greek spiritual figures, Orpheus and Pythagoras, are intriguingly connected with these areas.

Shamanic ideas and practices that originated in central and northern Asia may well have come south through the Black Sea trade route, becoming embedded in the spiritual traditions of Orphics and Pythagoreans. Previously, Greek religion had been largely a here-and-now affair with only a shadowy concept of the afterlife. "The abode of the dead, the dark and gloomy Hades, was somewhere far away beneath the earth."[9] Central Asian shamanism may have added the idea of a preexistent "spark" of soul within the body that could leave it in dreams or in a shamanic trance. (The Greeks, however, did believe that people received messages from the gods in dreams.) "Such an ontological self [existing separate from the body] appears to have started as a shamanistic idea, which migrated south from Scythia and Thrace into Greece during the fifth century before the Common Era."[10] Not surprisingly, the idea of a wandering soul fit well with teachings of reincarnation by Orphics and Pythagoreans.

The legendary shaman Orpheus has several connections with this area. Classical Greek stories set his life one generation before the Trojan War, in other words, "long ago," and made him the son of a Thracian king. (His mother was said to be one of the nine muses while in other versions of the story his father was Apollo.) A musician of miraculous talents, he joined the Argonauts, the crew of the hero Jason, who sailed in their ship *Argo* into various adventures on the coasts of the Black Sea during the quest for the Golden Fleece. But his most famous exploit was his descent into Hades itself to bring back his wife Eurydice. His harp-playing charmed the guardians of the Underworld into letting him pass even though he was not dead, but his quest was ultimately unsuccessful. In one version, he broke the prohibition against looking at Eurydice on the return journey, causing her to vanish and him to kill himself. In another, he left without her. In a variant version of his death, he was murdered by a mob of Thracian women.

By the sixth century B.C.E. a large body of mystical poetry was attributed to Orpheus including stories of the world's creation, the genealogy of the gods, and the soul's journey after death. One famous passage, speaking of those souls who travel after death by the "path of the well-head that is beside the white cypress" was incorporated by the English magician and author Dion Fortune into her rituals of Isis.[11]

In addition, an Orphic movement arose. Its members ate no meat, beans, or wine, and practiced no violence—a notable contrast to their countrymen, whose religion included animal sacrifice and whose warfare shaded off into piracy.[12] Several writers, including Plato, described Orphics as wandering magicians. They fasted, worked wonders, and undertook shamanic journeys. "Beggar priests and seers come to the doors of the rich and convince them that in their hands, given by the gods, there lies the power to heal…if a misdeed has been committed by themselves or their ancestors…and they offer a bundle of books of Musaios and Orpheus…according to which they perform their sacrifices [to deliver people from evil in the afterlife]; anyone who declines to sacrifice, however, is told that terrible things are waiting for him," wrote Plato in his *Republic*.

The man Pythagoras, by contrast, can be more confidently dated to the sixth century B.C.E.; he was born on the Greek island of Samos and lived mainly in the Greek colonies of southern Italy. While he is best remembered for teaching mathematical ideas—everyone learns the Pythagorean theorem in geometry—his mathematics was originally combined with many mystical ideas that the schoolbooks leave out. "The pre-Platonic testimonies point to a rather strange mixture of number symbolism, arithmetic, doctrines of immortality and the afterlife, and rules for an ascetic life."

Whether by followers of the Orphic mysteries, Pythagoras's ascetic philosophy, or initiates of the Dionysian mysteries, which also had shamanic elements, Greek ideas of the soul began to be transformed in a nondogmatic way. Plato, who lived from about 427 to 347 B.C.E., not only pursued the implications of having a preexisting, eternal soul, but moved further to asserting that ideas have a truer reality than their physical counterparts and manifestations and that the soul longs to move from the material plane into this realm of archetypes. "Through Plato reality is made unreal in favour of an incorporeal, unchangeable other world which is to be regarded as primary," wrote the historian Walter Burkert. "The ego is concentrated in an immortal soul which is alien to the body and captive in it. 'Flight from the world' is a watchword which actually occurs in Plato."[14]

Yet an alternative view suggests that Plato's "separate reality" was the gift of his experience at Eleusis, where a psychoactive preparation, similar to LSD, derived from ergot (*Claviceps purpurea*), a fungus that grows on rye, could have been used to heighten the spiritual effects of the ritual presentation of the story of the grain goddess Demeter, her daughter Persephone, and Persephone's sojourn in the Underworld—which brings us back to our theme.[15]

From Plato's time on into the early centuries of the Christian era was the heyday of the Mediterranean mystery religions: those of Orpheus, Isis, Jesus, Mithras, Dionysus, and the rest. It was a time of increasing urbanization and the concentration of political power in the empires of Alexander the Great, his successors, and then the Romans. No longer were all people content merely to sacrifice to the gods and then get on with farming, trading, or whatever; fascinated with the quasi-shamanic ideas of the soul, they sought forms of private practice involving ecstatic journeys. The parallels with our world are obvious!

In the minds of Jewish and Christian Gnostics these ideas became still more world-denying. Thus we arrive at a tremendous irony: what started as shamanism was modified by philosophy and influenced by Iranian, even Hindu and Buddhist ideas to produce the dualistic outlook blamed for much of what is wrong with the world today, the complex of associations in which body/female/material world is somehow "bad" and mind/male/spiritual world is "good." Thus one stream of shamanism becomes a stagnant swamp covered by a Gnostic mist.

But the streams flowing from primordial shamanism led other directions as well. From Scythia or Hyperborea another flows into Celtic Europe—it might be traced by the similarities between the "animal style" or zoomorphic Scythian art and Celtic interlaced animal figures. Carlo Ginzburg, an Italian historian whose works such as *The Night Battles* and *Ecstasies* represent the most original thinking on the witch-trial era (the Burning Times) in a generation or two, suggests that Asian Scythian and European Celtic animal style art represents a continuity of shamanic practice: "Indeed it has been proposed that in the struggles between animals, real or imaginary (bears, wolves, stags and griffons), portrayed by the art of the nomadic peoples, we should recognize a representation of the struggle between souls, transformed into animals, fought by the Eurasian shamans (alongside whom we might place, in the European sphere, the Hungarian *táltos* or the Balkan *kresniki*)."[16] Using Ginzburg as a guide, one may follow his linkages of "Siberian hunters, nomadic shepherds of the steppes of Central Asia, Scythians, Thracians, and Celts" to connect Central Asian shamanism with the nocturnal "flights" and the "flying ointments" attested by the witch-trial documents.

In *Ecstasies: Deciphering the Witches' Sabbath* Ginzburg exhaustively examines the lore of the "wild hunt" or "Diana's army," a throng of the dead (and/or the spirits of sleeping witches) who fly through the sky or pass through houses on their way to their rites and feasting. One of the earliest and most-quoted records of "Diana's army" was the *Canon Episcopi*, an ecclesiastical legal document of unknown origin often cited as evidence that pre-Christian Paganism coexisted with Christianity into at least the early Middle Ages. First publicized in about 906 by Regino of Prüm, Abbot of Treves (or Trier, a city in western Germany), who claimed that it had originated in the fourth century, the *Canon Episcopi* passed into the body of religious law. In essence, the canon stated that witchcraft, as commonly imagined, was a delusion and that it was *belief* in the reality of witchcraft, not witchcraft itself, that constituted heresy.

Its most famous passage reads:

> It is also not to be omitted that some wicked women, perverted by the Devil, seduced by illusions and phantasms of demons, believe and profess themselves in the hours of the night to ride upon certain beasts with Diana, the goddess of Pagans, and an innumerable multitude of women, and in the silence of the dead of the night to traverse great spaces of earth, and to obey her commands as of their mistress, and to be summoned to her service on certain nights...For an innumerable multitude, deceived by this false opinion [of those women], believe this to be true, and so believing, wander from the right faith and are involved in the error of the Pagans.

The period Ginzburg examines, stretching from the tenth to the eighteenth centuries at its extremes, included many such reports, however. In literary texts, he notes, processions of the dead were led by legendary male figures (such as King Arthur or King Herla, the origin of "harlequin," possibly identified with Woden/Odin) while the ecstatic women were led by a female figure.[17] But the witch trial documents (to whatever degree they are trustworthy, considering the circumstances) complicate the picture. "In some cases we find men who in ecstasy visited the Queen of the Elves (in whom we have recognized a variant of the nocturnal goddess); women who, like the *benandanti* of Friuli, watch the processions of the dead in ecstasy; men who…participated in the battles for the fertility of the fields."[18] Ginzburg traces variants of the Wild Hunt back to Roman times, but in areas of Celtic population, and suggests that this "Celtic pulp in a Roman rind" included a surviving cult of the Celtic goddess Epona, who was associated not only with horses and stables but with the world of the dead, and also a continuation of the cult of "the mothers," usually portrayed as three seated goddesses, whose statues were found throughout the northern Roman empire: Britain, Gaul, and the lower Rhineland.[19] Ultimately, Ginzburg suggests, the nocturnal goddess who leads the processions may be traced back to the "mistress of the animals" divinities found in many areas. "Moreover," he adds, "the ecstasies of the followers of the goddess irresistibly call to mind those of the shamans—men and women—of Siberia or of Lapland."[20]

Many explanations for the Burning Times have been offered: they represented a war against women midwives and healers, a war against an actual surviving Old Religion (the Margaret Murray theory), the growth of an actual Satanic religion (suggested by historian Jeffrey Burton Russell), and so forth. But I think it is undeniable that "psychotropic herbalism" played some part, simply because some of the recipes for "flying ointments" contained known psychoactive ingredients. In addition, some of these plants were potentially deadly in large doses, unlike the more benign peyote or psilocybin mushrooms. Consequently, it seems likely that some sort of tradition(s) for their safe preparation and use must have existed—but what this tradition called itself we cannot say.

The elements of midwifery and psychotropic herbalism come together in one particular instance, if the knowledge of how to safely prepare *Claviceps purpurea* had been passed down from ancient times. (Eating bread baked with ergot-contaminated rye can cause convulsions, cramps, and gangrene in the limbs, and the burning feeling associated with this poisoning led to it being referred to as "St. Anthony's fire.") In addition, ergot stimulates labor in pregnant women; midwives knew this, giving them the ability to hasten a difficult birth or to abort an unwanted baby, an action condemned by ecclesiastical (and sometimes civil) law.

And what about Cinderella? Her story makes an intriguing footnote to the quest for shamanistic elements in medieval, Renaissance, or early modern Europe. Beginning with an observation by the anthropologist Claude Lévi-Strauss, Ginzburg devotes a chapter of *Ecstasies*, "Bones and Skin," to the common theme of bodily asymmetry in shamans, gods, or spirits who move between this world and the world of the dead. This asymmetry may, for example, take the example of lameness, an injured foot or heel, or the loss of one shoe or sandal. For instance, the legendary Greek warrior Achilles, hero of the Trojan War, was (in one common story) dipped by his semi-divine mother in the river Styx, which flows through the Underworld. She held him by his heel, and that was the only place on his body where an enemy's weapons could hurt him. And, Ginzburg adds, although Achilles is normally thought of as wholly Greek, a Greek poem from the seventh century B.C.E. identifies him as "lord of the Scythians."

In a Christian context, consider how in *Genesis 32* the patriarch Jacob wrestles all night with "a man" (conventionally described as an angel but possibly to be understood as the Hebrew god Yahweh himself), winning the contest at the price of a dislocated thigh. In his novel *King Jesus* Robert Graves gives Jesus the same affliction as a sign of his sacred kingship: Graves also has much to say about lameness in *The White Goddess*, connecting mushrooms and the ecstatic god Dionysus, whose cult began in Thrace.[21]

In a ritual context, wearing one shoe or sandal also expresses the idea of being between two states, hence the admonition in some secret societies and magickal lodges that the candidate should be presented neither barefoot nor shod. Beyond that, "It is thought that the custom of wearing a single sandal was connected with ritual situations in which, through more immediate contact with the ground, the attempt was made to achieve a relationship with the subterranean powers [for example, in invoking Hecate]."22

Having discussed numerous other examples of "mono-sandalism," Ginzburg suggests that all fairy tales involving journeys and quests are shamanistic at their roots; that is, they are based on journeys to the world of the dead. "Anyone who goes to or returns from the nether world—man, animal, or a mixture of the two—is marked by an asymmetry," he asserts, even Cinderella. Her story (which in variations was told from Scotland to China) follows a classic sequence. She is forbidden to attend the prince's ball, gets help from a non-human source (her fairy godmother or an animal, depending on the version told), goes to the ball anyway and flees at midnight, leaving a slipper behind. After she is discovered and recognized as the only woman whose foot the slipper fits, she sees her step-sisters destroyed and she marries the prince. "Cinderella's monosandalism is a distinguishing sign of those who have visited the realm of the dead (the prince's palace)."23

But from "shamanistic elements" to shamanism is a long jump. Even if we could collect all the shamanistic elements in historic European witchcraft traditions, would that make modern Wicca a form of classical shamanism? I do not think so. In fact, as more Neopagan Witches study shamanism, some fundamental differences between Wicca and traditional shamanism emerge, not only in what operations are performed, but in their conceptions of the universe.

In *Shamanism: Archaic Techniques of Ecstasy,* his important cross-cultural study of shamanic patterns described in "Shamanism and Neoshamanism," the historian of religion Mircea Eliade described a cosmology common to a number of the northern and central Asian peoples, including the tribes who gave us the word "shaman." Among them is usually found a supreme sky god or creator, but this Supreme

Being has become over centuries a *deus otiosus*, a distant and detached divinity.[24] Eliade's technical term comes from the Latin word *otium*, meaning leisure. The only access through him is through intermediaries: "spirits," "messengers," "sons," and so forth, to whom the shaman must "ascend." (In the mythical past, this Supreme Being was closer to humans, but something happened to change this Golden Age relationship—so goes the frequent pattern.)

Another important figure, "the only great god after the Lord of the Sky," is the Lord of the Underworld, with whom shamans also communicate.[25] In Eliade's view, over centuries Asian shamans became more occupied with acquiring helpful spirits, being possessed by spirits, struggling with evil spirits, and dealing with a variety of divinized ancestors and lesser divine beings while the original Sky God was of less everyday concern. "In a general way, it can be said that shamanism defends life, health, fertility, the world of 'light' against death, diseases, sterility, disaster, and the world of 'darkness.'"[26]

Like the protohistorical Indo-European culture, these Central Asian shamanic cultures had few goddess figures: "The Turko-Tatar and Siberian peoples know several female divinities, but they are reserved for women, their spheres being childbirth and children's diseases. The mythological role of women is also markedly small, although traces remain of it in some shamanic traditions."[27]

As Eliade and numerous other researchers have demonstrated, shamanic traditions usually picture the cosmos divided into levels to which the shaman "descends" (via a tunnel or cave, for example) or "ascends" to by climbing a magical tree, being carried by an eagle, and so on. And as we have seen, such concepts were carried into the folklore of Western Europe, where travelers visit the Faery Folk "under the hill" or ride through the night with the goddess Diana.

But in Wicca as it has developed over the past half century, such ecstatic travel was downplayed in favor of ritual forms based on the circle, the four quarters, invocations of the deities, the sexual imagery of the central rite, and the working of magick appropriate to the time, followed by a ritual meal. That is not to say that trance work, with or without psychoactive agents, has not been part of twentieth-century Wicca. As Evan John Jones points out in "Sacred Mask and Sacred Trance," some potentially dangerous experiments were made in this century based on old witch-trial records. But as it has evolved, Wicca has been more about the sacrality of sexuality and the immanence of deity in the here-and-now than about ecstatic travel to other dimensions. "The great emphasis on sexuality in the rituals...is neither hedonistic nor exploitative, but genuinely sacramental, since it arises out of a search for communion and for community."[28] Some modern Witches strike an almost pantheistic note, for example, Starhawk in her metaphor-loaded descriptions of the Goddess and God of the Craft:

> To a Witch the world itself is what is real [as opposed to the Platonic reality of archetypes]. The Goddess, the Gods, are not mere psychological entities, existing in the psyche as if the psyche were a cave removed from the world; they too are real—that is, they are ways of thinking–in–things about real forces, real experiences.

> "Would you like to have a vision of the Goddess," I ask groups when I speak in public. When they nod, I tell them to turn and look at the person sitting next to them. The immanent Goddess is not abstract.[29]

Another contrast was noted by a Witch who commented in a recent discussion of shamanism as compared with the Craft, "It seems that shamans do much more of their work on the other planes while the Craft works more on this plane. We tend to call our Guardians, Watchers, Deities to our circle, rather than wander out to meet them."

In fact, many Witches celebrate and do magickal work without the use of trance or ecstasy at all, merely a state of heightened inner awareness while within the sacred circle. But few would deny the importance of a sacramental inter-

pretation of sexual energy, whether that is expressed symbolically, allegorically, or in the flesh.[30] Before the
neoshamanic renaissance, modern Witches were more likely
to characterize Wicca as a reborn fertility religion, although
in an overpopulated world the fertility aspect was frequently understood to apply to mental "children" and to other aspects of life and Nature.

The interplay of sexual energies seems by contrast to
play little part in traditional shamanic practice—which is
not to make a comment about the sexual natures of the
shamans themselves. The traditional shaman's important
journeying and curing is performed alone; he or she primarily interacts alone with the spirits or the gods—even if the
goal is fertility. Some Siberian shamans used to describe
their relationships with "female" spirits in sexual terms, but,
"The sexual relations that the shaman is believed to have
with his *ayami* [tutelary spirit] are not basic to his shamanic
vocation. For on one hand, sexual possession in dreams is
not confined to shamans; on the other hand, the sexual elements present in certain shamanic ceremonies go beyond
the relations between the shaman and his *ayami* and form
part of well-known rituals intended to increase the sexual
vigor of the community."[31]

I suspect that the eagerness with which many Neopagan
Witches have embraced the equation of the Craft with "European shamanism" has more to do with claiming primordial roots than with actually comparing their similarities
and differences. This claim was first made, to my knowledge, in the 1970s, an era when the renewed—and wholly
justifiable—political struggles of American Indians combined with one of our nation's periodic "back to the land"
movements, producing as a side-effect a renewed interest in
"the noble savage" and an upsurge in superficial interest in
Native religions. (Likewise, one contemporary Witch and
writer recently admitted to me that she knows how part of
her present interest in shamanism can be traced back to the
"cowboy and Indian" movies she saw as a young girl.)

But Witches, more than anyone, should be aware how allure and danger are combined in the "noble savage" stereotype, for "witch" is a very similar stereotype. Modern people have often viewed both tribal people and witches with a mixture of fear, respect, and ridicule. The witch is ridiculed for "pretending" to magickal powers and for being "primitive" and "irrational," but at the same time many people desire or fear those powers. As anthropologist Michael Taussig wrote of colonists' attitudes toward the Peruvian and Colombian tribes of the Upper Amazon, "Going to the Indians for their healing power and killing them for their wildness are not so far apart."[32] Modern Pagan Witches share the cultural stereotype of the "noble savage" because we were born into these times, yet, having sometimes been on the receiving end, we ought to be more aware of it than most people. Saying that Wicca is shamanism—which it is not although it may contain shamanic elements—is merely an attempt to grab something that has slipped through our fingers. It may serve as a political statement, as one way for the new, twentieth-century Old Religion to outbid Christianity, but it is not a defensible claim from the point of view of actual practice and cosmology.

Still, Wicca is nothing if not eclectic and open to borrowing. And, as Micea Eliade noted, shamanic ecstasy is a primary phenomenon. No one owns it. While shaped by historical influences, it is every culture's property. It is recoverable and reusable. The investigations of Felicitas Goodman and her students, summarized in "Shamans, Witches, and the Recovery of the Trance Posture," are just one example of the gains to be made by looking at old material with new eyes.

At the same time, the larger Pagan movement is growing so fast that at least some sympathetic observers believe it may be the fastest-growing religion in North America, even though relatively small in absolute numbers.[33] The growth in regional and national festivals, whose size and numbers zoomed upward in the 1980s with no end yet in sight, is one indicator that the coven of a dozen or fewer people is no longer the primary group model of Pagan practice. True communities are evolving, and a lively debate has arisen over whether and how Pagan clergy should be paid for their functions as planners, managers, counselors, ritual specialists, and religious functionaries. With this size comes an increasing division of the community into specialists and nonspecialists. Some people, for all their commitment to a Pagan worldview, do not wish to participate in the frequent, intense, small-group magico-religious practice of the Witches' coven.

This growth and this division are creating a niche for a Wiccan type of shamanism as the "techniques of ecstasy" are rediscovered and updated. (It has been suggested that computer-generated virtual reality, now used primarily for pilot-training and entertainment, could be used to mimic a shamanic journey or even the soul's journey after death, thus preparing people for that inevitable experience.) The Craft's increasing appeal and rapid growth cause some Witches to fear losing the intensity small groups generate; quite possibly, shamanic work will become a new method for increasing that inner experience as organizational forms expand around it.

Somebody is picking up that floating sandal and finding that it fits.

Notes

1. "Pantheon" comes from the Greek words for "all [the] gods." Some modern psychologists see the Old Gods reflected in the elements of the self.

2. Davíd Carrasco and Jane M. Swanberg, eds., *Waiting for the Dawn: Mircea Eliade in Perspective* (Boulder, Colorado: Westview Press, 1985), 48.

3. The philosophical schools of Athens, rooted in Classical Paganism, although developing in many different directions from it, lasted until 529 C.E. when Emperor Justinian suppressed them.

4. This is not to disallow individual exceptions. Buddhist monks, for example, may have reached Alexandria or other parts of the eastern Roman Empire, but their influence was not widespread.

5. One reason it is easy to over-emphasize the rational side of ancient Greek life is visual. We are so used to seeing all those chalky-white marble statues and buildings and their whiteness seems "cool" and "rational" in our symbolic vocabulary. But originally both the statues and the buildings were colorfully painted and gilded, something that the later Europeans who revived Greek and Roman styles did not realize at first, the paint having long since weathered away.

6. R. Gordon Wasson, Carl A.P. Ruck, and Albert Hofmann, *The Road to Eleusis: Unveiling the Secret of the Mysteries* (New York: Harcourt Brace Jovanovich, 1978). This large public religious event, held every two years at a sanctuary near Athens, began in the remote past and lasted at least until the fourth century C.E.

7. E. R. Dodds, *The Greeks and the Irrational* (Berkeley: University of California Press, 1951), 209.

8. Asiatic in origin, the Huns absorbed other races to the point that they had no definite ethnic or linguistic identity, particularly in their Western ranges.

9. Martin P. Nilsson, *Greek Folk Religion* (New York: Harper and Row, 1961 [1941]), 9.

10. Harold Bloom, *The American Religion: The Emergence of the Post-Christian Nation* (New York: Simon and Schuster, 1992), 51.

11. Dion Fortune, *The Sea Priestess* (New York: Samuel Weiser, 1978 [1938]), 221.

12. Consider how the hero Odysseus, homeward bound after the fall of Troy, first stops to raid and plunder the city of the Chicones, a Thracian people.

13. Walter Burkert, trans. John Raffan, *Greek Religion* (Cambridge: Harvard University Press, 1985), 299.

14. Burkert, 322.

15. Wasson, *et al.*, 20.

16. Carlo Ginzburg, trans. Raymond Rosenthal, *Ecstasies: Deciphering the Witches' Sabbath* (New York: Penguin, 1991 [1989]), 215.

17. To complicate the issue, processions of the dead were sometimes acted out—the origin of Halloween trick-or-treating by bands of "ghosts" and "witches."

18. Ginzburg, 102. For his study of the *benandanti* of Friuli, see his book *The Night Battles: Witchcraft and Agrarian Cults in the Sixteenth and Seventeenth Centuries* (New York: Penguin, 1985 [1966]).

19. Ginzburg, 104-105.

20. Ginzburg, 136.

21. Robert Graves, *The White Goddess* (Farrar, Straus, and Giroux, 1966 [1948]), 330-333.

22. Ginzburg, 232-233.

23. Ginzburg, 243.

24. Mircea Eliade, trans. Willard R. Trask, *Shamanism: Archaic Techniques of Ecstasy* (Princeton: Princeton University Press, 1964), 504-505. Through a series of connections, the *deus otiosus* may become the "god who disappears," causing a breakdown in the processes of life itself, creating the "wasteland" of Grail stories.

25. Eliade, 10.

26. Eliade, 508.

27. Eliade, 10. Anyone who thinks from this conclusion that Eliade must have been merely a limited, "patriarchal" thinker should then read the Great Goddess portions of his *A History of Religious Ideas* (Chicago: University of Chicago Press, 1978).

28. Aiden A. Kelly, *Crafting the Art of Magic Book 1: A History of Modern Witchcraft, 1939-1964* (St. Paul: Llewellyn Publications, 1991), 40. In the furor over Kelly's alleged betrayal of secrets and his suggestion that the rituals of Gardnerian Wicca reflected the sexual needs of its founder, Gerald Gardner, many critics ignored

this more important fact: twentieth-century Wicca is a new religion based on sacred sexuality.

29. Starhawk, *Dreaming the Dark: Magic, Sex, and Politics* (Boston: Beacon Press, 1982), 73.

30. For an introduction to the topic of sexual activity within a Wiccan framework, see Valerie Voigt, "Sex Magic," in Chas S. Clifton, ed., *Witchcraft Today, Book One: The Modern Craft Movement* (St. Paul: Llewellyn Publications, 1993), 85-108.

31. Eliade, 80-81.

32. Michael Taussig, *Shamanism, Colonialism, and the Wild Man: A Study in Terror and Healing* (Chicago: University of Chicago Press, 1987), 100.

33. Aiden A. Kelly, "An Update on Neopagan Witchcraft in America," in James R. Lewis and J. Gordon Melton, eds., *Perspectives on the New Age* (Albany: State University of New York Press, 1992), 136-151. Kelly estimated the American Neopagan population to be about 300,000 at the beginning of the 1990s.

Seeking Gitksan Shamanism

by Maggie Mountain Lion

Every Friday evening in summer, the dancers give a performance at the 'Ksan Indian Museum Village at Hazelton in
northern British Columbia. The speaker explains that the
format is based on the traditional potlach. It opens with a
welcome dance and includes dances depicting a shamanic
healing ritual, the throwing of power, and the dramatic
entry of a *naxnoq* (spiritual power being) in the form of a
grizzly bear.

"Potlach" is a word borrowed from the Kwakiutl people
of the coast and applied to an institution common to all the
First Nations of the Pacific Northwest. It means "give-
away." A potlach feast is held when a law is passed or an
agreement made, when a new chief is elevated, or to mark
any significant event. All the people are present to witness
what is said and done. They also witness the order of rank
and precedence, who sits in whose house, and all the protocols of this aristocratic culture. The chief who hosts the feast
gives lavish gifts to everyone present as payment for their
witness. These goods then become receivables; the other

chiefs are in his debt and must feast him in return. In a very real sense, this is a system of currency. The Indian agents had no understanding or tolerance of the idea that a chief demonstrated his wealth by what he could afford to give away. In 1884, an Act "further to amend the Indian Act, 1880, Section 3," stated that:

> Every Indian or other person who engages in or assists in celebrating the Indian festival known as the "Potlach"…is guilty of a misdemeanour, and shall be liable to imprisonment for a term of not more than six nor less than two months in any gaol or other place of confinement.

The same act also forbade the shamanic healing rituals. Ceremonial items were confiscated and many have never been returned. They may be found in museums and private collections. Although the ceremonies continued to be practiced in secret, this Act effectively cut the heart out of the West Coast civilizations. These provisions of the Act were not repealed until 1951, the same year that the Witchcraft law was repealed in Britain—an intriguing synchronicity.

I have been told that the last Gitksan shaman died in 1949, leaving no successor. She could not find a single young person who wanted to study with her. An elder who is also a chief told me that she was given an opportunity to study when she was young; she turned it down, and now regrets it. There are still healers, but one woman to whom I was referred politely but firmly refused to talk to me. I am *amsiwaa:* an outsider. However sympathetic and respectful, I remain on the outside looking in. I feel that I am closer to understanding their spirituality than most *amsiwaa*, because there are many obvious correspondences with my own Pagan practice, but I have barriers on my side, too.

I cannot tell them that I am a Witch, because that is the word the missionaries and anthropologists chose as the translation of *haldoygit:* a practitioner of evil magic. I prefer to talk to them about an ancient British culture that, like theirs, was matrilineal though not matriarchal, with totems and a clan structure, and a well-established spiritual tradition long before the missionaries arrived from foreign lands to the east. Because of what I do for a living, I judge it best to remain in the broom closet. I can sympathize with any *halaait* who feels the same way.

My home town stands at the confluence of two rivers. The Skeena ('Ksan) rises to the north of here, hangs a sharp right at the point where the Bulkley flows into it, and continues due west to its delta at Prince Rupert. Its name, 'Ksan, means Cloud Water, or River of Mists, and the Gitksan are the people of the River of Mists. They were the last people in all of Turtle Island (North America) to experience contact with people of European descent, in the last quarter of the nineteenth century; although they had heard about the newcomers from their neighbors and trading partners, the Wet'suwet'en to the east and the Coast Tsimshian from the delta.

The anthropologists write that the Gitksan are Tsimshian too. Their language is a dialect of Tsimshian. They have the same four clans—Eagle, Wolf, Raven and Killer Whale—but in the course of the migration up-river the Raven turned into a Frog and the Whale gave birth to the Fireweed.

"That's not true," a Gitksan woman firmly told me. "We are the Gitksan, and we have always been here."

When Europeans first began to explore the Americas, they must have been awed by the vastness of the land and the abundance of its resources, by comparison with the cramped, urbanized conditions of the Old World. There seemed to be no limit, and the need for conservation never occurred to them. We know better now, and it is surely no accident that the First Nations are experiencing a renaissance at this time when we need their knowledge of walking lightly upon the Earth.

In Canada, the Indian agencies and the missionaries worked together on a deliberate policy to eradicate the aboriginal cultures. Their methods were subtler than those employed by the United States, but just as effective.

Why didn't the Indians fight back? They certainly tried, but there are many reasons why they failed. They were not one great federation but many small nations who often went to war against each other. They had Stone Age weapons technology and no way to know the size of the problem they were dealing with. After the devastating epidemics of small-pox and measles and the introduction of alcohol by white traders, the populations were reduced to about one tenth of what they had been. At this point they were powerless to oppose road-builders, homesteaders, and the system of res-idential schools. I often compare their situation to that of Nazi-occupied Europe in the 1940s. There was resistance, and there was collaboration—often within the same family, with tragic results.

There is a myth which is widespread among the Native nations. It tells of the great love between Earth Mother and Sky Father, and of the four sons who were born to them. When the sons grew to manhood, they set out in the four di-rections. White Brother was expected to return some day, from strange lands across the sea, with tales of wonderful adventures and with many new things which would be ben-eficial to the people. When White Brother did indeed "re-turn," he was welcomed joyfully.

Because contact was so recent for the Gitksan, memory of the old ways is greener. I was introduced to a man who is 108 years old. Like most old people, he can remember his childhood better than the events of last week. He remembers stories that his grandparents told him about the precontact era. The Gitksan never forgot their *ada'ox*: the oral history of their clans and houses. In spite of the efforts of government, they have kept their system of hereditary chiefs.

The missionaries brought with them not only conflict between Christian beliefs and "heathen superstitions" but also conflict between the various denominations of Chris-tianity, which caused further rifts within villages and hous-es. They ran the residential schools to which the Indian agents sent children—often without their families' consent, and always without their informed consent. The children were beaten for speaking their own language and for any furtive attempts at traditional ceremony. Information about various kinds of abuse has only recently begun to surface. They were cut off from their own people and encouraged to despise their culture. The Native nations are now struggling with the consequences of these abuses.

On the authority of the notorious Act of 1884 (cited above), the various missions collected the totem poles together and publicly burned them as "objects of pagan worship." It seems not to have crossed their minds to ask the people what totem poles were about. If they had, it would have been explained to them that a pole is a sort of combined heraldic device and historical marker. Poles were erected to memorialize a chief or an important event. They were never religious objects. This is a common misconception; we get all our ideas about Indians from non-Indians sources, just as the general public gets its ideas about Witches from non-Craft sources.

There is a pole at 'Ksan which commemorates the agreement between the Gitksan nation and the Canadian government to set up the museum village. The topmost figure is a white man, conventionally depicted in tall hat and frock coat. The government representatives were pleased and flattered to be at the top. The Natives didn't trouble to explain to them that a pole is read from the bottom up! The whites made assumptions and were not about to be confused by mere facts, not unlike the preachers who are absolutely certain they know what goes on at a Witches' Sabbat even though they have never been to one.

I meet people who represent the whole spectrum of attitudes to religion. Some are devout evangelical Christians who will not permit their children even to learn which crests belong to their house. Many wish to preserve the culture as a reminder of their heritage but think of it in the past tense. A few are serious about reviving the old beliefs and practices, but they guard this from *amsiwaa*. As a Cheyenne medicine man said of medicine wheel sites on the prairies, "You don't talk about them because white people will go there and trash them."[1] Shades of Stonehenge! It grieves to me to be lumped in with such vandals.

Some Gitksan people can cope with the word pagan. A friend who has an academic degree is proud of her heritage. She described herself as a Pagan, and went on to tell me about the traditional Gitksan belief in reincarnation, which is still quite widely held. It appears to me that people who have broadened their horizons by travel or education are more inclined to value what they have at home while the simpler people know only that poles and crests are a part of their culture, but the missionaries liberated them from "superstition."

There is always the assumption that monotheism is a more highly evolved and somehow purer religion, not merely different but also better. Native religion is never assessed on its own terms but always in implied comparison to Christianity. In the *Jesuit Relations,* there is an account of a Huron who experienced a vision of a beautiful old man who came down from the sky, blessed him, and returned to the sky again. The *Relations* characterizes this apparition as a demon. Only Christians see angels.[2]

Shortly before the missionaries arrived, there arose prophets who foretold the coming of Christianity. There is a curious tale of a chief of the neighboring Wet'suwet'en people whose name was Bini. He lived around the middle of the nineteenth century. One day he disappeared, was found unconscious, and carried home. After he recovered, he reported that he had died and gone to heaven. God had sent him back to teach his people what they should do:

> You must chant my songs, for they are prayers; and you must make the sign of the cross. Things are going to change. You will hunt and fish for six days, but cease all work on the seventh.

Enter Father Morice of the Oblates of Mary Immaculate. A Christian Gitksan offered me this story as a proof that the people were supposed to abandon the old ways. A die-hard Pagan like me is not convinced. I want to know more details about Bini's disappearance, and how long his absence lasted. I think it may be just possible (but I have no way to prove it) that he had spent the time further east, at a mission.

I suspect but cannot prove that the spiritual traditions went underground and that remnants of them survived— even though they are always spoken of in the past tense. "Those who know do not speak."

There is anthropological evidence that shamanism among the Gitksan is very ancient, and a distinction is made between the shaman, an individual who is primarily a healer, and the initiates of the secret societies. It seems clear that the societies were imported from the coastal nations further south, some time during the eighteenth or nineteenth century—perhaps in response to colonization, like the Ghost Dance. Most people of good family were initiated into one or other of these societies. The initiation included an ordeal or vision quest, and possession is said to have been a feature of their rituals, which were closed to noninitiates.

By contrast, a shaman, a *swanaskxw halaait,* is perceived primarily as a healer. The office is not connected to rank or to house membership or to sex or to heredity, except insofar as a shaman's children and near relations are the most conveniently available apprentices. It is possible to inherit a shaman's power and ritual tools, even through a dream of the deceased shaman. Sometimes a man or a woman will decide to seek shamanic training. The great shamans, however, do not choose the power; it chooses them.

A shaman's first inkling of this choice is often an unsolicited vision and a loss of consciousness. He or she falls sick, and the sickness may persists for a long time. If he fights against the idea of becoming a shaman, his condition will grow worse, and he may die. I know personally of something similar to this happening to a member of another Native nation, a man destined for a priesthood who chose another way of life instead. He succeeded brilliantly in his chosen career, but the spiritual life of the people was impoverished and eventually he became ill and lost his gift. When a candidate for shamanism falls ill, he enlists the aid of other shamans to help him heal himself. By doing so, he acquires the power to heal others.

Those of us who have chosen—or been chosen by—a magickal lifestyle are inclined to believe this because it is analogous to our own experience. I think it is inaccurate to push the analogies too far, or to jump to the conclusion that the Craft and shamanism are essentially the same thing, but there is no doubt there are many correspondences between the two, and a knowledge of one furthers an understanding of the other.

Among the Gitksan, the initiatory vision typically involves the experience of death, often by drowning or by being eaten. The body rots away or is devoured until only the bones are left. The soul travels inside the earth, or under the water, perhaps to a cave inside a mountain, where he finds a house whose door shines as brightly as the sun. In this house dwell the *naxnoq:* the spirit beings from whom he gets his power. Sometimes it is freely given, but sometimes he must fight for it. Meanwhile his body lies in deep trance and the other shamans work to restore him to life. They sprinkle him with red ocher and sacred eagle down, and they sing their spirit songs.

He brings back with him a special song, which is his own personal property and may not be used by anyone else without his permission. He will also acquire a drum, a rattle, a soul-catcher, a fur robe, and a crown of grizzly bear or lynx claws. A Gitksan shaman, unlike those of other northwestern nations, never works in a mask.

Isaac Tens was a famous Gitksan shaman who flourished around seventy years ago. He told an ethnologist that at the age of about thirty he was out in the bush alone when he heard a strange sound. He looked up, and an owl swooped down on him, seized him by the face and tried to lift him. He lost consciousness.[3] When I heard this story, my skin started to crawl, because it reminded me of an evening years ago when I was called to the emergency room of the local hospital. My teenage son had been taken there by his friends. They had been walking after dark along a country lane, when my son passed out. He said a white ghost had appeared out of nowhere and swooped at his face. I suggested it might have been an owl, but he insisted that it was not. Whatever it was, he was badly frightened. The hospital staff assumed that he was "on" something. They tested him and found nothing. As far as I know, he has never experienced a follow-up to that event.

At the beginning of his or her career, a shaman sets off on a trance journey to find a spirit helper: *atiasxw*. The helper may be an animal, a spirit being, or even an object such as a canoe. Isaac Tens had an *atiasxw* which he described as an Otter Canoe. From his recorded account one gets the impression that the helper shape-shifted; that it appeared sometimes as an otter and at other times as a canoe. In its canoe form, it could take him on spirit journeys underwater or into the sky.

In this single example, there are three elements that we work with in the Craft. Astral, or out-of-body, journeying was an important part of the shaman's practice. He traveled in this way to find his spirit helpers and later, with their guidance, to seek knowledge and to retrieve lost souls. Spirit guides are not unknown to us, either, though they are not necessarily the same phenomenon as familiars. Shape-changing is frequently referred to in the transcripts of the witchcraft trials of Europe, where not only the helpers but also the Witches themselves were supposed to have taken on animal forms: "Oh, I shall go into a hare…All to fetch him home again."

Both shape-shifting and astral journeying are grounded in the belief that a soul is an autonomous entity. It can exist without the body, although the reverse is not true. It can incarnate more than once, exchanging one body for another. In a multidimensional reality, essence is not bound to form.

What is important is not "what you are made of," but "what you are."[4] In shamanic belief, living beings freely transform themselves and communicate with other species. When the salmon return to their houses in the sea, they resume their human form.

One shaman described how she became a rope made of light, which stretched from the remote past far into the future. She would rub herself against the knot in her patient's rope until it was smoothed away.

A shaman's first experiences of the power might be ecstatic, but he learned to control it in order to work with it. When he felt ready to claim his power, he announced his new status in the feast house by performing his song and his dance. The community witnessed and acknowledged his claim to power and his ownership of the songs and dances. He took a new name, for use only when performing shamanic functions. His public name, rank and seat in the feast house did not change. The shaman's sacred and secular identities remained separate.

One of Isaac Tens' songs, in translation, goes: "The Chief of the Salmon is floating in the canyon underneath me." The canyon is on the boundary between the Gitksan and Wet'suwet'en territories. There used to be a huge boulder in it. Every year, when the salmon people ran upriver to spawn, they would stop for a while to dance at this rock. The people took the opportunity to catch many of them while they were dancing. It was crucial to collect all the bones and put them back in the river so they could reincarnate and return to dance again the next year. About forty years ago, the Department of Fisheries, in its superior wisdom, decided the dancing rock impeded the salmon run, so they blasted it to smithereens (a slight exaggeration: the town of Smithers is 68 km. away!). After that, the salmon hurried upstream without stopping to dance and the fishing village had to be abandoned.

I was once asked to undertake a shamanic trance-journey, along with two other priestesses, to find a spirit helper for a sister. We used a drumming tape, and I remember thinking that the drumming was intrusive and preventing me from getting into trance. At the next instant, it seemed, I was floating about the canyon—above the rock, which I never saw in ordinary reality—and there were many silver salmon leaping around it. I cannot know, of course, if it really looked as I saw it in my trance, but the vision was very clear and precise and quite unexpected; I was far away from home at the time. I brought the salmon back for my sister, and only afterwards did I find out that she loved to swim.

Marie-Francoise Guedon[5] makes the distinction that while possession was a typical feature of the secret society rituals, the shaman usually used only light trance—a dissociation state—in the healing rituals, remaining aware of both realities at the same time. He remained in control of his own mental state and of his spirit helpers. They were servants, not masters.

It is believed that a *haldoygit* cannot shape-change and has no spiritual helpers. They are the practitioners of evil magic, men and women who work alone and in secret. It is forbidden to talk about them, I am told, and nobody knows who they are. Their motive is malice, and they work with the universal elements of folk magic: hair and nail parings, poppets, and so on. The anthropologists and the missionaries translated *haldoygit* as witch, of course. It is remarkable that these beliefs are so widespread. Even people who deny the validity of the old spirituality believe in "witchcraft." It is always useful to have an Other to blame for one's bad luck. I know a woman who is a high chief, a respected elder, and a practicing Catholic. Someone with whom she quarreled spread the rumor that she was *haldoygit*. If such a rumor reached my ears, it must have been all through the community first.

The society values the shaman because he is seen primarily as a healer. He performs an important service to his community, unlike the *haldoygit* who is antisocial. But the process of becoming a shaman transforms the individual and his worldview in ways similar to those in which Craft training and initiation have transformed me. This transformation is not sudden. A process of gradual change is initiated and continues. I am acutely aware of the abundant life force surrounding me, and I know I can draw energy from it and direct (or bend) the flow of that energy. I think the shamanic experience is like this and, if that is true, then service to the community as a healer must be secondary to personal growth.

According to Gitksan tradition, an illness may be caused by an evil influence, by a foreign body, or by soul loss. Any of these may be the result of *haldoygit* magic. A soul may become weak. It may wander away and be unable to find its way back. It may be scared away by a trauma of any sort or stolen by a rival. If they are understood not literally but metaphorically, these explanations are not totally at odds with the diagnoses of modern Western medicine.

Disease is thought of as an entity, and some powerful healers can see it. There is a story of a shaman who entered a house where several shamans were dancing. He saw a ghost dancing among them and predicted that one of them was going to die. Sure enough, one of them died a few hours later.

On one occasion years ago, I saw a grey cloud hover over a person and slowly envelop her. She lost consciousness and when she recovered she had no dream or trance memory. "I was just gone," she said. If I had known then what I have learned since, I would have recognized that cloud as the illness which manifested shortly afterwards and eventually caused her death. There was probably nothing I could have done to prevent it. I mention the incident to demonstrate an independent experience of seeing a disease.

Among the Gitksan, when a person fell ill, the family would ask a shaman to perform a healing ceremony. The principal shaman usually enlisted the help of several others to assist him. They prepared themselves by fasting and sometimes by purgation also as well as by ritual cleansing and sexual continence. They put on their fur robes and claw headdresses and entered the house where the patient was lying. The whole family would be present. The shamans painted their faces and those of everyone in the house with red ocher. They put eagle down on their headdresses so that it was shaken over people as they danced. The ocher is for physical health and the down for spiritual. The use of a red earth element and a white spirit element brings to mind the symbolism of the alchemists.

The shaman began to sing his healing songs, accompanied by rattle and drum. The drum was made exactly like a *bodhran*, a circle of birchwood with a skin stretched over one side and crossed thongs in back to hold it by. As they danced, everyone joined in the singing. The patient was also expected to participate as much as he was able. Sometimes a person healed in such a ceremony would go on to become a healer too.

After a soul had been retrieved, it might be weakened by its ordeal. The shaman would blow gently on it as though it were an ember or hold it in his mouth for a while. If he had diagnosed the condition as the intrusion of a foreign body, he would suck the affected part until he got it out. He showed the object to the patient and to the other people present, as proof of the cure. It might be a small crystal or a sliver of wood or some other small thing. European observers are quick with their accusations of trickery and dismiss the whole business as a fraud. The shaman would probably say that simple folk need to deal with the concrete. He made use of the placebo effect.

Sometimes a drama was enacted, using a puppet to represent the disease entity. In difficult cases the shaman might enter a trance state and go to the world of the *naxnoq* for instructions. During the influenza epidemic of 1915, a shaman from the village of Kispiox received a prescription from an entity named Disease Woman, which he then sent to all the villages.

It was in Kispiox that a friend of mine attended a healing ceremony when she was a little girl in the 1930s. The patient was her mother who, as she lay on her sickbed, saw a skeletal hand at the window. She was taken to the house of healing, which was in the bush at a little distance from the village, because the old ways were still outlawed at the time. There were several shamans present. They danced and drummed and shook rattles while all the people sang. At some point during the ceremony, the patient saw the same skeletal hand again. She recovered completely and lived to an advanced age.

My friend's recollection is that of a child observing the mysterious goings-on of the grownups, which nobody explained to her. Children were not usually present at such ceremonies, she told me. I suppose they might innocently betray the illegal activity. She added that the house was later raided by the police.

It is important to note that shamans expected to be paid for performing healing rituals, usually on a sliding scale according to the seriousness of the illness and the patient's ability to pay. There are even accounts of shamans who were not satisfied with the payment offered and made the patient sick again! Recovery was not expected to be instantaneous, but if the patient did not improve after a reasonable period of time, or if he died, the shaman returned his fee.

Although healing rituals were the most important part of the shamans' practice, they also used local plants as herbs of protection, purification and healing. There is no evidence that plants were ever used to alter one's state of consciousness; this was done by drumming, singing, dancing, fasting and, probably, by breathing techniques. Plants are still used in the traditional ways as medicine, but what we would call the "magickal" uses of them were discouraged and either died out or went underground.[6]

One of the most valued of all the medicinal herbs is devil's club (*Oplopanax horridus*), which is a member of the ginseng family. The stems are gathered after the first snowfall of October. The inner bark is used in infusions and decoctions. It may be chewed or used in a poultice. It can be dried for storage. Devil's club is used in the treatment of rheumatism, ailments of the respiratory system, stomach ulcers, diabetes and some cancers, as well as for dressing open wounds. An elder from the village of Kitwancool claimed to have cured his arthritis by chewing devil's club every day for a month. It is sometimes mixed with other barks, such as those of alder, mountain ash or spruce, because it is so strong. In combination with the root of the yellow pond lily, it is used to treat tuberculosis. It is often taken as a general tonic, and it is also used for spiritual purification, in hunting rituals, and as a smudge to protect against *haldoygit* and other evil influences.

The yellow pond lily (*Nuphar polysepalum*) is abundant in the local small lakes. The rhizome is the part used. In May, they are often found floating on the surface, where beavers have dug them up. The rhizomes are sliced and skewered on sticks, like shish kebab, to dry. The dried slices may then be powdered. An infusion is made from the slices, or the powder may be sprinkled on food. This plant has been used in the past as a contraceptive, and it was believed that too much might make a man impotent.

The roots of Indian hellebore (*Veratrum viride*), which the Gitksan call *mulgwis,* are gathered in the fall and dried for storage. This is an herb of purification as well as healing. It is used as a smudge to purify a house and to banish evil spirits. It can be added to the water used for laundering clothes, and it is used in purification rituals before setting out on hunting or trapping expeditions. Some people carry a piece as a good luck talisman. It must be gathered by someone who is in a properly respectful frame of mind. A brief prayer is said and an appropriate small offering is left in its place.

Not far from here there is a rehabilitation center for chemical addictions, which is run by and for Native people in their traditional ways—or as near to their traditional ways as they can remember. One of their most useful tools is the sweat lodge. The Gitksan sweat lodge was always a solitary practice. One of the elders told me she remembers seeing an old man trudging through the snow to his private sweat. The children mocked him, and her mother reprimanded them. They should respect what he was doing, she said, because it was a holy thing. Nowadays the Gitksan are relearning the sweat lodge ceremonies from the Cree, whose tradition is for a group sweat, led by a pipe carrier. My friend who works at the center has had this training. She was surprised and pleased, she told me, when someone called her a medicine person, because she had not presumed to claim that title for herself. She finds the sweat very powerful; it connects her as nothing else does to the ancestors. Once, in the total darkness, she opened her eyes and saw the green auras of all the other people in the lodge, then she saw tiny stars dancing among them. At first she thought they must be sparks from the fire, but her teacher assured her she had seen spirits.

She described to me how a coworker had stumbled upon a healing technique which was shamanic in nature. A patient was choking with grief. The healer kept hitting his back, urging him to cough it up. As he coughed, a strong smell of garbage came out of his mouth; a smell so foul the healer gagged. Then the patient began to weep. As the tears flowed freely, his grief and anger were released and his healing begun.

In one especially powerful healing session, the people present could all hear a woman weeping. The staff thought she might be a former patient who had died shortly after leaving the center. My friend smudged the room with *mulgwis*, and the weeping went away. She smudges frequently with *mulgwis*, and with sage (*Artemisia*, not *Salvia*), which is a Cree tradition, to keep the place cleansed of the negative energy which is released there. She has recently begun the habit of smudging herself daily (again, a practice borrowed from her Cree teachers). She finds that she is more aware, more sensitive, and even that her aging eyesight and hearing are improved. She emphasizes the need for the healer to cleanse and replenish her own energy. A Sarcee man told her: "When you leave [the healing circle], take your spirit with you—all of it."

Although she claims descent from shamans and a belief that the ability is inherited, she told me she doesn't know of any shamans now practicing among the Gitksan. She is rediscovering and relearning ceremonies and techniques which "feel right." Here, again, is a comparison with our own experience. Probably we have all, at some time, had that insightful moment when we think: "Ah, yes, it must have been like this." It's not evidence; not the kind that convinces scholars and skeptics, anyway. It is valid only for the person who receives the insight, but it works.

Nowadays one still hears Gitksanamxw spoken in the post office and general store. It is being taught in the schools now, but there are few fluent speakers among the young people, while the elders have difficulty explaining the old ways in English. At a function I attended, a respected elder was asked to give an invocation. She prayed in Gitksanamxw and afterwards I asked her what she had said. She thought for a minute and then replied, "It doesn't translate." The language is complex and hard for English speakers to learn. There are layers of meaning which one would need to grasp in order to achieve a deep understanding of the spiritual aspects of the culture.

Take the word *halaait*, for example. It means spiritual or psychic power, and it also refers to the person who wields such power. It is usually translated as "healer," but there is a lot more to it than that. Guedon speculates that it may be related to a root word meaning "to spin." That sets off a whole train of associations for me. A *halaait* raises power by, among other things, dancing, and this puts me in mind of the circle and spiral dances of the Craft.

While any spiritual practitioner may be called *halaait*, a shaman, as we have defined him in this discussion, is a *swanaskxw halaait*. *Swanaskxw* means wind, breath, spirit: life. A shaman restores health by sucking, by blowing, or by spitting water, as well as by singing. The shaman mask, which was danced in the potlach but never in the healing ceremony, is always characterized by a puckered mouth.

One of the shaman's ritual tools was a "soul-catcher," which is usually a hollow piece of bone carved or painted with a face at either end and incorporating the hole as the mouth in the design. He used it to blow through.

He prepared himself by fasting and purging, so that his physical body might become a clear channel for the *halaait* power. (One famous shaman of the past was called Mouth at Each End.) Modern Gitksan healers use the laying-on of hands, which is clearly an adaptation to the ideas of the missionaries, who were not comfortable with orifices.

Is shamanism a religion? It depends on your definition. Guedon decides it is not, on the grounds that it does not incorporate "a formally recognized and accepted body of beliefs and moral principles, nor does it control the moral state of a community."

I do not know if Dr. Guedon practices a religion, but it is likely that she grew up in an environment with at least a background of Judeo-Christian culture. She assumes that a religion has a formal credo and it is supposed to control social morality. A spiritual path which does not aspire to either of these things is not a "real" religion. This verdict will certainly sound familiar to Neopagans.

Shamanism is a spiritual discipline which begins with an initiation into alternative realities and results in a transformation, which may be manifested in this mundane reality by means of the ritual raising of power. Similar, though not identical, claims may be made for the Craft. By my criteria, sha-manism is indeed a religion.

The people who want to restore the old ways are working with the fragments of a broken oral tradition. It will never again be what it was, but it may evolve into something appropriate for the modern context. In this, too, I see a similarity to the Neopagan movement.

Academics are not the only people who have trouble with the notion of other realities. Experience in that mode is explained away. The culture is then devalued as a kind of self-defense. To accept the challenge of these ideas involves changing the way one looks at the world. This in turn necessitates changes in one's value system and priorities. It is difficult and frightening. Those of us who call ourselves Witches with a capital W have already been through something like this, and our personal experience validates for us the shamanic journey.

Notes

1. Andrew Nikiforuk, "Sacred Circles," *Canadian Geographic* July-August 1992.
2. Diamond Jeness, *The Indians of Canada* (Ottawa: National Museum of Canada, 1932).
3. C. Marius Barbeau, *Medicine Men of the North Pacific Coast* (Ottawa: National Museum of Canada, 1958).
4. Marie-Francoise Guedon, "World View and Shamanism," in Margaret Seguin, ed., *The Tsimshian: Images of the Past: Views for the Present* (Vancouver: University of British Columbia, 1984).
5. Ibid.
6. Leslie M. Johnson Gottesfeld and Beverly Anderson, "Gitksan Traditional Medicine: Herbs and Healing," *Journal of Ethnobiology* 8:1, 13-33.

About the Author

Born in England, Maggie Mountain Lion has lived in Canada for nearly forty years. She first visited northern British Columbia as a tourist and was so attracted by the area that she settled there, living in a town inhabited mainly by First Nations people. She works in a school and has three cats and three grandchildren.

© Malcolm Brenner/Eyes Open (photography)
and Zelda Gordon (collage composition)

Where New Pagans and Modern Cultural Beliefs Collide

by George Dew (Kahóte)

An Amerind (American Indian or Native American) friend of mine, Tony Shearer, recently pointed out over coffee that the Spirit Worlds are "rushing toward us all the time right in front of us" regardless of our genetic heritage or spiritual path if we can merely relax and allow ourselves to open up without placing false visualization barriers and overly complex ritual procedures between ourselves and the Presences.

Less than a week before I wrote this, one of my beginning students came to class and reported the following experience. Leaving a crowded shopping mall, he did a simple "Sky above and Earth below, I greet you" ritual, not intending to communicate with the Earth Mother or any other deity, but merely to stabilize and ground himself. He was confronted by a person-high Eagle form that gave him a warm friendly mental greeting and then vanished—all in the middle of a shopping center parking lot at midday. This can be a typical kind of experience if we, as Tony suggested, quit worrying about religiously doing this or that rite with its visualizations and motions, and just be with the Earth.

The student's experience partly answers the question why the interest in Earth Religion continues to grow. While mainstream religious systems promote at length the idea that "ordinary humans" may have contact with deity-beings and the "higher levels" only through the efforts of a priest or by some "special dispensation" by God, the majority of Earth religions teach that virtually any person may have direct personal contact with deity(ies) at virtually any time without need of intercession or help by a priest or priestess; the only requirement is that the person is undertaking to be connected to the Earth.

In addition, most Earth religion paths train everybody to perform all the rites that might be needed in a practitioner's usual living so that the need for priestesses or priests only arises when there are group rites or teaching to be done or special and unusual individual circumstances to be dealt with, the individual's personal relationships with deity and the spirit-realms thus being truly a personal matter between the individual and deity.

Unfortunately, I have encountered too many instances where a supposedly "higher-level" practitioner—priestess, priest, teacher, sweat-leader, or whoever—has not broken her or his mainstream conditioning and, as a result, has been unable to accept the fact that someone not yet "properly initiated" or "ritually prepared" may have had a real communication with The Mother or one of her agents.

As a case in point, less than a year ago a lady came to consult with me after the following experience. She had attended two or three Wiccan introductory meetings and then had been invited by a friend who was studying Amerind ways to visit a *Yuwipi* healing gathering conducted by a traditional Amerind practitioner.

This ceremony involves the gathering together of one or more persons in need of healing plus their relatives and friends in an enclosed area, either a sweat lodge or a relatively large and private room in a barn or a house. The area and the attendees are ritually cleansed, the area is darkened, and prayers and invocations to the Spirit Worlds are made. Then the healing operator is wrapped and bound in hides or blankets to conduct direct communications with the invoked Spirits relative to the desired healings for the designated persons for which the ceremony is being performed.

To return to the story, while she was sitting in the pitch-dark of the crowded room, listening to the prayer chants of the other attendees, and noticing a lot of energy effects and mysterious noises, the lady was suddenly confronted visually by a large owl-form that empathically gave her answers to some spiritual questions she had had for some time and then physically stroked her with its wings before disappearing into the darkness after telling her she could call on it for guidance in the future.

None of her previous Christian and social background nor her brief meeting with Wicca nor what her friend had told her about the *Yuwipi* having prepared her for such an experience, she was understandably shaken by the experience. After the *Yuwipi* was over, she approached the Amerind practitioner about what happened to her. Satisfied as to her experience's validity, he told her that she now had owl medicine if she wished to use it and gave her several contact procedures to use for later private communications with the owl spirit. What he could not grasp, as a traditional practitioner, was her Christian-influenced reaction of "I'm not worthy!" and "But I didn't earn it!" nor was he unwilling to stop the other, mostly nonwhite participants from expressing their own disbelief at this "outsider's" experience.

When she sought further guidance from the Wiccan priestess who had given the introductory lessons, she was told that what happened could not possibly have happened to a noninitiate, much less a mere visitor to an Amerind rite. Even if she had been a Wiccan initiate, she would have had to be an initiate of at least second-degree attainment.

Consequently, by the time she talked with me, her underlying belief that she was not spiritual enough to have "earned" not only the attention of but a gift from deity had

combined with these negative and unchallenged evalua-
tions from both the other *Yuwipi* participants and the priestess. The combination created a situation that required
almost six months of counseling plus some hands-on magickal training until she could happily and effectively incorporate Earth-religion practices smoothly and productively
into her life and regain the "coming home" feeling she had
had at the time that she attended her first Wicca classes.

Intellectually, people find the traditional Earth-religion
viewpoint that each individual is "all right" for being human
and being on the planet regardless of his or her devoutness to
be attractive. But it is emotionally difficult to internalize this
viewpoint in the face of mainstream standards that subtly
and pervasively communicate the idea that in order to be
"spiritual" or "worthy" of spiritual communication, we
must somehow become something Other than what we are.

Thus, when we get ourselves in one or another situation
where we are open and grounded—be it an esbat, sabbat,
sweat, vision-seek, or merely some nonspecific grounding
or centering procedure—and have a "face-to-face" with the
Mother or one or another of her agents, we have great emotional difficulty accepting that we did "deserve" the contact,
regardless how much we may have hoped for it, and in spite
of the fact that its happening is evidence of our "deserving"
in the eyes of whatever beings were involved.

For traditional practitioners more or less uncontaminat-
ed by mainstream culture, the student who had the experience with the eagle spirit and the lady who had the owl
experience did deserve what occurred, or it would not have
happened, regardless of whether or not priests or anyone
else—including the recipients—could see or explain exactly
how it came to be deserved or earned.

As a summary of the discussion to this point, if you decide that Wicca or some other Earth religion feels right
somehow for you, that feeling is probably accurate; however, that does not mean that at the point where you are beginning to truly connect with the Earth and the Mother, you

will not have one or another experience that may be a real shock to the unrecognized, inculcated beliefs that you got by osmosis merely by existing in this place and time. This is true regardless of your genetic heritage—white, red, yellow, black, or tan. If you were not raised in a more or less traditional tribal environment of some kind, truly "getting back to the earth" may well include some surprises, no matter how right it is as your personal path.

One of the more difficult things for a modern North American who gets involved with any form of Earth religion—Wiccan, Druidic, Amerind, or any other—is the difficulty of crediting the manifesting of spirit beings, call them divine or otherwise, as real and actual in the external environment, especially if they manifest without your having done some complex or age-old ritual "by the book." In traditional teachings, if you experience some manifestation in your external environment, then that did happen as perceived without regard to whether or not some authority could explain "the whichness-of-the-what" of it in terms of the known mechanisms of the material side of the Universe.

As an eight-year-old ranch kid in northwestern Wyoming in the mid-1940s, I had been impressed with the idea that sheer survival in the mountains depends on one's trusting the evidences of one's own senses. Therefore, I was sure that whatever "thing" larger than me that one evening leapt across a small campfire at me as I was looking across the valley in the dusk after a long day working as part of a haying crew was not merely a fantasy. My horse, tied to a tree some thirty yards away, was seriously upset and wanted to leave forthwith, clearly indicating he also had experienced that presence as reality, whether or not it had a physical body. It was almost four decades later that an Earth-guardian spirit more or less humorously answered, "Woke you up so you could get Here, didn't it?" when I thought to inquire if that event had been for some purpose of the Mother's.

Because of most urban dwellers' cultural backgrounds, Wiccan groups (depending on the group, of course), may be

easier on your systems than undertaking to jump into
Amerind or other tribal practices, since many of the Wiccan
groups, particularly those tracing their lineage to Alexandrian or Gardnerian approaches, have some preinitiation procedures and contemplations that will help you identify and
modify some of the aspects of your social conditioning that
might otherwise get severely jolted by real experiences with
the Mother and her agents.

Another concept that can be both fascinating and trou-
bling for a modern person is the matter of learning and
using "magic," or "magick," as many practitioners now
spell it in order to differentiate it from stage magic. According to many tribal traditions, two sciences came into being
at the time of Creation: religion, which is the study of humanity's relationships, collectively and individually, with
those other spiritual beings who are part of the spiritual
ecology of our environment; and magick, which is the study
of spirit abilities and the applications of those to the handling of the energies of Air, Fire, Water, and Earth in both
our daily affairs and our religious communications with
deity, a science often referred to in older traditions as being
necessary to the effective practice of any religion.

If we take the view that deities are spirit beings who have
evolved to a higher and different level of existence than that
of humans, then if human prayers and invocations and so on
are to, in fact, reach the intended recipient, these messages
must be sent in a directed manner with particular energies.
Just as if you were to undertake to telephone someone, you
must set up certain energy frequencies in the telephone system that will cause the intended recipient's telephone to
ring and establish an "energy bridge" with your telephone.

The ancients were also aware that in order for our level
and the deity levels to interact without seriously disturbing
the balances between the various existence levels, we need
to make the energies of this level available to deity for use in
communicating and acting in our levels in order that our
level not become overcharged and the deity-levels drained.

In this connection, you might find it interesting that some esoteric Christian traditions view the "Lord's Prayer," given by Christ to the disciples, as an instruction in how to pray: what energies to take in, how that is to be done, how the energies are to be "programmed" so as to carry the message, and how the energies are to be released so they will go to the intended recipient. It is only superficially a suggestion as to what one is to pray for or about.

Traditions that discuss magick as the science necessary to effective religious practice also teach that it is proper to use magick in everyday life for self-balance, self-protection, healing, and providing of necessary food, clothing and shelter for oneself and for one's community, with this being done either by individual procedures or by group rites and rituals. depending on the need and the circumstances.

While tribal peoples learn to consciously recognize and handle the basic Air, Fire, Water, and Earth energies as just a normal part of life from the time of conception onward, our cultural system has a history of negating and invalidating not only existence of the energies themselves but also our human competence to handle them. It expends large amounts of energy suppressing the knowledge and practice of magick—up to and including in some cases torturing and killing anyone who manifested abilities in magickal technology. All this leads to an almost inborn avoidance of the conscious developing of one's natural human magickal awareness and abilities.

Several years ago, I was struck by the response of a Central American shaman, interviewed in the magazine *Shaman's Drum*, that summed up the situation as I have experienced it. The interviewer asked what the shaman thought of the practice of magick in North America, and he replied that it terrified him because in North America, no one believed in magick, so no one understood it, and everyone was doing it.

Too many modern Wiccan priestesses and priests lack sufficient real magickal training to even enable them to perform effective religious rites, much less utilize magick effectively on a moment-to-moment, day-to-day basis. A few years ago, several of my more experienced students were invited to what was advertised as a traditional Wiccan Hallowmass, to be led by a supposedly well-trained third-degree priestess and priest, the ritual to be a "full-cast challenge circle" open only to experienced Witches.

Such a procedure is usually only used when there are very important and high-energy rites to be performed. Participants wait outside the ritual circle while it is first cleansed by the operators with the energies of Air, Fire, Water, and Earth; then the operators construct energy walls, one with each element, enclosing the circle, following this by drawing on the floor or ground with a knife (athame) or sword an electric-blue energy line with an entry left temporarily unsealed at some point in the perimeter, usually at the northeast, the purpose being to wall off the circle from the external environment in both the material and the spiritual levels of the Universe.

The waiting participants then approach the entry from outside the circle, are stopped there by a knife pointed at the heart, and asked one or more questions that must be answered correctly in order for them to be allowed into the circle. The challenge generally used to ensure that no one who has issues with other participants or who has reservations about participating will be in the circle. Once all are within the circle, the "door" is closed by completion of the electric-blue energy-line across the gap.

If you are not familiar with the Wiccan ritual calendar, Hallowmass is not just a New Year's celebration usually involving the invoking of the presence of the Goddess into the body of the priestess. It is also supposed to be the last time for the participants to communicate with and bid farewell to the spirits of any departed family or friends who have "passed over" during the year. The spirits of the departed are supposed to appear outside the ritual circle. In the Wiccan view, the delicacies of both of these procedures require a fully cast ritual circle. The invocation of guardian presences

(Watchtowers) is not only important religiously but also magickally mandatory for the safety of all concerned.

At the Hallowmass rite to which my students had been invited, it became obvious that although the motions of circle-casting had been done, no real energies had been laid down by the operators, and that the Watchtowers were merely thought-form projections (visualizations) of the operators instead of being actual invoked guardian presences. Thus, there was no protection of the ritual area and participants against unwanted negative energies and improper intrusion into the circle by ghosts and other nondivine spirits.

As the ceremony progressed, not only did the ghosts of two departed suddenly appear *inside* the circle trying to attach themselves to their living relatives, but the out-of-body spirit of a living exhusband suddenly showed up in the circle and undertook to attack his exwife. These manifestations were perceived by at least four participants, in addition to the three participants actually attacked. To make matters worse, the high priestess and high priest were apparently completely unaware of the intrusions until other people who had some real magickal training banished the intruders with "Get out!" commands reinforced by energy-bolts thrown from their hands.

If the circle had been cast with real elemental energies, it should have kept the various spirits outside where they properly belonged; and if not, real Watchtowers would not have permitted either the ghosts or the spirit of the estranged living exhusband to enter the circle.

Reconstructing the experience with my students, I verified that the operators had made all the right motions and said all the right words and so on that were called for in casting the circle "by the book;" however, they clearly had not done so from a viewpoint wherein magick, the Watchtower presences and other spirits were real outside of their own visualizations and intentions (read hopes). While such a "form without content" disaster is regrettable, it is a logical byproduct of the intense cultural brainwashing against the reality of spirits and magickal technology that I have been discussing and which the ritual operators had obviously not escaped from in the course of their practice—regardless of its duration.

Regrettably, modern Wiccan practice in general seem to be deteriorating in the direction of doing the procedures in the direction of "form without content" as a result of buying unconsciously and without question our culture's "scientific" viewpoint of the nonexistence of nonphysical beings and real magick and so on. If not reversed, this deterioration will soon lead to Wicca being as spiritually unfulfilling as mainline Christianity, as far as the public is concerned.

Much of the appeal of traditional shamanism and other tribal practices these days, to Wiccans and to others, lies in the fact that their native practitioners, while in some ways having their own "cookbook" problems, produce real magickal and spirit-contact phenomena, mainly as a result of their not having accepted the viewpoint that the effects are solely dependent upon their ability to visualize and project the desired manifestations for the participants to experience, but rather depend upon the operators' ability to handle the appropriate energies and "dial the right number on the telephone," as it were, with real elemental energies in order to contact real external beings.

Several years ago I unexpectedly was invited by an Amerind sweat-lodge leader to participate as an elder in an "elders' lodge," a sweat being held for the purpose of "debriefing" a white woman as a completion of her four-day vision quest. Though the cleansed and purified area in which the lodge was located was unmarked and extended a radius some one hundred yards out from the lodge—out of sight of the lodge—there was distinct energy change when I crossed the area's boundary. The actual wind directions and temperature were different inside the area from outside it, just as one would experience in a properly cast Wiccan circle.

During the ceremony inside the lodge (Boy, is it dark and hot in a good sweat!), there seemed to be plenty of room for all the participants right up to the time when the sweat leader began doing invocations to a wide array of spirits, at which point the lodge began feeling really crowded. The darkness became filled with vague indescribable colors and energy-forms—mostly in what we normally think of as the ultraviolet spectrum. I had sensations of being periodically touched and brushed against on my face, chest and back, even though none of the human participants was moving. These effects persisted until the leader thanked the spirits for attending, at which time the lodge became adequately roomy again.

Aside from the leader, all of the half dozen people reported experiencing similar effects, and three said they were suddenly confronted by visible and identifiable (to the participant) animal or bird forms that gave them messages, much in the way of the owl spirit and the woman at the *Yuwipi* Ceremony I described earlier.

In my own and others' experience, while the Watchtower presences in a Wiccan ceremony do not usually behave in the somewhat rowdy manner of spirits in a sweat lodge or a *Yuwipi* ceremony or some of the other tribal rites, the energy effects and the feeling of presence at each of the four directions where they are supposed to manifest is much the same if the invocations are done to real beings rather than to projected visualizations, with these beings more often than not manifesting a detailed visual only for specific participants with whom one or another Watchtower would have private conversation, again like the spirits I mentioned in connection with the *Yuwipi* and sweat-lodge ceremonies.

In the interests of effective magickal religion, more practitioners on the Wiccan and other Earth-religion paths must develop renewed interest in learning and using the technology of real magick, regardless what of our modern scientific establishment may have to say about how real or not the elemental energies and the deities may be. This concerns you, the reader, should you decide to follow or be already following such a path.

Any Earth religion is a matter of daily living of the path. It is not a matter of application only in coven or at ceremonies; it is a way of life that one must "eat, breath, and sleep." Hence, I would suggest that modern Wiccans, both female and male, need to devote a lot more energy and effort than has occurred in the last decade or so to recognizing and undoing their social conditioning and "walking their talk." Whether we consider the Celtic, Pictish, Druidic or whatever other tribal peoples' systems, or even the Classical Greek, Roman, or Egyptian systems, it seems to me that the real keys to their effectiveness for their practitioners lay in their day-to-day "walking their talk" and in their basic energy awareness and energy-handling moment by moment, whatever activity they were engaged in.

Today, modern Wicca has the most potential currently available for helping us heal ourselves and Mother Earth— if Wiccan priestesses, priests, and practitioners can bring themselves to do the personal work needed to get past the conditioning against the reality of the spirit realms and magickal technology.

One last block to modern Wiccans "walking their talk" is an often unconscious assent to attitudes of male supremacy. Even as various Pagan traditions teach the primacy of the feminine in combination with the rites being conducted toward and in the name(s) of the Goddess, too many priestesses let their priests be the actual "power behind the throne" in covens and rituals, and too many Wiccan women just cannot seem to make themselves assert their rights with men—husbands, sons, bosses, others. There also seem to me to be too many devout Wiccan men who still sabotage women in unthinking and habitual socially acceptable ways.

Destroying one's social conditioning seems like a large order at first glance; however, it seems to me that it might become a lot smaller if more Wiccan practitioners would study basic magickal technology and thus tap into their natural basic human capacities to consciously know and manipulate the basic Air, Fire, Water, and Earth energies "hands-on" from moment-to-moment. Aid is available for anyone who accepts the reality of the Goddess, the Watchtower presences and others of the Goddess's agent-spirits in the external environment.

By doing the "deconditioning," one becomes much more adaptable to the Mother's environment and much less in need of protection from it, to say nothing of practical matters like getting along without conflict in high-energy situations or in getting rid of fevers, healing body damages rapidly, and minimizing sprains, burns, headaches, and so forth with minimal need for the plethora of medications and supportive treatments promoted by modern medicine.

From my own experience, it is really nice to be able to warm oneself in cold weather and cool oneself in hot weather, or to not have blisters from spilled hot liquids or bruises from smashed toes or fingers, or to not get "wired" if someone "blasts" me with high-energy emotional tensions, or to be able to "pass through" or "dump" energies from sources such as televisions, computers, microwave ovens, fluorescent-light ballasts and so on...and on...and on.

When it comes to communicating with the Mother, her guardians, land spirits, totem spirits, and other beings in our spiritual ecology, a little bit of conscious awareness and basic energy-handling so as to be actually harmonious and connected with the Earth wherever you are will go a long way toward your having real spirit-contact experiences such as I have mentioned earlier, with no need for visualizations or projections or complex ritual procedures. Additionally, your magickal and religious workings become really effective instead of being the "form without content" type of thing such as the Hallowmass fiasco I described, to say nothing of your increased probability of surviving the planetary energy-rebalancing processes that seem to be rapidly increasing in intensity in the current decade.

Before I finally "vanish into the sunset," I feel the need to say a little bit about old-time shamanic practice also. As far as I have been able to discover, every tribal group had a special name for shamanic practitioners as different from the healers, seers, priestesses or priests, and visionaries, each of whom was something of a specialist in some aspect of shamanic practice. There are almost one hundred different tribal terms for shaman given in Mircea Eliade's *Shamanism*. The shaman was expected to be more competent than average in both magickal technology and religion, competent as a healer, seer, and ritualist, and also to be able to find or suggest solutions to new or unusual situations not resolvable by the group's past traditions, plus being able to comprehend and assist with the health and well-being of the entire group viewed as a single living organism in the Mother's ecology, both physical and spiritual. Thus in the ancient systems, the shamanic initiation or the break-through experience was only a part of becoming a shaman. Surviving the initiation or having a break-through experience only told the tribal elders and other practitioners that the person *might* become a shaman; there were additional years of learning and exploration to accomplish at apprentice and journeyman status, often over the course of several incarnations, before one was able to perform as a "master" or "adept" or "big shaman."

It is one thing to be a priestess/priest, healer, or psychic and it is quite another thing to be a shaman, at least according to worldwide old traditions, which basically say that a real shaman is a more competent than average magician, theologian, historian, social and individual psychologist, metaphysician, sociologist, economist, ecologist, political scientist, and physical science student and researcher. I bring this up in that it seems to me that there are all too many people in the Earth-religion community, Wiccan and otherwise, who are claiming "shaman-status," while at the same time refusing to become conversant with the many areas of knowledge that would permit them to actually perform the complex role of shamans as described in old traditions recorded by historians and ethnographers. With that thought, I say, "Take care and be well—and good hunting!"

About the Author

Born in 1935 on a ranch in the mountains of northwestern Wyoming, the Rev. George Dew (also known as Kahóte) has been involved with some aspect of psychic, magickal, and Earth-religious practice since the age of eight, when he had his first major encounter with a spirit being. Since going public with the founding of the Seven Arrows Congregation of the Universal Life Church in 1975 in Denver, Colorado, in order to teach magickal and Earth-religion technologies, he, in partnership with copastor Rev. Linda Hillshafer (also known as Nahóta and Môrag na Beinne), has coauthored handbooks published by the church and known to the Earth-religion community throughout North America and Western Europe. For ten years he also edited a national monthly magickal newsletter, *Thunderbow,* now no longer published.

© Zelda Gordon

Nobody in Here Now but Us "Neos":

A Neo-Jungian Perspective on Neoshamanism's Inner Journey

by Daniel C. Noel

Just as there is no Paganism in modern Western culture that is not a "neo" phenomenon, a recent reconstruction that can only be approximate, so there is no shamanism in modern Western culture that is not a "neo" movement. While the latter may look to non-Western indigenous cultures' supposed shamanic practices for models, it generally does so through outsiders' eyes—eyes, moreover, that are clouded by (at best) envious yearning or (at worst) colonialist acquisitiveness.

This lack of clear vision, along with isolated instances of Western seekers who do actually apprentice themselves to non-Western shamans, can delude neoshamanism into forgetting its reality as a Western enterprise built upon various modes of imagining. Its cross-cultural and counter-cultural fantasies began with Carlos Castaneda's fairy tale of hallucinogenic learnings at the feet of a fictive Yaqui sorcerer. (I use "fictive" in the sense of not necessarily denying all reality to the noun it modifies, the way fictional would and, likewise, imaginal rather than imaginary.) There may be parallels with modern Wiccans sometimes fantasying (even fabricating) a personal lineage leading back to ancient European people and practices that were *not* neo. But, overall, the modern Craft movement seems healthily aware of its imaginal status as a more or less invented tradition.

I raise these points at the outset in order to establish neoshamanism's immersion in imagination and its distance from the reality of tribal religions. Even the creation of the word "shamanism" from the Tungus (Siberian) word *saman* is a result of what I would call the comparative or comparativist imagination of modern Western scholars like Mircea Eliade, finding similarities in the religious and healing practices of various indigenous peoples while often overlooking the dissimilarities that may be more significant. Thus all shamanism, considered as a constructed "ism," might technically be describable as neoshamanism, but for our purposes, let neoshamanism be said to begin with the publication of Carlos Castaneda's *The Teachings of Don Juan* in 1968.

All the above leads up to my more specific discussion of imagination at work in the visualization practice—usually called journeying—of neoshamanism. What I say about journeying will be informed by my larger sense (itself shaped by Jungian psychology) of the centrality of modes of imagining in the theory and practice of neoshamanism. (Given my revisionist leanings, I should probably be called a "neo-Jungian" but I will for now suppress that unwieldy label.)

There is something else I should say before beginning in earnest: My conviction about imagination's key role in neoshamanism does not have to be read as a judgment that recent Western attempts to simulate native shamanism are false or fraudulent. Indeed, drawing heavily as I do upon the positive view of imagination presented by Jungian psychology—"imagination is reality" proclaims the title of one book examining the work of C. G. Jung and successor James Hillman[1]—I see the imagination as neoshamanism's hidden treasure, not the skeleton in its closet. Ironically, neoshamanism so far has failed to find this treasure, neglecting to see past its credulous reading of Castaneda to the fictive power of the imagination that fueled the success of his hoax. Neoshamanism neglects to see through its fantasies of literal contact with literal spirits, animal allies, or celestial teachers who are taken to be factually real.

Now, twenty-five years from its Castanedan birth, neoshamanism needs to come of age and achieve an active self-awareness about its true identity as a potentially valuable imaginal enterprise of "power and healing."

Neopagan Witchcraft, I have said, seems to be a crucial step ahead of neoshamanism in this regard, having achieved a degree of what Aidan Kelly calls "theological maturity."[2] Still, as I explore modes of imagining in visualization practice, the reader may be alerted to possible areas of unawareness in Neopaganism with its magical rituals and pathworking, no less than in neoshamanism with its "journeying."

From a Jungian perspective a key distinction here would be between passive and active imagination, with the issue of ego-control emerging as relevant to both neoshamanism and Neopaganism. Let me explain by setting forth the most pertinent points in that perspective's development as first presented by Jung and later extended by Hillman. From that perspective, then, I will try to assess neoshamanism's inner journeys before closing with a few questions, as an outsider, about Neopagan visualization.

C. G. Jung's Art of Active Imagination

In his book *Healing Fiction* James Hillman calls the Jungian method of active imagination—dialoguing with an image from a dream—"the healing art."[3] Before examining what he means by that phrase, let us briefly survey what Jung himself had to say about how active imagination can be healing—and how it can fail to be healing if misconstrued.

A major way it can be misconstrued, according to Jung's earliest formulations, is by confusing it with either Freud's free association technique or with a passive relationship to the flow of fantasy images. These two confu-

sions probably amount to the same thing, or at least overlap, while a third possible misconception, taking active
imagination to be a "guided visualization" exercise (where
the one receiving the exercise is not providing the guidance), may be a special case of passive imagination, one that
will concern us later on.

If we look at Jung's first statements on the active imagination process, we find that for him it is not "free" but "focused," not a passive "going with the flow" but a delicately
willed interaction. A possible analogy might be with the
parachutist who descends not in a total free fall, a passive
plummeting, but rather, with chute opened, in a more two-
sided relationship to the elements of air and gravity. In this
analogy, pulling the ripcord could be likened to the initial
engagement, i.e., simply selecting and visualizing the image
and then working with it—the downward dialogue.

As early as 1921, Jung distinguished in his book *Psychological Types* between active and passive fantasy, adding that
while the latter, in its passivity, is antithetical to consciousness, "active fantasy is one of the highest forms of psychic
activity. For here the conscious and unconscious personality
of the subject flow together into a common product in which
both are united."[4] This notion of a "common product" of the
conscious and unconscious mind—which might be a synonym for Jung's goal of selfhood—echoes his earlier discussion of the "transcendent function" in the key 1916 essay of
that title. In this essay he also began to sketch out the actual
technique of active imagination, suggesting how one might
achieve the equal conversation he recommended between
the ego and the fantasy images of the unconscious.

In early essays like these Jung discussed active imagination without using that exact term, which he began to do in
the mid-thirties. By the autumn of 1935 in his Tavistock Lectures, "On the Theory and Practice of Analytical Psychology," he not only settled upon the name "active imagination"
for his method but also suggested that the word "imagination" by itself implies an active, purposeful creativity. He

then comments further that "active imagination" means that the images have a life of their own and that the symbolic events develop according to their own logic—that is, if your conscious reason does not interfere.[5]

In various places Jung emphasizes that first, after the initial visualization, the image must be given free play and must be accepted as if fully real, though nonliteral. Only then should the conscious ego participate—on equal terms—in the inner dialogue with the unconscious as manifested by the image. For that reason Jung spoke of the need to relax "the cramp in the conscious mind" so that "one can let things happen" in the unconscious as the first stage of the process.[6] And for that reason also, interactive imagination may be a better name for his method.

In fact, the ego's activity in the interaction—its "mastery" of this healing art—resembles the "creative letting-be" of the Christian mystic Meister Eckhart or the Taoist meditative practice of "action through nonaction," as Jung himself noted in his "Commentary on *The Secret of the Golden Flower*," a Chinese alchemical text.[7] He reemphasizes the interactive process in his description of a patient who, "through her active participation…merges herself in the unconscious processes, and she gains possession of them by allowing them to possess her."[8]

Clearly the ego must not dominate the process or dialogue—it could as easily and accurately be called a dance in which the ego does not always lead. Thus, the "activity" in active imagination is two-sided.

For Jung and his most orthodox disciples such as Marie-Louise von Franz and Barbara Hannah, "healing" occurs because a new midpoint of selfhood is achieved; a new harmony or *unio mentalis* within the personality takes place through a process that avoids free association and passive fantasy while, nevertheless, allowing for the nonliteral reality and purposeful activity of the imagination, orbiting, as it were, around the focal image with which one is in dialogue.

From the Reality of the Imagined (Jung)
to the Deliteralization of the Real (Hillman)

If we look now at the heterodox Jungian James Hillman's
view of active imagination, we find that (as in most areas)
he offers a new twist on Jung's formulations. For Hillman,
active imagination is the healing art no less than it was for
Jung, but the meaning of "healing" differs in ways that
point us back to issues of neoshamanic practice.

In Hillman's opinion, active imagination heals the psychological disease of literalism, the literalism of pure "spiritual" goals and concrete "material" facts as compared to the
middle realm of ambiguous imaginings where the psyche or
soul natively operates. Therefore, the healing art of active
imagination deliteralizes, seeing everything from psyche's
"as if" perspective, finding the confounding fiction or fantasy behind every so-called solid fact and spiritual revelation.
For such an art, passive imagination would be losing oneself
in the fiction or fantasy without seeing it as fiction or fantasy, as nonliteral, as imaginal.

While Hillman's approach to active imagination may
seem to discard Jung's goal of balanced wholeness, the two
are connected by Jung's conviction that fantasy's bad reputation (and by implication that of all modes of imagining)
stems from "the circumstance that it cannot be taken literally."[9] Elsewhere Jung discusses the difficulties of the fanta-
sy/reality distinction in psychological experience. These are
the difficulties that Carlos had to face in the Castaneda tales
and that neoshamanism has yet to face by exploring the implications of its having been born out of the reading of his
fiction. They are the difficulties that I believe prompt Hillman to stress actively imagined fictions as healing.

Jung begins his discussion on a familiar note: "the fantasy," he says, "to be completely experienced, demands not
just perception and passivity, but active participation." But
then he goes on to point out an obstacle not generally dealt
with in the Jungian tradition before Hillman's radically

imaginal revisionings, namely, that "it is almost insuperably difficult to forget, even for a moment, that all this is only a fantasy, a figment of the imagination that must strike one as altogether arbitrary and artificial. How can one assert that anything of this kind is 'real' and take it seriously?"[10]

Clearly, he implies that one *should* forget that this is only a figment or fantasy, merely make-believe—or perhaps instead that one should forget the "only," the "merely"—and take it seriously as "real." However, Jung also acknowledges that we "must not concretize our fantasies," must not take them literally.[11] He sees us all caught in what he calls "the scientific credo of our time," which has a "superstitious phobia about fantasy," disallowing fantasy's reality since only the literal is seen as real.[12] Then he takes a further turn: "But the real is what works. And the fantasies of the unconscious work…" So the question becomes how can we work with them, work with them as realities in order to heal? Jung decides that "while we are in the grip of the actual experience, the fantasies cannot be taken literally enough" although "when it comes to understanding them" we must overcome "the tendency to concretization."[13]

These are difficult and delicate maneuvers indeed! One must experience the fantasy–image as more than the mere figment our scientific credo would call it, taking the image rather as real, literally so, it seems, in the experience itself, but nonliterally so in the interpretive moment immediately thereafter.

Jung's pivotal discussion looks ahead to Hillman and to neoshamanism in one more way. Referring to a patient who had fantasized watching his fiancee commit suicide in an icy river, Jung elaborates that:

> thus, my patient is not experiencing the suicide scene "on another plane" (though in every other respect it is just as concrete as a real suicide); he experiences something real which looks like a suicide. The two opposing "realities," the world of the conscious and the world of the unconscious, do not quarrel for supremacy, but each makes the other relative.

He then adds, somewhat sarcastically:

> That the reality of the unconscious is very relative indeed
> will presumably arouse no violent contradiction; but that
> the reality of the conscious world could be doubted will be
> accepted with less alacrity. And yet both "realities" are psy-
> chic experience, psychic semblances painted on an in-
> scrutably dark back-cloth. To the critical intelligence,
> nothing is left of absolute reality.[14]

The literal world and the nonliteral world are, then,
equally real, but neither is absolutely so. In my reading,
Hillman's approach presupposes Jung's reasoning quoted
here, but in the decades since Jung wrote, the terms of the
discussion have shifted, and Hillman takes a new step.

James Hillman's Healing Fictions

Hillman handles the idea of the relative reality of the literal
world of conscious perception being equal to the nonliteral
realm of unconscious images by calling for a general deliter-
alization. He sees through the scientific credo of our time,
with its superstitious phobia about fantasy, as being itself an
imaginal fantasy. The healing strategy now is to realize that
nothing, not even literal fact, is absolutely real and to begin
to work much more respectfully with the relative reality of
the nonliteral, the fictive, the imaginal.

This is Hillman's version of the healing art of active
imagination: to actively see the fictive power informing
every reality. "A 'healed consciousness,'" he writes in *Healing Fiction*, "lives fictionally."[15] Such a consciousness lives
in active cooperation with the unconscious, and "the unconscious produces dreams, poetic fictions; it is a theater…Like dreams, inner fantasy too…has the compelling
logic of theater."[16]

Healing Fiction further connects active imagination and
the healing power of fiction (or theater) with a chapter titled
"What Does the Soul Want." For once, Hillman describes
particular cases, in this instance active imagination dia-

logues reported by four of his patients. "These dialogues," he decides, "demonstrate less a hypothesis or even a set of facts, than they show a way of therapy, a method, taken from Jung, of actively being engaged in imagining...So, our first attempt with 'What does the soul want?' does not yield a substantial answer, what it wants, but a methodical answer, how [to] discover what it wants."[17]

Here Hillman explicitly links active imagination with healing fiction while just as explicitly applying all this Jungian theory to neoshamanism. He observes that "the method of inquiry is like writing fiction," although, recalling that a passive spectator must play a role on the stage of his or her own psychic theater, he notes an understandable difference, namely:

> the active intervention in the fiction of the interlocutor him—or herself. These dialogues demand that one take a role oneself in one's own story, all the while attempting to play the role of the main character, the first-person singular, "I," as close to social realism as possible, much as Carlos Castaneda, for instance, maintained his guise of social realism by playing the anthropological interviewer in his imaginary dialogues with "Don Juan."[18]

Assessing Neoshamanism's Non-Jungian Journeys

The first ramification of Jungian active imagination for neoshamanic visualization practice, then, is that to follow in Castaneda's footsteps one must emulate his practice—not in the desert with Don Juan ingesting datura or psilocybin but at one's desk writing social-realist fiction. Except, of course, this would be neither a literal desk nor a literal act of writing. Rather, it would be an inner, imaginal creation, nevertheless taken nonliterally to be a reality in which one, as the ego, participates in a healing dialogue with some similarly real, autonomous focal image. How does this compare with neoshamanic journeying?

To answer this question we must bring another character into the discussion. Sometime in the 1970s Michael Harner, a credentialed and credible anthropologist who had
served on Castaneda's doctoral committee, circulated a letter saying that the latter's research was "110% valid." When
his own 1980 book, *The Way of the Shaman*, came out in paperback in 1982, it carried Castaneda's stamp of approval: a
cover blurb declared, "Wonderful, fascinating...Harner really knows what he's talking about." And Harner seemed to
return the compliment (or to invite the blurb) in his introduction, where he wrote that "the books of Carlos Castaneda, regardless of the questions that have been raised
regarding their degree of fictionalization, have performed
the valuable service of introducing many Westerners to the
adventure and excitement of shamanism and to some of the
legitimate principles involved."[19]

Unfortunately, despite quite a few references in the balance of his book, Harner never examines the "degree of fictionalization" of the founding father's sacred scriptures.
Consequently, this primary how-to handbook of neoshamanism, subtitled "a guide to power and healing," never
unfolds the radically imaginal lessons available by ponder-
ing the implications of how the fictive power of Castaneda's
fairy tales hoaxed their many readers. Had it done so, those
lessons would have intersected James Hillman's Jungian insights on the healing art of active imagination.

Like most neoshamanic writers, Harner draws approvingly on the historian of religions Mircea Eliade's definition
of shamanism as an "archaic technique of ecstasy,"[20] where
ecstasy involves "standing outside of" (ec-stasis) one's body,
one's ego-consciousness, one's "ordinary reality" (to use a
term Harner borrows from Castaneda). Although this definition might be harmonized in major respects with active
imagination in the Jungian sense, Harner does not do so—
even when coming very close. Here is how he describes the
classic shaman's ecstatic journey: "His experiences are like
dreams, but waking ones that feel real and in which he can

control his actions and direct his adventures."[21] In addition to raising the issue of control that we have yet to examine, the terminology of this passage suggests that Harner may be familiar with Mary Watkins's *Waking Dreams*, an extremely valuable survey of theories and practices of visualization that highlights the active-imagination practices of Jung and Hillman.[22] However, Watkins's significant title does not appear in his bibliography, and he comes no closer than this to taking advantage of the potential Jungian contribution to neoshamanism.

But to be fair to Harner, let us rephrase the question posed a few paragraphs ago as follows: Do his influential neoshamanic methods, chiefly the drumming-induced inner journeys, perhaps in their own fashion honor and interact with the imagination as fully as the Jungian approach that I have been promoting?

After reading *The Way of the Shaman* in the mid-1980s, I inferred that Harner's instructions on how to journey with the accompaniment of monotonous drumming provided a version of guided imagery to those who wanted an experience loosely simulating the classic shaman's. Shamanic imagery culled by Harner from his own anthropological fieldwork and reading—and distilled, somewhat debatably, into the generic blend he calls "core shamanism"—provides the would-be neoshaman with guidance plus several strict procedural cautions. For example, no "voracious nonmammal" or insect can be one's "power animal."[23]

Harner's guided imagery exercise could be considered equivalent to the first stage of a Jungian active imagination process, the stage wherein the image or images are permitted to arise and perform their own independent actions. But this exercise would remain at the passive level, a kind of spectator relationship to the preapproved shamanic images. Or, more accurately, it would prescribe what kind of interactions were permissible.

In a short essay written in 1988, Harner showed that he would disagree with my inference about his core shamanic journeying technique. At first he exults that "evidence of progress in this return to our shamanic roots can be seen in the fact that now shamanic journeys are being labeled as 'guided imagery' or 'visualization' and are even accepted in some official medical circles. Nevertheless," he continues, "it should be noted that the real shamanic journey goes well beyond what is called 'guided imagery.'"[24]

While I could agree that this last point was probably true for the classic shaman's ecstatic flights in an indigenous culture, it remained to be seen how this could be the case for the neoshamanic journeys that Harner had described in his guidebook and was now leading in his workshops. It seemed time for a trip to one of these weekend events.

At a Journey Workshop

Accordingly, in July 1990 I drove from my Vermont home to the Omega Institute in the Hudson River valley to participate in the basic Harner workshop, "The Shamanic Journey of Power and Healing." With some one hundred people seated on the floor in two concentric circles I listened to Michael (as he encouraged us to address him) for parts of three days and experienced several times the journey I had read about.

I have not the space to describe all the details of a rich weekend. Suffice it to say that I found the experience to be a positive one but probably not one that went "well beyond what is called 'guided imagery.'" I was not only impressed by the impact and autonomy of the images that I encountered in my experiential journeying—impressed enough to keep them private—but also pleased that Michael expressed respect for Jung as a kind of shaman. Still, there was not as much sensitivity to the range of Jungian ideas as there could have been.

When the terms "imagination" and "fantasy" were raised (and I was grateful that they there) Michael neatly dodged any discussion by saying that these words were part of theories of what is happening in our journeys whereas his intention for the weekend was to "leave the baggage of theories behind." Except, I could not help thinking, that he scarcely left behind the baggage of his own explicit and implicit theories, which seemed needlessly beholden to "the scientific credo of our time" and which inevitably became ingredients in the guidance structuring our imaginal exercises. In any case, Michael more than once met inquiries about the psychological meaning of shamanism with such responses, appealing to our supposedly direct experience of "spirits" in contrast to abstract concepts like "the unconscious" which involved conceptual speculation that he preferred to leave to others.

When a woman asked him how someone would know the difference between a visualization created by his or her imagination (already a narrow view of imagining) and the reality of his "Shamanic State of Consciousness,"[25] he said "people who have done guided imagery say it is qualitatively different."

I asked Michael myself whether the people who felt that way had published their findings anywhere, but he said that he did not know of any publication on the matter.

I was therefore surprised when, a year after the workshop, the summer 1991 issue of Michael Harner's *Foundation for Shamanic Studies Newsletter* appeared with an article claiming that same allegedly qualitative difference between guided imagery and the journeying I had experienced the previous summer.

The article was by Leilani Lewis, Ph.D., a clinical psychologist and Harner–trained "shamanic counselor" who offers the following list of comparisons, some not objectionable, some unacceptable:

- The shamanic journey uses drumming to induce the experience whereas guided imagery uses relaxation techniques.

- Journeying is free-form as opposed to having step-by-step guidance by another person or a recorded voice.

- Shamanic journeying involves a sense of "go to, travel to…" whereas guided imagery involves "Imagine going to…"

- Shamanic journeys are empowering; guided imagery features "dependence on [an] ordinary reality guide."

- On shamanic journeys people encounter a celestial teacher or power animal rather than an "inner advisor."

- The journeys lead to an Upper World or Lower World rather than imagery of "a special place in nature."

- In the Shamanic State of Consciousness one encounters spirits separate from the self rather than "parts of [one's] inner self" in the guided imagery experience.

- Finally, the shamanic journey is a "real" experience versus the "imaginary" one on the guided imagery trip.

What can be made of this series of comparisons? If we equate "shamanic journey" with Harner's neoshamanic approximation of the indigenous shaman's ecstatic experience, setting the latter aside, we find several debatable points. To say that neoshamanic journeying is "free form," with no outside guidance, stretches the facts because it ignores the instructions given prior to the journey, instructions that amount to a specific "shopping list" of assigned encounters and approved interactions.

Likewise, the idea that guided imagery tells people to imagine going somewhere "imaginary" while the Harner journey involves real travel to a real Lower World or Upper World loses sight of the fact that these locations are themselves imagined fictions, however nonliterally real. That is, although the guided imagery emphasis may be on the unreality of the exercise, it is possible to avoid this implication altogether and at the same time acknowledge the central role of images, whether drawn from classic shamanism or occurring spontaneously.

Leilani Lewis believes that "the primary difference between the two methods is how they are each conceptualized."[26] But I am persuaded, finally, that conceptualizing both experiences by comparison with the active imagination process of the Jungian tradition makes better sense of each.

Seen from this perspective, the Harner method involves mainly passive imagination, a somewhat more subtly guided imagery exercise that nonetheless unduly limits its conscious or active dialogical relationship to its own importantly imaginal components because it has not yet found conceptual resources to validate the autonomous reality of the imagination upon which it is (unknowingly?) dependent.

How Much Should Imagining be Controlled?
A Question for Neopagan Practice

From a Jungian viewpoint on active imagination, developed throughout the twentieth century through clinical observation as to "the scientific credo of our time" with its "superstitious phobia about fantasy," the Harner's and other neoshamans' visualization practice is not without value but seems too passive for its participants, too guided by its workshop leaders. In light of the radically independent reality Jung and Hillman accord the images of the unconscious psyche—the outer limits of which may extend infinitely beyond the self—neoshamanism's so-called spirit entities can seem slightly coddled by the caution with which those on the inner journey are instructed to approach them.

It is as though the neoshamanic concept cannot cope with the full, untrammeled, often fearsome reality—the shamanic reality—of the spirits it claims are more real than "mere images" and must soft-pedal its journey encounters for Western consumers who fear anything that is not marketed for fun and/or problem-solving profit. Put even more starkly, these are issues of control, control of images and imagining, and it is my outsider's sense that they may pertain critically to Neopagan as well as neoshamanic practice.

Granted, in Mircea Eliade's canonical definition of the classic shaman the ingredient of control is a strong and positive one: shamans are masters of ecstasy, in control of the assorted spirits they encounter. Thus neoshamanism appears to appeal to impressive authority when its inner journeys are set up to privilege control over spontaneous activity.

By implication this Eliadean *imprimatur* could conceivably be extended to tendencies towards control in Neopagan pathworking or ritual magic. Surely, as both Starhawk, an insider, and Tanya Luhrmann, an observer/participant but finally an outsider, attest, much of Wiccan and Western ceremonial magical visualization is precisely a matter of control.[27] Based on my comparison of Jungian and neoshamanic attitudes and procedures, the question I would like to pose, in closing, to Neopagan readers is: How much should imagining (and its products) be controlled?

This is not a rhetorical question but a genuine one that leads to others. Do we grant more reality to images (or imagined spirits) by seeking to dominate them—our fear of their chaotic vitality providing a backhanded endorsement of their existence—or by dancing with them in an interactive relationship of equals that allows imaginal entities[28] to act as real "others," animated by their own apparent subjectivity. Eliade's definitive work can and should be reevaluated: despite his own Jungian affiliations, did he unwittingly project Western inclinations (or masculine ones) toward ego-control onto Tungus practitioners and thence, from Siberia, onto the entire indigenous world? Only a thorough revisioning of Eliade's writings could hope to answer this question.[29] But even if neoshamanism has less authoritative grounds than it currently assumes for circumscribing the spontaneity of its visualized entities, does Neopaganism even depend on the same sort of presumed authority to continue its controlling practice?

Perhaps not. Perhaps the magic it remembers or invents is central to its identity and simply requires an attempt at total control not necessary to neoshamanism's continuing development so that my misgivings about an excess of control are irrelevant to Neopaganism. This is an issue of power and of whether Neopaganism—unlike, in my Jungian view, neoshamanism—must use essentially technological means to gain it. Again, I do not now have the answers to these puzzles and problems, which may also interconnect, in our scientific age, with the search for legitimation, the persuasions that so preoccupy the social anthropologist Luhrmann in her large book on "ritual magic in contemporary England."

At all events, as I ponder this possible difficulty for Neopagan visualization practice, I am put in mind of a figure whom many Wiccans and Western magicians have greatly venerated over the years. I am reminded of how Merlin used his magic at the end, voluntarily relinquishing its controlling power, according to some accounts, yet continuing to call out from his invisibility, inviting us to imagine, to yield mindfully to imagining.

Notes

1. Robert Avens, *Imagination is Reality* (Irving, Texas: Spring Publications, 1980).

2. Aiden Kelly, "An Update on Neopagan Witchcraft in America," in J. R. Lewis and J. G. Melton, eds., *Perspectives on the New Age* (Albany: State University of New York Press, 1992), 148.

3. James Hillman, *Healing Fiction* (Barrytown, New York: Station Hill Press, 1983), 78-81.

4. C. G. Jung, *The Collected Works*, Vol. 6, Bollingen Series XX, trans. H. G. Baynes and R. F. C. Hull (Princeton: Princeton University Press, 1971), 428.

5. C. G. Jung, *The Collected Works*, Vol. 18, Bollingen Series XX, trans. R. F. C. Hull (Princeton: Princeton University Press, 1980), 171.

6. C. G. Jung, *The Collected Works*, Vol. 13, Bollingen Series XX, trans. R. F. C. Hull (Princeton: Princeton University Press, 1967), 17.

7. Ibid, 16.

8. C. G. Jung, *The Collected Works*, Vol. 17, Bollingen Series XX, trans. R. F. C. Hull (Princeton: Princeton University Press, 1953), 223.

9. Ibid, 291.

10. Ibid, 216-217.

11. Ibid, 217.

12. Ibid.

13. Ibid.

14. Ibid, 218.

15. Hillman, 80.

16. Ibid, 36-38.

17. Ibid, 93.

18. Ibid.

19. Micheal Harner, *The Way of the Shaman: A Guide to Power and Healing* (San Francisco: Harper and Row, 1980), xvii.

20. Mircea Eliade, *Shamanism: Archaic Techniques of Ecstacy*, Bollingen Series LXXVI, trans. W. R. Trask (Princeton: Princeton University Press, 1964).

21. Harner, 21.

22. Mary Watkins, *Waking Dreams* (Dallas: Spring Publications, 1976, 1984).

23. Harner, 78, 81. Compare Hillman's outrageously supportive attitude toward imaginal insects in his essay "Going Bugs," *Spring: A Journal of Archetype and Culture* (1988), 40-72.

24. Micheal Harner, "What is a Shaman?" in G. Doore, ed., *Shaman's Path* (Boston: Shambhala, 1988), 11.

25. Harner, *Way*, xiii and *passim*.

26. Leilani Lewis, "Coming Out of the Closet as a Shamanic Practitioner," *Foundation for Shamanic Studies Newsletter* 4:1 (Summer 1991), 5.

27. See Starhawk, *The Spiral Dance* (San Francisco: Harper and Row, 1979), 141, 147; and T. M. Luhrmann, *Persuasions of the Witch's Craft: Ritual Magic in Contemporary England* (Cambridge, Massachusetts: Harvard University Press, 1989), 104-106, 258-261.

28. See Edith Turner, "The Reality of Spirits," *ReVision* 15:1 (Summer 1992), 28-32, where the author, an anthropologist, argues—against the majority in her field—for the reality of "spirits" as more than "imaginary," approvingly describing a journeying en-

counter at a Harner workshop as well as field experiences in Zambia and Alaska, but finally opts for Mary Watkins' Jungian-phemomenological approach to the issue in *Waking Dreams* and adopts her terminology, changing Watkins' adjective "imaginal" (which Watkins gets, as I do, from Henry Corbin by way of Hillman) to a plural noun, "imaginals," which she then uses to describe what she had started out by calling "spirits ." Would that the "theology" of Micheal Harner and his neoshamanic colleagues could mature in the direction of Turner's perceptiveness.

29. I am talking about such a revisioning in my own ongoing work. Meanwhile, I am struck by the extent to which a respected psychologist like Charles Taft could be carried along—and carry along many others—in a fantasy of controlled dreaming attributed to a Malaysian tribe, the Senoi, who did no such thing. See G. William Domhoff, *The Mystique of Dreams* (Berkeley: University of California Press, 1985).

About the Author

Daniel C. Noel (Ph.D., Drew University) is professor of liberal studies in religion and culture at Vermont College of Norwich University in Montpelier, Vermont, where he has facilitated the educational growth of adult learners in the Adult Degree Program since 1981 (and before that in the same program, when it was at Goddard College, since 1972). He is the author of *Approaching Earth: A Search for the Mythic Significance of the Space Age* (1986) and editor of *Seeing Castaneda: Reactions to the "Don Juan" Writings of Carlos Castaneda* (1976), and *Paths to the Power of Myth: Joseph Campbell and the Study of Religion* (1990). He is currently working on *Merlin's Cry*, a study of modes of imaging in the making of a modern Western shamanism, and *Soul and Earth*, a collection of "Jungian perspectives on planetary survival." He publishes regularly in academic and Jungian journals, lectures widely, and leads travel seminars to sacred sites in the British Isles and the American Southwest through World and Image, 45 Liberty St., Montpelier, Vt. 05602. Telephone 802-229-5031.

© Ashleen O'Gaea

The Second Gate:

A Perspective on Witchcraft and Shamanism from Arizona's Crystal Cave

by Ashleen O'Gaea

In the search for a transcendent level of knowledge, it has long been part of human endeavour to enter a symbolic womb of darkness and learn within its space. Many temples, caves, burial chambers and "vision pits" have been constructed and used for this...Here again the link between birth and death is clear, as there is often no firm distinction between "womb" and "tomb" in...the chambers, or in the states that the participant is expected to experience. Initiation rites...often require the candidate to be shut up in a dark vault...in order to die and be reborn to himself.[1]

> *Lord of Adventure, Horned Helm*
> *admit us to Your magic realm.*
> *Embrace us in Your mortal reign:*
> *take us through the Gates again*[2]

Perhaps because Wicca is initiatory, many in the Craft are looking for the personal sort of vision-journey that is a shaman's initiation. For a generation or so, shamanism has been a popular (if somewhat insensitively appropriated) model of initiation's ordeal, especially in terms of the Native North American vision quest. We have come to the Chiricahua Mountains to make such a journey into Crystal Cave.

It is the spring equinox. At the equator, the hours of day and night will be equal. Here at a latitude of about 35 degrees north, we have to compensate for the planet's angle to calculate the balance, but we can feel spring and rebirth in the air and see it in the delicate green buds everywhere around us.

Camp established at Sunny Flat, we sing brightly and in fair harmony around the fire this first night out, and we laugh heartily at the expression on the first-timers' faces when they hear *Waltzing Godzilla*.[3]

"There are two deaths anyone can undergo: the death of the body and the death of initiation; and of these deaths, the death of the body is the lesser."[4] We eat well tonight, for tomorrow, deep in the Mother indeed, we will approach death—and claim rebirth after our ordeal.

Crystal Cave is about three miles away and maybe three-quarters of a mile above us in the rhyolite mountain. We will go there after breakfast tomorrow. This descent is our way of celebrating the holiday, one of the quarters on the Wheel of the Year. There are fourteen of us: Canyondancer, Rock, Feather, Red and her three-year-old daughter, Peanut; Lady Day, the two twenty-somethings, Questor, Greenhelma, Morgen, O'Gaea, and two newcomers, Wren and Padraic.

We will not cast a circle, for out here we are in one already. In the first fully dark room of the cave, there will be a ritual blessing though, one we wrote long ago and have used for several years. Early tomorrow, we will enter the cave, where we will die and be reborn. Symbolically, by plan; but the risks of "lesser death" are real.

• • •

In the morning we drive to the wash from the campground, but even though our vehicle has four-wheel drive, we walk from the mouth of the wash. We do not take much with us: helmet, two more lights each, canteen, camera, maybe a snack for after. We creep over some scrabbly little hills, reality becoming less ordinary by the moment. Is that a slight sparkle in the air, or some chemical reaction between sweat and sunscreen?

As the trail demands more and more of our attention, we talk and pause less often. We start a steep climb, up another three hundred yards from the bed of a tributary wash: it will take us half an hour, maybe, to get to the first Gate. The entrance is locked.

"The standard payment...for shamanic initiation was... a muzzle-loading shotgun."[5]

We put down a deposit with the Forest Service, and they mailed us the key. We never had to give anybody a shotgun, but last year Canyondancer had to drive the 130 miles or so down to Douglas to pick up the key. Like everything else about the cave (and initiation and many other magical quests), just getting permission to attempt it takes some effort.

The first Gate is protected by a tubular metal baffle around the lock. Canyondancer undoes it, swings it open, and steps through, bent double, into a small chamber. Following him, we take off our sunglasses, stretch our helmet-elastics under our chins, and test our lights. A canteen slung under one arm and a camera over the other shoulder, we head down and to the right.

"For a journey to the lower world the shaman usually visualizes an entrance into the earth. Common entrances include images of caves..."[6]

Visualization, of course, is moot right now: we are well and truly in a place that is no place, in a time that is no time. One difference between this and shamanism is that we come down here on personal quests, not on missions for patients. We're not shamans, or even aspiring shamans; but the cave experience is such a familiar metaphor for shamanism that the similarities of parts of the Craft to parts of shamanism are starkly apparent to us.

• • •

The first passageway is easy, almost like stair steps. The other lights seem small, and it is hard to tell if we are underground, under water, or in space; maybe there is not much difference anyway. Whatever it is, going into it is obviously death, coming back is rebirth. It will feel like that to us. It does every time.

The similarity of this Sabbat observance to shamanistic adventure is inescapable, but it is the spirit of adventure we share, not the rites or world-view of classical shamanism. We think of the Celtic myths, so many of which involve underground or underwater passages, and mystical worlds that can only be reached through mounds or tunnels. We think of the part blindness plays in myths and stories around the world. We think of labyrinths and mazes. And we share the altered perception of reality that every hero must discover or endure. That Witches and shamans approach the alteration differently only matters some of the time; that the Craft and shamanism both expect us to approach is important all the time.

Michael Harner drank psychoactive plant mash to ready his consciousness for his first shamanic descent. What activates our psyches today is the cave's extraordinary environment. Our perceptions cannot not change. We could restore a more-or-less ordinary perception by aiming all our lights across one wall at the same time. But we don't.

Today's descent is the eighth for some of us, the first for others; Morgen and the twenty-somethings are here their second time. And our equipment is as varied as our experience: there are some specialized caving helmets, some generic hardhats, a bicycle helmet, and one from the army surplus store; Padraic has no headgear at all.

He understands that this will make it more dangerous for him. What is easy to claim is not worthless, but it is held in less awe; if we want that sense of awe in our lives, we accept some risks. The reversal of polarities between dimensions turns risks here into inspiration on the magical planes.

Deepening his opportunity to receive inspiration, we promise somberly not to leave him alone if he gets hurt and we have to go for help. He is inspired to do brilliantly, and never knocks himself once.

"Thousands of years ago," Don Juan told Carlos, "by means of seeing, sorcerers became aware that the earth was sentient and that its awareness could affect the awareness of humans. They tried to find a way to use the earth's influence on human awareness and they discovered that certain caves were most effective."[7]

It's easy to be sapiens—or sentience—centric, until not only our ideas but our experiences of sentience (which seems to translate into worth and authority) are challenged. The cave challenges us: mineral formations aren't supposed to be alive, much less sentient, but this cave has a personality and we are in no position to argue that it can't have. Recognizing (literally *knowing again*) that "the hills are alive" means that we can't dismiss their rights and sensibilities so easily. Coming to this canyon and the cave influences our human awareness, all right, and expands it very effectively. If we are not careful, some would say, and if we are careful, we say, our awareness could expand to include the whole universe.

The main floor of the cave is our immediate goal, though, and to get there, we cross an apparent abyss dotted with jutting boulders. It is easier than we expect it to be. Then we see the narrow, interrupted ledge sloping down a twenty-foot, irregularly bulging boulder face. Someone is already inching across, looking very small where each of us will be in just minutes. A single helmet's light looks like an isolated star in the night sky.

Below the traverse is a roughly circular floor, only gently sloping...west? The only directions here are left and right, up and down. Each of us has ourself and the cave for reference points. Dozens of passages take off in all directions from the main floor. There are spray-painted arrows over some holes; most of those holes look too small to get into, but we will disappear through some of them anyway.

When the last two of us have got down to the main floor, we instinctively form a circle that is more of an oval, following the shape of the floor. It is time for the blessing.

I read the Old English, not sure if I'm pronouncing it correctly. It's been years since I studied this long-since evolved language, but our heritage is partly Anglo-Saxon, so we try. My original translations are lost, leaving me only these phonetic crib notes, but it sounds ancient, and it "shivers me timbers" well enough. Everyone else reads the responses in modern English. Their voices are powerful and resonant.

Afterward, we turn off our lights. It is actually, proverbially, too dark to see our hands in front of our faces. We could be a group of good friends, hearty campers, or we could each be alone in the cave with a thousand spirits, hearing their breath, feeling their movements, or both.

The Blessing of the Crystal Cave [8]

(pronounced) Onshay that laikt een oosah yond-likten that shada-helm oosah for-yurdan.

The light within us shall illuminate the many darknesses around us.

(pronounced) Onshay oora fetkth yewitt oaf that oon yedollek een thees ye-dollek clayofah that we may onfee thad thah on-ye-dolleks whella oosah for-yurdath.

In this finite cosm we embrace the several infinities that surround us.

Onshay oora yellid-ye-kind on-springan frohm thees forsainlik cars oonder whereh we standath,thoor oosah ond frohm oosah, to anbwyn that sikth of oor sayfas ond freedness.

Our primal humanity rises from the neglected stones beneath our feet, from us and through us, to clarify the vision of our hearts and minds.

Nimah that streng-thu of shada-helm, the streng-thu of sekt ond sailness; ond we hib habbath mit oosah, hereh thees dyeh ond when we gaith frohm thees rooma.

We claim the strength of darkness, the strength of peace and silence; and we will have it with us now and when we go from this place.

Een thah nahm oaf that Eortha, befarath een sekt.

In the name of the Earth, we go in peace.

• • •

"Without overly forcing the evidence, we can view the whole of paleolithic figurative art as the expression of ideas concerning the natural and supernatural organization of the living world (the two might have been one in paleolithic thought)."[9] There are no bison or horses painted on these walls, no reciprocity suggested, but only crudely painted names of vandals, whose trouble to reach these indescribable niches only to deface them is unfathomable.

GARLAND is written in red and practically unaffected by the wire brush we've brought to try to erase it; an LL is over there and MIKE WHITLOCK scrawled across another wall. The concepts about the world that these vicious scrawls admit are scary ones, and trouble us more deeply than any danger from the sharp outcrops or bottomless pits in here.

I can't help likening these daring feats of vandalism to more noble quests of myth and legend though, and I wonder about a lot of things back in town and in the rest of the sociopolitical world. As above, so below, after all. "What is quite critical is the extent to which [a] belief system allows profound insights, transformations of consciousness and identity and a renewed sense of being within the world."[10]

Modern civilization generally discourages those sorts of creativity and any sense of identification with (rather than power over) the world. Witchcraft does allow—delightedly promises and anticipates!—insights, transformations, and renewal, and shamans require them as well. We hope that even if we cannot clean up the paint mess, we can at least restore some of the psychic trust, some of the mutual respect, people and caves used to feel.

• • •

"Only the shaman can make this journey to the depths...thus, while the ordinary human being lives as a more or less helpless pawn of the spirits, it is the shaman alone who can contract and control them."[11] This is not what we believe. We think we can all be our own shamans and priest/esses. "Approximately nine out of ten persons have the capacity for the visualization necessary to the shamanic journey."[12] That is what we believe; otherwise, we would not be here.

Shamanism is not the emphasis in our practice of Witchcraft. In the cave, on this physical journey, for all its shamanistic elements, the only spirits we have to tame are our own. We are aware of the presence of others, and we are aware of their metaphorical (other-dimensional, Otherworldly) nature, too.

Yet Wicca's Anglo-European heritage does contain shamanistic stories and tendencies. We ourselves camp as many sabbats as we can. We do, in fact, commune with spirits and with rocks and sticks and…for us, the landscapes Here and There merge easily, as they do for our mostly Celtic forebears. (We know it is meant to be like that, by the evidence of our having the *corpus callosum* connecting the right and left halves of our brains.)

We do not aspire to be shamans; our aspiration is to adventure in our own heritage and tradition, with our emphasis on the integration of the worlds rather than on their separation: we trust that when we wander into the woods where the trees are the thickest,[13] adventure will come to us as we follow our curiosities and hunches. This sort of adventuring is different from classical shamanism's mission-oriented journeying. But sometimes Witchcraft and shamanism meet, and the cave is one of their rendezvous.

Canyondancer says that a few of our fellow cavers "have gone way the wrong way," and that this is the passage we want to take. We are headed for some long, low, and narrow rooms that are entirely lined with undamaged crystal formations. Once we're through the difficult entrances, we look around and find ourselves inside a geode.

"Shamans have long used their quartz crystals for seeing and divination. Not surprisingly, bone game players sometimes carry a quartz crystal for luck. The crystal ball with which people in our culture are familiar, at least by name, is simply a polished descendant of the old shamanic crystal."[14] And of the curved mirror of space in which the Goddess saw Herself? These curved crystal walls also reflect us each in ways we have not previously seen ourselves.

Right now we need to keep our attention on the physical plane, but when we're back in camp, and for the rest of our lives, lying here now will take us on many journeys. The communication link need never be broken. Religion means "relinking." The cave relinks us with all time and all space, with the void, and with the creation that comes from the void. In here, where we cannot see anything; really, we can see everything.

"Shamanic enlightenment is the literal ability to lighten the darkness, to see in that darkness what others cannot perceive."[15] We may not have divined or seen a map of the cave's tunnels, but the crystals have illuminated other truths, differently for each of us. And they have inspired Morgen and Questor...

There are two keys on the ring the Forest Service loans people, because there are two Gates in Crystal Cave. We have been through the outer First Gate many a time. We have never found the Second Gate, and the boy and his uncle want to find it.

It will be wonderful when they do, a sort of *National Geographic*-style celebration; and then they will hear of another Gate, or squint downstream toward the next bend. In the cave, it's the Second Gate we seek; on the stream back at camp, we Just Want to See What's Around the Next Bend. May there always be an undiscovered Gate, another bend that calls us on around it, whatever wonders the opened Gates reveal.

We have heard of the Second Gate from many people. People who have never seen it speak of it in hushed tones, with awe and reverence; their eyes get wide even in the bright sunlight in the wash below the cave. People who have found it, unlocked it, and lowered themselves through it say, "It starts to get interesting once you get through the Second Gate."

• • •

Our fellow cavers come back, pretending to be annoyed with their mistake. But they are not sorry they went where they did, for they've seen some crystals now. They were dusty, and there were heavy calcite deposits at their bases, so it looked as though they were mounted in cement, but they were wonders nonetheless.

We descend feet first, on our bellies, down the correct tunnel. We do not stand up again for a long time. Sometimes

we can crawl on our hands and knees, sometimes we worm
along on our backs, and then turning a corner or wiggling
through a hole in the ceiling puts us on our bellies again.

We do not shed our layers of clothes or gear as we descend like the Goddess does. Instead, we shed our conventional perspectives on the world until, at bottom, it is just
us and the cave, the individual and the infinite, the mortal
and the eternal.

"Entrances into the lowerworld commonly lead down
into a tunnel or tube that conveys the shaman to an exit,
which opens out upon bright and marvelous landscapes."[16]
Is this what Morgen and Questor and the rest of us would
find beyond the Second Gate? Is this the same tunnel we go
through when we are born, the same one we go through
when we die? There is always the Gate we come through to
get here; and there is always the second Gate, the one you
go through when you leave.

Once before Questor and his uncle have sought the Second Gate in Crystal Cave. They only know that it is "off to
the right from the main floor," and down one of several
small tunnels. We have heard that ropes are helpful. We are
apprehensive, but compelled; knowing about that Second
Gate, we are "neither bound nor free," ready for whatever
initiation the cave and—we like to think—life has to offer.

This year they almost find the Second Gate. Morgen
thinks he sees a metallic glimmer in his light, but it is getting
late, and we need to think about going out. It is better to suffer the lesser death of the body than to enter the Circle with
fear in our hearts; it would tempt lesser death to attempt the
Second Gate with such exhaustion in our muscles.

We are as covered with goose bumps as anyone would
be on a Yule midnight out-of-doors and deprived at some
moments of all our senses. The thunking of our helmets is
almost rhythmic; our own heartbeats fill in the gaps. We become unaware that there is no drumming.

"The folklore of Britain abounds in stories of underground passages, few of which have been proved to exist,

and most of which are physically unlikely to do so."[17] A physically "impossible" landscape is a sure sign of nonordinary reality. We have to ask whether the impossibility is the landscape's or ours. Not knowing how something is possible does not make it impossible except personally, and then only if a person insists on knowing how something works before she will accept that it does. Our ideas about possible and impossible are changing as we move around in here.

I heard Carlos Castaneda speak once, and his books have brought me to some precious experience. We live where he writes about, and we have entered caves like those of which he speaks, seen the shimmer of magic over some of the same expanses of mesquite and mirage.

Yet here in Crystal Cave, I expect to see Merlin, not the Mexican sorcerer. Though the creosote bushes conjure them down on the desert floor, in the cave I think not so much of Don Juan and Carlos as of Wulf and Brand, their Anglo-Saxon counterparts in Brian Bates's *The Way of Wyrd*.[18] The cave in those tales is an underground chamber like this one, where the forges of death and rebirth roar and surge.

It is not forge-like down here; it is a constant sixty-eight degrees Fahrenheit. But the clank of helmets and the occasional gasp or groan is consistent with hard work, and there is no sense of passing effortlessly through these tunnels as shamans do in their underground travels.

We relate to the land when we are on the surface, and to our own elements when we are beneath it. We half expect to see Apache ghosts among the trees when we are poking about in the canyon. But in the cave, in this place that could be anywhere, at a time that could be any time, night or day, this century or any other, we are fiercely ourselves, fiercely all our ethnic generations, fiercely the whole universe.

It is, of course, not just the depths and narrows and darknesses that galvanize us. It is the crystal current we all feel, "the mysterious earth currents which thrill the clay of our bodies."[19] Here in the cool darkness and mystery we associate with death, the clay of our bodies is fully attentive, fully alive. This wry awareness is something else Witches and shamans have in common. Like Don Juan and Wulf, we smile and feel ruthless.[20]

• • •

We are about 250 feet under the surface of the Earth. The entrance to the cave is at about 5,700 feet, so we are standing inside the planet at an elevation of about 5,400 feet. The sight of another caver's helmet light, alone in absolute darkness, can make us think we're floating in Space or deep in the Ocean.

It is mind-boggling, and we can't think about it for more than a few seconds at a time. The disorientation can lead to panic, which is dangerous, like coming up from a dive too fast and risking the crippling pain of the bends. One can't look back at Eurydice, one cannot trust fanged insects, and one must not panic in the cave.

We have been underground for a long time now. Forever, maybe; someone's watch says three hours. It is time to head up and out, back to camp to start the small cooking fire we'll need for lunch. One by one, we ascend a steep tunnel, climbing almost straight up, as if there were a ladder.

For a moment, each of us is entirely contained in isolation. It crosses our minds that these walls are not as soft as the sides of the birth canal they resemble, the absence of contractions and our eagerness to be reborn notwithstanding. Mountains are born of tremendous contractions, too, forced out through narrow birth canals, shoved up from warm, liquid magma-wombs, thrusting and exploding into life much as we are pushed into the world by powerful matrix movements.

We look at things differently here; we look at ourselves differently here, too. Although we are not scared, we are in a life-and-death situation. We have a very clear sense of what requires our attention. When we get back outside, we have to sort again through sights and sounds we used to take for granted, recognizing the environment, recognizing ourselves within it, reevaluating from that life-and-death perspective.

The changes this instinctive reevaluation will make in our lives might be subtle, or a long time coming, or immediate, or dramatic. The only sure thing is that coming here, doing this, will change us: She changes everything She touches.

Going up is hard. We are tired, and everybody has taken some wrong turns. Canyondancer, Morgen, and Rock are trying to figure out which color arrows to follow out of the labyrinth. They find the tunnel, their shouts echo back down, and lights blink like a carnival to point out the passageway, sending us a little more energy that we can all use.

On the way in we talked; now we are quiet. We are hoping only to be symbolically reborn in celebration of Ostara. The cave does not need to be a literal Gateway to the Otherworld, not this time.

Two women are helping the three-year-old across the flat-fronted boulder that rises above the back of the main floor. Peanut has been very brave—and patient—and now she is ready to Go Out. Her mother and Lady Day are easing her across. Once past its upper edge, the going is easier, and through impatient and a little scared, the Peanut does fine.

She is disappointed that neither Mom nor Lady Day is sure how to open the Gate to the World of Light, but at least there are chocolate chip cookies in one of the tote-bags. Presently the Peanut herself discovers the Secret of the Gate's Lock and lets the three of them back out into the sunshine. They scramble for sunglasses.

This cave is in Arizona, under 9,000-foot mountains. They are spectacularly beautiful and literally entrancing.[21] There is little distinction among the dimensions here, and much communication. The crystals themselves beckon and hypnotize.

Witches and shamans have walked here before us and will walk here after we are gone. Only a hundred years ago these Chiricahua Mountains were an Apache stronghold, and as far as we can see in any direction the mountain has been peopled for tens of thousands of years. Farther north, Pueblo cultures left magnificent castles behind.

"The entrance to the underworld in the circular *kivas* (ceremonial chambers) of the Zuni Indians...is a hole located in the floor. Such *sipapu* holes were common in prehistoric *kivas* of the Puebloan peoples, but absent from those of some present-day pueblos. Interestingly, at Zuni, where the *sipapu* survives in the circular form of the *kiva*, so do the shamanistic medicine societies."[22] Our Circles are round, our ancient forms survive, and we survive with them. We approach the Circle primarily as a microcosm, but as also an entrance to other dimensions, just as the circles associated with birth and death—and Gates in the cave—are entrances to other dimensions. As above, so below.

Outside the cave, light bounces off (out of?) the crystals studding the rocky mountain top, and we can feel that light tingle like moving air against our skin. "Quartz crystals are in a sense 'solidified light' involved with 'enlightenment' and seeing...The association of quartz crystals with...celestial phenomena is a significant one, connected not only with light but with the sun."[23] When everybody is standing outside and stretching, getting used to the light and to standing up again, Canyondancer locks the Gate and we all go a few hundred yards more up the mountain until we are standing on the roof of the cave.

Crystals are strewn about here like gems fallen out of a giant's pocket. "Peoples as distant from one another as the Aborigines of eastern Australia and the Yuman-speakers of southern California and adjacent Baja California consider the quartz crystal 'living,' or a 'live rock.'"[24] So do we; these crystals are so alive for me that I feel like inviting them back to camp for lunch. Other times when I have been here, some of them have explained things to me, and once several citron-tinged crystals offered themselves as "healing rods" for friends of mine. They were of comfort.

Huge slabs, covered with perfect points sparkling in the nearly noon-time sun, stick up out of the ground, dazzling our eyes and charging our spirits. "The quartz crystal is considered the strongest power object of all among such widely separated peoples as the Jívaro in South America and the tribes of Australia."[25] The twenty-somethings have claimed one for an altar on the astral, it being too big to carry off even if that were allowed. But what more appropriate altar could there be than crystal, this stone that at once embodies the Moony depths of Earth and the glittering light and soul of the Sun?

"In modern physics the quartz crystal is also involved in the manipulation of power. Its remarkable properties early made it a basic component in radio transmitters and receivers (remember the crystal set?). Thin wafers sliced from quartz crystals later became basic components for modern electronic hardware such as computers and timepieces."[26] This chapter is written by, as well as about, crystals!

"While all this may be coincidental, it is one of the many synchronicities that make the accumulated knowledge of shamanism exciting and often even awesome."[27] Conversation about shamanism these days usually refers to primal cultures, South American gatherer/hunters, far-Northern ice-dwelling tribes, far-Eastern high-mountain Asian cultures, Amerind woods-and-plains traditions. In those terms, we are not shamans, for our vision of ordinary reality is very different, and thus our Lowerworld is similarly different. (As above, so below, literally.)

What we, Witches, have in common with shamans is the concept of other dimensions and the idea of intercourse and influence between or among them. We share an acceptance of other natural forms as "a people" or "tribes" or "clans" or "houses." We also share a reliance on our instinct and intuition. We just don't describe the environment in the same way, which puts us in some significantly different places. Not better or worse, just different. Like flowers in a wild field, like the different shapes crystals take.

Everywhere, though, it is the equinox, and our deaths and rebirths have rebalanced, reinitiated us. Remembering that Rhiannon Ryall has told us that caves were used as initiation sites in the West Country when she was growing up,[28] thinking this must have been the custom of many cultures for tens of thousands of years, we guess our ancestors walked similar tracks back to camp from caves such as this one.

The Mystery is pervasive, the more so for looking so ordinary. Trees. Rocks. A few fluffy clouds in a sky as blue as a PC screen,[29] and birds. Laughter, footsteps, familiar faces, people who have known at least some of each other for quite a while. Like the cave that extends unmeasured distances down and into the Earth, which is not evident just in looking at the mountain, there is a hidden depth in all of this, in the bird song, in the wind's whisper, in everybody's eyes.

Like the crystals that glitter subtly through the dust and despite miners' and vandals' ravages, the depth and breadth of life, the universe and everything glitters in our changed awareness. Shafts of light not only dapple the floor of the wash, but also conjure in our minds images of webs and threads and other interconnections.

In the morning, one last fire keeps us thawed until the sun rises over the hill and spills into camp. Breakfast is cereal; the stove is already packed away. Breaking camp takes enough energy to ground us at last; neither the hot, bumpy ride past the American Museum of Natural History's Research Station back to camp, nor the mundane dinner rituals could settle us yesterday.

A cool breeze brushes past us and we look back toward the cave, though we cannot see that cliff face from this site. Our eyes are focused on the colorful mountains, red and gold, but we are remembering the cave and looking deep inside ourselves. Where there are crystals too, now we come to think of it.

Notes

1. Gilchrist, Cherry, *The Circle of Nine* (London: Arkana, 1991), 102.
2. From Campsight Coven's *Book of Shadows*.
3. It's a song we learned from the Department of Folksong on Garrison Keillor's radio show, *A Prairie Home Companion*.
4. This is traditionally confided to initiates; Campsight's version is taken and a little bit adapted from the Farrars' work, who got it from Dion Fortune's *The Sea Priestess*.
5. Harner, Micheal, *The Way of the Shaman* (San Francisco: Harper and Row, 1980), 10.
6. Walsh, Ross, M.D., Ph.D., *The Spirit of Shamanism* (Los Angeles: Jeremy P. Tarcher, 1990), 143.
7. Castaneda, Carlos, *The Power of Silence* (New York: Simon and Schuster, 1987), 120.
8. From Campsight Coven's *Book of Shadows*.
9. Leroi-Gourhan, *Treasures of Prehistoric Art* (New York: Harry M. Abrams, n.d.), 174.
10. Drury, Neville, *The Shaman and the Magician: Journeys Between the Worlds* (London: Routledge and Kegan Paul, 1982), 19.
11. Walsh, 147.
12. Walsh, 155 (quoting Harner).
13. In *The Masks of God: Creative Mythology* (New York: Penguin Books, 1968), 540. Joseph Campbell, quoting from Albert Pauphilet, talks bout the Knights of the Round Table who "entered into the forest, at one point and another, there where they saw it to be thickest..." because they're looking to find their own adventures rather than following established trails.
14. Harner, 141.
15. Harner, 28.
16. Harner, 32.
17. Bord, Janet and Colin, *The Secret Country: An Interpretation of the Folklore of Ancient Sites in Britain* (London: Paul Elek, 1976), 24.
18. Bates, Brian, *The Way of Wyrd: Tales of an Anglo-Saxon Sorcerer* (London: Butler and Tanner, 1984).
19. Bord, quoting Kipling.
20. According to Don Juan in nearly all of Castaneda's books, "ruthlessness" is that perspective which allows no self-pity. As far as

I know, it's a term from Don Juan's personal vocabulary, rather than an academically accepted anthro-psychological term.

21. For more about Cave Creek Canyon, read the Arizona chapter in *Sacred Sites*, ed. Frank Joseph (St. Paul: Llewellyn, 1992).

22. Harner, 35.

23. Harner, 140.

24. Harner, 139.

25. Harner, 139.

26. Harner, 141.

27. Harner, 141.

28. Ryall, Rhiannon, *West Country Wicca: A Journal of the Old Religion* (Custer, Washington: Phoenix, 1989), 21.

29. Really. It seemed ironic to compare the natural sky to the artificial screen in a discussion of Pagan perception, or it could be argued that nature has nothing, philosophically, to fear from technology, and that we have managed to make technology a semisentient lifeform in our minds, and so we might as well give up the prejudice and see about making a productive citizen of it. But the real reason for saying the sky was as blue as a PC screen is that it was and most people don't imagine as dark as that unless it is specified.

About the Author

Born in the Pacific Northwest, O'Gaea now lives in the legendary Old West, sharing a home in Tucson with her HHP (husband and high priest) Canyondancer, their teen-age son Questor, three cats, and uncounted garden wildlives.

Like Canyondancer, O'Gaea is an enthusiastic proponent of camping as sacred and re-creational. With Campsight Coven, they spend as many sabbats as they can "at camp" all over eastern Arizona and western New Mexico, hosting an annual five-day Beltane retreat and, of course, the annual Ostara trek to Crystal Cave.

Sacred Mask and Sacred Trance

by Evan John Jones

A rich and diverse group of symbols and concepts illustrate the beliefs and ideas of the Craft. "The castle that spins between two Worlds" and "The rose beyond the grave" refer to the journey the soul takes after death. Or consider the figure of Pan, half goat and half man, the old horned god as the divine king figure, visualized again as Herne, leader of the Wild Hunt, or the mythos of "the roebuck in the thicket," or the other images which so many of us take for granted as being part of Craft tradition.

Where did these ideas come from and why did they take on the forms that they have? Did somebody somewhere sit down one day and say, "This is how it will be"? Or is there something more behind them? Quite simply, I believe that many traditional Craft images and the concepts behind them evolved from a mystical trance–state vision technique which is now defined as "shamanism."

To approach this shamanistic art, we must start with the basic premise that everyone alive today is a shaman. Everyone who has ever lived was a shaman; everyone who has yet to be born will be a shaman. In fact, because of the way the human nervous system works, it is physiologically impossible for a human being not to be a shaman. No matter who they are, what race, color, or creed, without exception, everyone has the ability to enter into what we have chosen to call "first-state trance," the basic tool of the shaman.

While various techniques produce this trance, and the soul or spirit takes on different images once free from the body while in it, first-state trance involves four distinct and separate levels of consciousness. Each level produces its own distinctive geometric pattern in our inner vision. Stage One manifests itself as circular bands of light on a pitch-black background (Figure 1). During Stage Two, the bands of light are replaced by an irregular circle of flashing zig-zags against the same dark background (Figure 2). In Stage Three, a grid-like formation or horizontal and vertical lines builds up in the center of the zig-zag pattern (Figure 3).

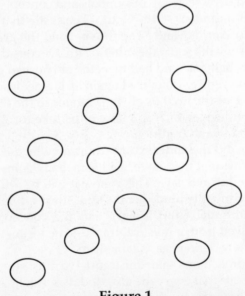

Figure 1

Figure 2

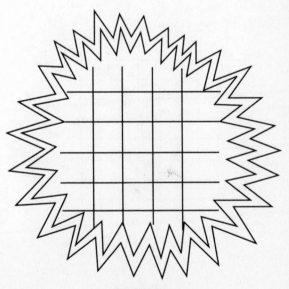

Figure 3

And in the final stage, Stage Four, the shamanistic technique comes into play, and this is the hardest part of all. Now the shaman must impose the "key" to the objective he or she is aiming at while in a trance state (Figure 4). This objective may be an ecstatic vision of the Godhead with mystic messages and prophecies. Or perhaps the shaman wishes to release the soul or spirit from the body to seek out the world beyond the grave. Strangely enough, in these instances the soul rarely retains the shape of the body; rather it transforms itself into an animal form. Thus, it is the shape of this animal or bird that the shaman superimposes on the grid as a key to spiritual shape-shifting.[1]

The Craft tradition within which I work (its full name being The People of Goda of the Clan of Tubal Cain) bases its shamanistic journeys on the concept of freeing the soul from the body, thus leaving it free to reach the Otherworld by crossing the river between this world and that. As we comprehend it, the shaman's journey is a pseudo-death, similar

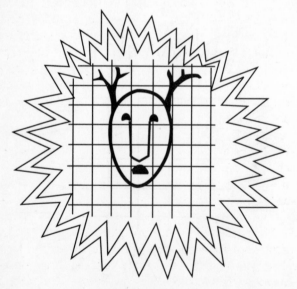

Figure 3

to the one-way passage made by the souls of the dead. But to be honest about it, since European shamanistic Witchcraft virtually died out, we at first were not completely certain that we were on the right path. Then confirming evidence began to come from the last place we expected, South Africa.

The Bushman culture of South Africa reaches forward from a distant past to the present time, and some of its members still practice the rites of their ancestors. They can still interpret the records left by their ancestors in the form of rock paintings. It took a long time for South African archaeologists to come to examine and catalog these prehistoric paintings, and when they did, they discovered that a sizable body of evidence about Bushman culture was still *in situ*—not to mention tucked away in university basements and private collections. Not only are some modern Bushmen still using the same imagery and techniques as their ancestors, they are able to look at a cave painting from a thousand years or more ago and explain its religious and magical meaning.

Far from being random drawings as first thought, the bulk of these paintings have certain themes running through them. They are now recognized as pictorial representations of a series of concepts illustrating this culture's ideas of spiritual development. Unlike European religious art, these paintings showed the method used to reach out and meet the totem spirit of the Great Eland, visualized as the god of the herds.

As migratory hunter/gatherers, their lives were intertwined with the herds of eland (a large African antelope), and their tribal totem spirit was the Great Eland. Little wonder that with time the protecting deity of the herds came to be visualized as the Great Eland that dwelt in the Otherworld. In addition, often when the Great Eland was portrayed, it was shown against a grid or surrounded by a circle of zig-zag lines, exactly the same geometric patterns as in the last two stages of first-state trance as we observed them in our own workings. The paintings also sometimes show an eland surrounded by archers while another goes on to show the dying beast. Human figures are linked to the dying eland by a "chain," and, oddly enough, fish are drawn in the background.

Modern-day reports of Bushmen ritual help explain these images. When the shaman reached a certain stage of trance, he began to mime first wading in a river and then swimming—flat on his face on the ground. The people explain his actions and their connection with the rock paintings as follows. Tribal shamans are portrayed with elongated skulls because the spirit leaves the body through the top of the head, while the chain-like connection between the shaman and the Great Eland shows how he draws power from the dying god in the workings of their ancestors. The fish have two meanings: they contain the ghosts of the ancestors and they also symbolize the river that the shaman had to cross to reach the Otherworld where the Great Eland dwells. Hence he mimics wading and then swimming as his soul crosses this river on another plane.

Many past civilizations have believed that a river or stretch of ocean separated the world of the living from that of the dead, a belief matched by a strong Craft tradition of a river between our world and that of the dead and the castle of the Goddess. Like the Bushman, we too believe that the shaman's soul, once free from the body, can cross this river to seek out the Godhead. This concept is so central to our mythos that one specific working, that of the "Castle," brings together all its elements in one ritual.

This ritual begins with three circles cast one inside the other. The outer circle represents life and is always marked with salt. The next circle represents death and is marked with the ash of two woods: willow, symbolizing mourning, and birch, symbolizing rebirth. The innermost circle is the river. Marked with a mixture of water, vinegar, wine, and salt, it represents the boundary between this world and the spiritual one.

Starting at the outer ring and working inward, the magician symbolically goes from life to death and across the river to the castle of the Goddess. The soul of the shaman and the soul of the dead make parallel journeys: to quote the late Robert Cochrane, "Sometimes called the [river] Lethe or time, it is the beginning of power, the river which the witch has to cross in spirit to seek out the power and wisdom of the Goddess."[2]

Having accepted the concept of a river between us and the Otherworld which one day we all have to cross in death, we should also realize and accept that there is another way of doing so: to cross the river in first-state trance as in the case of the shaman-witch. Unlike the Bushman, we do not see the Godhead in animal form; instead we have the old Horned God and the Goddess. Indeed, in many ways we have been conditioned to see the Godhead through the eyes of those who trod the same path long ago, and the images that they used to seek out the mystic universe beyond this living world are still with us. In the European tradition, the main function of the shaman-witch was to seek out the Old Gods while in trance to determine their will and to enlist their aid for the future wellbeing of the group or clan—and also to appease and obtain the supernatural aid of the ancestors to keep the group safe in a hostile world. To do this, the shaman would use certain techniques, sometimes including hallucinogenic drugs—something I have never agreed with. In the first instance, the use of these drugs is illegal in most countries. Second and perhaps more important, how can you be sure you are experiencing a true vision and not a drug-induced one? Even with plant-based drugs, I am willing to bet that the old shamans experienced some fatalities. The true opening up of the spirit to the Godhead has always been achieved through an act of willpower; there are never any shortcuts.

All trance workings rely on a basic technique to separate the soul from the body through the twin media of dance and breath control. With the dance, which starts slowly and gradually speeds up, the idea is to stamp the feet monotonously and hypnotically, either in one spot or in a circle. As the dance gets faster, the shaman becomes progressively shorter of breath, thus bringing about altered oxygen levels in the bloodstream.

The body's actual changes follow a distinct pattern. First, everything follows the rhythm of the dance; as the trance deepens, there is a sensation of divorced reality. Everything seems to be taking place on two levels. The dancer feels that she or he can look down and see her or his body going through the same actions on this other level. This is followed by blackness, which is only broken by the floating circles of light which seem to fill the entire vision. These are replaced by repeated circular flashing zig-zag patterns constantly changing color and getting brighter all the time. Finally, in the center of this pulsating pattern, the dancer starts to see vertical and horizontal bands of light starting to form a grid. It is at this stage that the shaman-witch superimposes the shape his or her soul will take on while in trance state.

To really describe what happens next is perhaps the hardest thing of all. It has to be experienced and lived through before someone can really understand the effect it has. I cannot speak for other Witches even though what they have described to me tallied with what I have experienced; therefore, I will have a go at putting into words what my first trance-state working felt like. Strangely enough, the whole thing seemed to work on two levels. One moment I was me; the next, I became me within an owl. I knew who I was and that I had retained my human form. Yet at the same time I consciously knew that there was an outer skin or shape that was the owl. I also had the distinct impression that there was a gap of six to nine inches between us. When I looked at the world beyond, it was like looking out with my own eyes into the owl eyes and through them to see what was going on outside. In a sense there were two of us: one was the owl, and the other was me inside the owl, a distinct case of two separate identities intertwining and having to act as one, yet at the same time remaining two separate entities. Even though separated by a gap, I could see and feel the feathers on the owl's body while at the same time having to respond with the same feelings and actions as the "owl me."

Perhaps the scariest thing of all was finding myself perched on the branch of a tree looking down at my own body stretched out flat on the ground with the rest of the group gathered around me. All of a sudden I found myself being propped up by one of them while the masked figure of Stag was talking to me, quietly bringing me back to this world. It must have taken at least ten minutes for me to gather enough energy to stand and eventually to walk away from the site. Even then, for some hours after, I had the distinct impression of two persons being in the same body. Eventually, that impression faded, leaving only the vivid memory of what had occurred.

Something else that should be made crystal clear: as this was my first experience of trance state, I received no startling revelations or great prophetic visions. Everything I have gained from first-state trance workings came later. First I had to learn to control and direct the tool that I have been given, something that took a long time.

By now, you may wonder what owls have to do with trance workings. The answer is quite simple: European tradition has always had it that the shaman-witch while in trance state undergoes a soul transformation into either an animal or bird form. Just why this happened no one can really be sure. There are lots of theories, including the idea that it stemmed from the animal totem guardian of the clan or tribe. In the same light, we should reexamine the old witches' claims of changing into animals, usually to attend a meeting. The records of the witch trials of late Middle Ages to early modern period prove this one of the charges brought against the accused.

During the Aberdeen witch trials of 1598 (which resulted in the burning of twenty-four men and women), the accused were to have gathered at the market cross of the burgh and to dance around the cross under Satan's orders.

Some of them, including a woman named Bessie Thom, were also accused of changing themselves into other shapes such as cats and hares. In a 1658 trial at Alloa in Scotland, the catalog of crimes went even further to include witchcraft, shape-shifting, and the murder of "Cowden's bairns" (children) while in cat form.

A peculiar thing about this trial was the evidence given by Jonet (or Janet) Blak and Kathren Renny, who were also part of the coven. They said that only certain members became cats and that there was no visible change in the appearance of these cat-witches. This leaves us with two contradictory claims and nothing to explain why.

Ann Armstrong, a member of a Northumberland coven testified in 1673 that the "Devil" of the gathering changed one Ann Bates into various animal forms. The Guernsey witch Marie Bequet claimed that when the "Devil" came to her, he always changed her into a bitch, and so the list goes on and on. Time and time again, the witches' claim of shape-shifting was brought out.

Since apparently not all witches had this ability, we could possibly conclude that a two-tier system operated in former covens, hence the ability of some to see themselves as animals.

The Nordic Pagan tradition offers a specific type of witchcraft called Seior witchcraft, a specific form of ecstatic divinatory practice that reached its development during the Viking era. It was associated with the cult of the Vanir, the older part of the Norse pantheon. The Goddess Freya, one of the three Vanir deities (Freya, her brother Freyr, and Njord), was portrayed as riding in a wagon or chariot drawn by cats, thus making them sacred to both her and the Seior witches. These witches or sorceresses were credited, on the dark side, with the ability to blast cattle, raise storms, and damage crops—the same crimes the historic witches often stood accused of.

Reconsidering the evidence of the witch trials, we might ask why those victims were accused of shape-shifting, an accusation absurd on its face, unless perhaps what "shape-shifting" really meant was once common knowledge, its meaning only becoming distorted with time.

I suspect that the true meaning of shape-shifting indeed gradually became misunderstood, from being true only in a spiritual sense to being a seemingly nonsensical accusation that someone physically was transformed into a cat or other animal. Rather, this accusation represents the remains of a long shamanistic tradition of soul shape-changing while in trance state, a tradition that had been slowly dying over the centuries. But even though it was practically moribund, its relics offered sufficient clues for us to establish some of the animals and birds sacred to the Craft that would have provided ideal vehicles for soul transformation while in trance, plus some of the reasons why they were appropriate.

Stag would have been a primary shape, even though more Celtic by tradition than Anglo-Saxon. He is by far the oldest, as witnesses by the famous cave painting of a man covered by a deer hide performing a ritual. Translated into shamanistic terms, the painting shows a robed and masked figure that in first-state trance would visit the Otherworld as a stag to seek out the stag-god of the wild herds. By going bodily through the motions of the hunt and kill, his soul would be doing the same in the Otherworld to show the God what was needed.

The Celtic God-figure Cernunnos, often viewed as god of the herds and their fertility, was originally a hunters' god before the early Celts changed to a predominately pastoral culture. But though the god's image would change, the way to meet him face-to-face would not.

Another shape would be that of Goose, who was not so much a god but the messenger of the Goddess. On the rare occasions when we see the goose pictured in a Craft context, it is nearly always at the feet of the Goddess, gazing up at her with adoring eyes. The mythos of the goose makes an allegory of a natural fact in order to illustrate an tenet of the faith. Even today there is still some magic in standing on the edge of an estuary watching wild geese fly in to winter over in the British Isles. Today we know where they came from and the vast distances they fly to get here, but earlier inhabitants of this country did not. All they knew was that the geese turned up at the onset of winter and stayed until spring. In the past, winter frequently was the time of death for the old, the young, and the weak, so in time the legend grew up that the coming of the goose brought death. When the geese departed for unknown places, they took with them the souls of the winter's dead, returning with them to the Goddess's realm. Consequently, when a shaman needed to reach out to the ancestral spirits, what better way than to assume the shape of the bird that carried off their souls?

Two other masks that represent the Craft tradition and are worthy of being included in shamanistic rites are those of the Hound and the Hare. The Hound belongs to the mythos of Herne as the Horned God mounted on the Night-Mare. Some Witch covens maintain a tradition that at the end of the Candlemas rite the members become the Hell-Hounds of the Wild Hunt. Snapping and snarling at the heels of the Night-Mare, they follow the old Horned God in a wild midnight ride over the countryside, chasing the souls of the dead back into the Underworld. This hearkens back to the old theme that the shades of the dead left their domain at night to haunt their descendants. It then became the job of the witch-priests and priestesses to bind these spirits to their own world by magical means, something still reflected in the Candlemas rites even though now more symbolic than a supernatural defense against supernatural activity.

In the same vein, through the mask of the Mare we see one of the main myths of the old witch tradition. The Night-Mare is the dread steed of the Horned God, the instrument for driving hostile souls back into the Underworld as well as a symbol of divine retribution. This ill-omened animal was long associated with fear, haunting, and the Underworld, hence the bad dream that awakens us in a cold sweat of fear still is called a nightmare.

These are only four of the many animals and birds associated with the European Craft which became symbols within a certain strata of the faith. Other cultures would have developed other symbolic forms as key elements in their beliefs, things that are alien to us and also useless in a shamanistic sense because we are not steeped in their tradition. But one thing that has not changed is first-state trance and the four steps it follows. The final step is crucial: in it we superimpose on the grid the mask of the form our soul will take on when free from the body during a trance working.

When any group follows a shaman-witch tradition, the maximum number of people involved would be thirteen, in effect making it a cult within a cult. Why only thirteen? As arbitrary as this number may seem, there is a practical reason for it. Experience has shown that the more people are in a circle "pacing a mill," the harder it is to get them all working together—especially on a dark night. Keeping the number of a magical group down to thirteen makes life easier all around. Having fewer than thirteen does not invalidate the concept; in fact, it was probably more traditional for a group to have two or three members who were shamans than a full thirteen. The number thirteen seems to be a modern convention, which has the added attraction of letting any group that wants to follow this path gradually grow into it.

The first thing, then, that a would-be shaman-witch must do is to adopt an animal mask and personality for the rites. The masks most familiar to me are those of Stag, Fox, Boar, Goose, Owl, Raven, Squirrel, Hare, Hound, Cat, Ram, Mare, and Swan. Arbitrary as this list may seem, these were the ones my group settled on, and everyone involved with our workings would know and understand why they were chosen and the particular Craft mythos that led to them being chosen. In fact, the mask could have been that of a duck-billed platypus, providing it has some relevance to the person concerned. The mask is nothing more than the illusion that is imprinted on the grid at the start of a trance journey. To be honest about it, the shamanistic rites have been and always will be somewhat theatrical. They are a total illusion that in the end becomes a total reality. The mask, when worn, is an outward and visible face of that illusion being presented to the world while inwardly acting as a key to the inwardly changing shape of that spark of divinity, that core essence, of the shaman's soul.

Today the climate of opinion about the Craft is changing, bringing about a renewed interest in the shamanistic elements of the faith. But by the time this happened, the shamanistic side of the Craft was almost dead. Anyone wanting to follow that particular path has two options: either to try recreating something from the past or using material from other cultures, neither option being what I would call ideal. Now, if one accepts the basic premise that shamanism is basically breath control with chanting to take the shaman through the four steps of first-stage trance, anything beyond this can be created on the spot just as our group has, and this new creation will have same validity as some practice worked for a thousand years. We revived the technique of animal masks and found that this old technique worked well with new masks. We chose our masks for their Craft connections, then researched everything we knew about the mythos of each animal.

To be honest, the idea of creating a series of coven masks was not ours in the first place; it came from another, older gathering I had worked with in the past. As a point of interest, we feel that three masks in particular are the most important: the Stag, Raven, and Squirrel. These are the nearest thing to coven officers the masked rites have. King Stag is the group's leader, the one who carries the staff of office in the circle. Stag also never enters into first-state trance because he is the observer, the one who calls for an end to the trance and ritual.

The mask of Raven recalls his aspect of taker-of-the-souls-of-the-dead as well as his aspect of Trickster. A special rite for Raven involves taking the rest of the gathering through a spiral dance to a marked spot called the Tower, symbolizing carrying off the souls of the dead to the castle of the Goddess.

Squirrel is the group's shaman-seer, living in the branches of the World Tree *Yggdrasil*, whose roots are in the Underworld and its trunk and branches in the Upper World. Like its real-life counterpart, the soul of Squirrel has the ability to use the tree as a ladder while seeking knowledge from both realms.

Admittedly, it is hard to come to terms mentally with what is going on. If you would be a shaman, you must come to grips with the idea of who you are as opposed to what you are, then let the persona in the mask totally dominate your whole being. Let our own personality recede into the background while the "illusion" that is the mask becomes the reality that is the rite, thus freeing your soul from the body to seek out the Godhead. Because being a shaman-witch is such a highly individualistic endeavor, no one can really show you how to do this; only you can tell which is the right mask.

Having found one, you must grow into it and make it your own. One of the best ways I have found to do this is to hang the mask from your personal forked altar stang[3] and just sit there contemplating the implications of taking it off the stang before actually removing it and putting it on. Through this process, you can see your self symbolically receiving from the Horned God, whose servant you are, the gift of shape-shifting into the form that the mask represents. The mask gives you the power to travel beyond this world to the realm of death and the world beyond death where you come face-to-face with the Godhead in a form or shape you can comprehend.

As an analogy, imagine that you are in a square tower. You can see the four walls, walk around them, reach out and touch them. You know that something is beyond these walls, but you can only guess what is outside. You can only know for sure if you go through the door, walk around the tower, and look at each wall in turn. If you imagine the inside of the tower to be life, the walls as the barrier of death, then you can only see the other side in death. Yet the true shaman is the one who can see both sides of the walls at the same time. The first-stage trance is the pseudodeath that the shaman endures in order to gain the foresight and magic that was once vital to the life of the tribe.

Today, perhaps, we are no longer governed by the forces of nature in quite the same way. We no longer have to grow our daily bread; we leave the production problems to others. Instead, the trance should be used to reach out beyond the boundaries of this world. Otherwise, we can spend hour upon hour in discussion, advance all sorts of theories, even paint pretty little pictures of our concepts, but how can we live them? How do we find the Castle that spins without motion between two worlds to live out its meaning? How do we follow the path of the Rose beyond the Grave and see the wastelands bloom again with our own eyes? How do we experience the spirals of existence, seeing in them the creating of many of our cherished beliefs? How do we trace the path that in the end everyone must trace, then return bringing with us the spiritual knowledge so gained? Only through trance, the oldest working tool used by humanity in its search for the Godhead.

Notes

1. European tradition points to the use of animal masks in shamanistic rites, but other cultures using first-state trance developed their own "keys," and these might take other forms. Despite the use of different "keys," the use of first-state trance as a shamanistic tool is in no way invalidated.
2. Letter to William G. Gray.
3. The forked stang is, of course, also a stylized image of the Horned God.

About the Author

Evan John Jones first came into contact with Witchcraft and the occult during the 1960s, a time of great change in Britain which stemmed from the repeal in 1951 of the Witchcraft Act. By 1960, Witchcraft as a subject was firmly placed in the public mind. His interest in Witchcraft both in theory and as a practical system of belief has never wavered. Ex-regular Army and an engineer by profession, he was later forced to retire by ill health. He is married and now lives in Brighton, not far from the Downs where he first experienced the magic of the Witches' circle. Evan John Jones is the author of *Witchcraft: A Tradition Renewed*, edited by Doreen Valiente and published by Robert Hale in 1990, with a North American edition published by Phoenix Publishing in 1990 and a Brazilian edition published by Bertrand Brasil S.A. in 1992.

© Zelda Gordon

Obtaining a
Power Animal

by G. A. Hawk

Obtaining a power animal as an inner plane friend or ally
and then maintaining and strengthening this contact is the
foundation of all successful shamanic work. It provides a
much-needed counterpoint and grounding for all inner
journeying and all spiritual practices. In the absence of such
grounding, it has been noticed that psychics and mediums
tend to become physically unbalanced, sickly, or grossly fat
(e.g., Dion Fortune, H. P. Blavatsky).

Shamanic practice disregards belief or faith as largely irrelevant and focuses on personal experience, empirical evidence, and the pragmatism of results that make a difference.
Both drumming and dancing with your power animal effectively take you into the shamanic state of consciousness and
raise shamanic or magical power. In turn, this power is essential for the effective practice of magic: the deliberate production of positive synchronicities.

Dancing and Drumming to Enter the Shamanic State of Consciousness

1. Obtain a one-sided drum (a seventeen-inch diameter is ideal) and a decent beater.

2. Completely alone, in the privacy of your home, in almost complete darkness, you are going to drum and dance for a minimum of fifteen minutes.

3. The dancing can be freeform or a two-step in a clockwise circle. Keep your eyes almost shut, open enough that you can avoid colliding with nearby objects.

4. The drumming *must* be a regular, monotonous sonic input at a fairly fast pace. It is extremely important that you refrain from introducing any tune or patterning.

5. While dancing, focus entirely on a total awareness of feelings or sensations inside your body. The objective is to extend awareness beyond head-consciousness to the rest of your body. How do your arms and legs feel on the inside? How does your back feel? Monitor any sensations or feelings in the heart area. Feel anything in your solar plexus or lower abdomen? The objective is not to scan area by area, but to attain and hold total body awareness from the inside. If the inside of your body begins to feel illuminated with a white or golden light, that is fine. You are doing a shamanic version of the famous Buddhist mindfulness exercise. If thoughts interfere, let them go, and return to full body awareness. If done properly, this focus on internal body awareness quiets the chatter of the mind.

Commentary: If you examine these instructions, you will see that they are designed to keep your body moving, in high arousal, while the regular and monotonous sound of the drum takes your mind into low arousal (delta or theta). The shamanic trance is different from various forms of meditation, in that it requires dissociation: the mind goes into low arousal while the body is kept active and in motion.[1]

Preparation for the Visionary Journey

There is a drill or preparatory technique that seems to facilitate access to the shamanic state of consciousness. This technique was first described by G. M. Glaskin as part of a past-life regression procedure.[2]

1. Massage your feet and ankles for two minutes. Pay particular attention to any sore spots on the ankles.

2. Lie down, close your eyes, and use the soft flesh of your palm to massage your forehead over the area of the third eye (between and just above the eyebrows). Use a circular, clockwise motion. As you do this, visualize a vortex of golden energy, rotating clockwise, and centered on this area (one minute).

3. Use the fingertips of both hands to massage your temples in a circular motion (two minutes).

4. Relax, arms to the sides, legs uncrossed, eyes closed. Imagine that your feet and ankles are extending by two inches. This extension of your energy field is often signaled by a definite sensation within one minute. Shift your internal awareness to your head and neck. Imagine that they are extending by two inches. Shift your awareness back to your feet and ankles. Imagine that they are extending by twelve inches. Back to your head and neck. Imagine that they are extending by twelve inches. Back to your feet and ankles: extend forty-eight inches. Back to your head and neck: extend forty-eight inches. At this point you may have a feeling that your feet are touching one wall of the room, while the top edge of your hair is touching the opposite wall.

5. Expand your energy field to fill the room and continue doing this until you feel that the front edge touches the ceiling. This is often perceived as a faint sensation of cold, somewhere above your abdomen.

An Inner World Map or Experiential Cosmology

Worldwide shamanism tends to divide the inner world into three major domains: Upper World, Middle World, and Lower World. The Upper World is made up of sectors or regions that are experientially above us. The Middle World is made up of regions that are experientially adjacent to our ordinary reality. The Lower World is made up of regions or levels that are experientially below us. Here the terms "below" and "above" are descriptive and not evaluative. The Lower World is "just as good" and the Upper World.

For people raised in Western Civilization, it is important to understand that the Lower World is not Hades or Hell. The notion of a Lower World filled with demons and torment was the bizarre invention of those Nazis of Antiquity, the Assyrians, around 1000 B.C.E.[3] From the Assyrians, this anal-sadistic fantasy passed to other Near-Eastern groups and eventually to Christianity.

The various levels of the Lower World are the home of the power animals. These power animals are good and powerful beings. They are the immortal archetypes of the various animal species (including those whose last physical exemplars were exterminated by humans).

Wicca, as a Pagan nature religion, and shamanism, as the visionary spiritual technology of the hunters and gatherers, share a common interest in circumventing or reversing two thousand years of contempt for the body, and exploitative contempt for nature and the rest of the animals. We celebrate sensuality, sexuality, and pleasure (but not necessarily human reproduction, for this has become a serious threat to the viability of plant and animal life on Earth). Unlike the religions of the Father, we know that animals have noble and good spirits and these spirits are sometimes better than those of humans.

A Visionary Journey to the Lower World

You will need a good-quality tape player (with Dolby noise reduction) and a good-quality drumming tape. The drumming tape (often advertised as "drumming for the shamanic journey") should contain nothing but a high-quality recording of regular, repetitive, monotonous drumming, with no words, tunes, or patterns. I use a double-drum tape and a single-drum tape which uses a water drum. Experiment until you find the one that works best for you. The obvious places to look are your local occult or metaphysical bookstore and ads in the pages of a journal such as *Shaman's Drum*.

You will need a mask or bandanna to cover your eyes and insure total darkness.

To journey to the Lower World you will visualize entering a tunnel that goes down. The entrance to this tunnel has to be a point of departure in ordinary reality: some place which you have seen or visited. Your options are variations on three basic entrances: a cave, a tree with a wide trunk, or a hot spring. Select your entrance on the basis of familiarity and gut feeling.

The purpose or mission of your journey will be to find a power animal and establish contact. Strictly speaking, the power animal will find you; and if you are wise, you will accept gratefully, provided that the archetypal animal is part of one of the suitable categories. Generally speaking, all mammals and birds are excellent. Snakes are borderline but clearly acceptable, as long as they are not associated with slime or do not attack you. An example will help to clarify this. On the one hand, a former student of mine is very happy with his power animal: a thirty-foot boa constrictor.

On the other hand, a nest of slimy snakes would be most unsuitable. Fish (e.g., a shark) are also borderline, but acceptable if they do not attack you. *Insects are unsuitable and unacceptable* as power animals. The reason for this is that parasitic intrusions that infect the human energy field take the form of insects, slimy snakes, or sludge. Furthermore, tame or captive animals are unsuitable as power animals. Thus a horse would be an excellent power animal, provided that it is a wild horse. Western people are most likely to get as power animals wild eagles, falcons, owls, lions, tigers, panthers, wolves, boars, seals, sea lions, otters, bears, bisons, monkeys, apes, or elephants.

Be prepared to accept whatever suitable archetypal animal comes to you and agrees to be your power animal. You should only reject or ignore entities in the unsuitable categories. The power of a power animal does not depend on our preconceptions. A wild ram or goat is just as effective as an eagle, lion, or tiger.

The Journey

1. Lock the front door, disconnect the phone, and make sure of total privacy. Since darkness is needed for shamanic work, evening or night is the best time. Turn on your drumming tape at a suitable volume. Lie down on your back, in darkness, eyes covered, arms and legs uncrossed. Begin to remember and visualize your point of departure in ordinary reality.

2. From here on, you are going to describe your entire journey *out loud*, as it happens. This is very important in order to produce the dissociation which is peculiar to the shamanic state of consciousness. Furthermore, speaking your journey out loud dramatically increases the reality of the experience.

3. If you are starting from a familiar cave, visualize it in detail and describe it out loud. Establish internal sen-

sory awareness. Touch the walls. How do they feel? What are the colors? How does the air smell? What is the temperature? Touch the ground on which you stand. If you are starting from the wide trunk of a familiar tree, describe it out loud, touch and smell the bark and leaves.

Now, imagine an open door on the trunk and go inside. Once you are inside your cave or tree, look for a tunnel that goes down. In the case of the tree, this will be the inside of a giant root which plunges into the earth. If you are in a cave, this will be a tunnel which you have never seen before. Make any size adjustments as needed; for instance, if the tunnel is too small, reduce your size. Remember, you are describing everything out loud.

4. Walk into your tunnel and touch the walls. As soon as the ground begins to slope, you can sit and slide. Usually, there is some form of minimal indirect lighting. Let the sound of the drum propel you forward. Some people just flow downward at top speed: feet first, head first, it does not matter. Do whatever feels comfortable.

5. Once you are moving inside the tunnel, look ahead for an exit which usually appears as a point of light. If you see it, head for it. If you have trouble finding an exit, then go ahead and imagine (deliberately visualize) an exit as a point of light and head for it. (This procedure is quite proper because—in alternative language—you are entering a sector of the astral plane or the Jungian collective unconscious. And there, as occultists know, what begins as deliberate imagination quickly becomes reality.)

6. As soon as you come out, stop, scan the scene, and describe everything out loud as you perceive it. Establish sensory awareness. Where are you? Is it day or night?

Is it warm or cold? Are you in a desert, at the sea shore, in a land of snow and ice, in a tropical rain forest? What is the ground like? Touch it. Any rocks? Touch them. Smell the air. Is there any wind? Can you guess the time from the approximate position of the Sun or Moon? Do you see any trees, plants, or vegetation? What sounds do you hear?

7.   It is possible, though unlikely, that you may come out into blinding light or total darkness. If that happens, then close your inner eyes and scan your environment using your other inner senses (e.g., hearing, touch, smell). Your first move should be to touch the ground and find out whether you are standing on rock, sand, soil, or shallow water. If you scan patiently, it is very likely that when you open your inner eyes, you will begin to see the scene in the front of you.

8.   The next thing to do is to stand up (in your shamanic inner world), open your arms and call out, "Will my power animal please come to me." Repeat this out loud three times while scanning the scene from side to side, looking for signs of animal life or motion. Continue to describe everything out loud. If nothing is happening, say, "Nothing is happening." It is possible but unlikely that an animal will come to you without your having to search. If no animal shows up, then begin walking. As you walk, pause every few steps and call out, "Will my power animal please come to me." The scene may change suddenly: for example, you were walking in a desert, and now you are in a rain forest. These sudden changes are likely to bring you closer to your objective.

9.   Eventually, you will encounter an animal of one of the suitable and acceptable categories. Face the animal and ask out loud, "Are you my power animal?" Repeat this two or three times. There are three possible responses: the animal gives you a "YES" answer in words or ges-

tures, the animal gives you a "NO" answer in words or gestures, or the animal does not respond (e.g., the animal stares at you in silence). No reply is the equivalent of a "NO" answer. Thank the animal and continue your quest. Remember, you are still describing everything out loud.

Commentary: At this point you probably want to know how you can tell whether what you are experiencing is something more than make-believe or deliberate, conscious visualization. The typical question is: How do I know that this is real and that I am not making it happen? There are two criteria for the authenticity of the shamanic state of consciousness: First, you begin to experience a "high," produced by the release of beta endorphins in your brain. Second, unexpected events happen that take you by surprise. This second feature tells you that what is happening in your journey is not the result of conscious ego make-believe. Depending on your framework and model, you are contacting an alternate reality in the shamanic inner planes or in the Jungian collective unconscious.

10. Eventually, you will encounter an animal who says "YES", it is willing to be your power animal. If in doubt, ask again, and obtain a second confirmation. At this point you are likely to feel some positive emotion. You might want to touch or hug the animal. By all means do so, and thank the animal for its willingness to be your power animal. Follow this with a short visit, either on the spot, or in the animal's lair. In the context of this visit, ask your power animal to give you a signal (e.g., a gesture, a sound) which you can use to call it to you in a hurry or in an emergency. If at any point the communication becomes confused, repeat your question and say "Please explain in a manner that I will understand." Remember, you have been narrating the entire encounter out loud.

11. A power animal is not a pet and is not a deity. A power animal should be treated with utmost consideration and respect as an equal, as a dear friend from another species, which is precisely what it is. Any other kind of treatment (for example, using it as a carrier or mount without its permission or being invited to do so) will result in the loss of the power animal. You may want to ask your power animal to help you change into a fellow animal, so that you can run or fly with it at its speed. Power animals are not subject to the limitations of ordinary reality. For example, an elephant power animal can swim in the ocean (or inside the ocean), can travel inside the earth, or can fly in the sky. Furthermore, power animals are indestructible and immortal.

12. You are now ready to end your visit. Thank your power animal and ask it to take you back to your tunnel. At the entrance, say goodbye, regain your human form, enter the tunnel and let the sound of the drum bring you back up to your entrance in ordinary reality. Let the scene fade, and get up.

13. Ordinarily, as part of your weekly practice, you will do shamanic dancing with your power animal only once, before entering the inner planes to do a journey. However, this time, since you have just obtained a power animal, it is important to dance with it to strengthen the bond which you have just forged. Using a live drum (or your drumming tape) dance with your power animal for about fifteen minutes. To do this, give your agreed signal (sound or gesture) and bring the power animal to you. You will either see it in the darkness or feel its energy or both. Now begin to dance, repeating the signal call at intervals, alternating this with deliberate awareness of the inside of your body, as explained earlier. Dancing your power animal on a weekly basis is what you do for it. The power an-

imal seems to enjoy feeling once again what it is like to be in a material body. In addition, during the rest of the week, you may want to give your signal call to allow the power animal to share in some of your daily activities. However, for most people, the latter does not seem to be a full substitute for the weekly dancing with your power animal. Therefore, shamanic dancing, as described, is essential to strengthen and maintain the contact.

In summary, your weekly practice should be to start by doing shamanic dancing with your power animal, using a live drum, for about fifteen minutes. Follow with the Glaskin procedure. Finally, journey with your power animal to the Lower World, Middle World, or Upper World in pursuit of a particular purpose or mission. Shamanic dancing is the most important part of this routine; and if necessary, it can be done as frequently as every night. The Glaskin procedure is optional; if it continues to enhance your journeys, then use it. Journeying for yourself should be limited to once or twice a week.

Some Benefits of Having a Power Animal

You can now travel safely anywhere in the inner planes. You can obtain a teacher guide in the Upper World. You can travel to that sector of the Middle World where many of the dead are temporarily confused, lost, or stranded and offer help. Your power animal will protect you from harm, neutralize any malevolent or demonic entity, and provide you with completely reliable information and advice. I strongly suggest that you incorporate your power animal into any Wicca ceremonies, magical rituals, or occult pursuits in which you may be involved.

As the power of your power animal begins to flow into your life, you will experience an improvement in mood (depression tends to disappear), and an enhanced ability to cope. There will be an increased sense of control over what happens to you. It is also likely that your luck will improve. Protect your newly acquired shamanic power by not talking about it. Do not reveal the identity of your power animal (except when talking with others engaged in the same work, and then for a good reason).

Call on your power animal to help you in practical, everyday difficulties and emergencies. You may want to have it with you as protection during a journey, avoiding a driving citation, facing a stressful interview, or taking an important examination. In this area, perhaps the most important activity is doing magic with your power animal.

Some Suggested
Improvements

While it is preferable to use a live drum for dancing, for journeying you may want to use a drumming tape in a small, high-quality player, and listen to the drumming through earphones. This will allow you to journey at irregular hours of the night when it is illegal to make noise and keep others awake.

As you journey and narrate the journey out loud as it happens, you may want to tape record your journey. This will require a separate player-recorder and an extension microphone. The extension microphone should be placed a few inches away from your head. After the journey, play back the tape, and discover how much detailed information you have previously lost thanks to a measure of instant amnesia. If you want to keep a permanent record of your journey, you can transcribe it from the tape into a journal.

How to Do Magic with
Your Power Animal

Magic is the deliberate production of positive synchronicities. You do something in the inner planes, in an altered state of consciousness, and eventually this produces a desired and expected result in the objective external world. This irrational sequence seems to lie outside all currently accepted scientific paradigms. In other words, we know that it does happen, but we do not know how it happens. As practitioners of neoshamanism, we honor personal experience as the touchstone of reality and do not worry too much that the irrational half of reality remains largely unexplainable.

There is agreement among major contemporary ritual magicians that a successful magical operation depends on three fundamental factors: effective visualization, a successful focusing of the magical will, and a suitable altered state of consciousness. Effective visualization must focus on an image of the final desired outcome. (You never tell the inner powers how to go about doing their job.) The magical will is not willpower or self-denial. In the phrase of Peter Carroll, the magical will is unity of desire; and this means that you focus the desires of your entire being on a single outcome. A suitable altered state of consciousness is one that raises power and puts you in contact with the relevant inner forces. Here the shamanic state of consciousness, achieved by dancing and drumming, seems to be more powerful and effective than most other forms of magical ritual or ceremony, when the latter are used alone.

It is perfectly proper to do magic to improve your material conditions, enhance your pleasures, and increase your happiness, achievements, and fulfillment. However, if you want to avoid serious trouble, *you must remain ethical*. For example, in the area of love magic, it would be ethical and proper to do magic to "get a woman (or man) who is right for me, and with whom I can share great pleasure and happiness." It would not be ethical to use magic to try to make a specific woman (or man) fall in love with you. In the latter case, even if you succeed, the outcome is likely to bring you pain and unhappiness.

Additional important considerations are that you avoid hubris, remain humble, and not overreach. For example, if you are unemployed, it makes sense to do magic to get a job that is commensurate with your intelligence, education, and training. However, if you do not own a car, it would be stupid to do magic to obtain a $40,000 Lexus.

Inner world operations such as magic are not an excuse for outer world passivity. On the contrary, you must make all necessary moves in the ordinary external world. For example, if you need a job, you must apply for work at every opportunity, and then do magic to tip the balance in your favor.

Select the wording of your magical request with care and make sure that it says precisely what you mean. Furthermore, it must be for something that is important to you. Be very careful in selecting that final desired outcome. Once it happens or comes to you, you have to accept it. Furthermore, you have to begin to enjoy it or use it. Enjoying it or using it, "anchors" the outcome in external reality.

After suitable preparation, as described above, you do magic with your power animal in the following manner:

1. After drumming and dancing, journey to the Lower World and visit your power animal.

2. Face your power animal and ask that it bring you a single, desired outcome. It is important that you make this request both in words and by visualizing the final desired outcome. As the late Franz Bardon said, the language of the inner planes is made up of images, not words. Repeat your request two or three times.

3. Thank your power animal and inquire whether there is anything it wants to tell you.

4. Say goodbye and return from your journey.

5. Repeat this operation at weekly intervals until you get the anticipated results. In the intervals, think about something else, and don't talk about it.

Obtaining a Sigil

You can further strengthen your bond with your power animal by obtaining its sigil. A sigil is a visual design or symbolic image which is used for communication with the inner planes or collective unconscious. This is effective, because the language of the inner planes is made up of images. A given sigil may represent a message or part of a message. A sigil can also be the unique signature or emblem of an inner plane entity or spirit.

In this century, the foremost practitioner of sigil magic was the British painter Austin Osman Spare (1886–1956). (An excellent book on sigil magic is the one by the German magician Frater U.. D., *Practical Sigil Magic*.[4] In the West, sigil magic is traceable to the work of Henry Cornelius Agrippa (1486–1535) and other Renaissance magicians; however, its real origins are found in shamanism. In her investigation of Siona shamanism in the Amazon rain forest, anthropologist E. Jean Matteson Langdon has described how the Siona shamans use psychedelics (mostly *yage*, *ayahuasca*) to obtain specific designs which are later used to establish contact with particular spirits.[5]

We are concerned with a procedure that exactly parallels the one used by Siona shamans. If a sigil can be the signature or emblem of a particular entity, then your power animal has its own unique sigil. We are going to use monotonous sonic input to enter the shamanic trance and obtain the sigil directly from the power animal. It is very important that you avoid all conscious construction or ego interference and that the sigil be obtained directly from the power animal in the collective unconscious. The sigil may or may not suggest something about your power animal. On the following page are some examples of possible sigils:

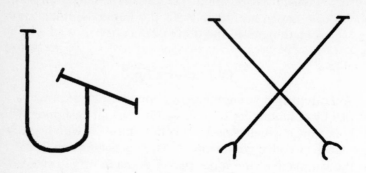

These particular sigils are only examples and useless for any practical work. The sigil that you obtain is your very own, it is the personal emblem of your power animal, and it can be used by you and no one else.

In your next journey to the Lower World ask your power animal to give you its sigil. An alternative procedure is to sit at a desk while listening to your drumming tape. In darkness, with eyes closed, visualize a clear white field the size of a drawing sheet or board. Then give your signal or gesture and call your power animal. Say, "Please give me your sigil so that I can use it to call you in an emergency." Repeat if necessary. The sigil should appear on the white field. Take a good look at it and memorize it. Thank your power animal and say goodbye. Open your eyes, turn on the light, and draw the sigil in the notebook in which you record your journeys. The sigil is private and should be kept secret. The purpose of this secrecy is to avoid loss of power.

From now on, when you dance, journey, or face an emergency, you can visualize your sigil in addition to giving your signal, call, or gesture. This is the most effective way to establish instant contact with your power animal.

Since the shamanism of the hunters and gatherers is the remote source of the occult tradition in both East and West, it follows that contemporary practitioners of the Craft can enhance the effectiveness of their ritual practice by incorporating shamanic procedures. This means using a drum to enter the shamanic trance, obtaining a power animal, and weekly dancing with your power animal. It is only with your power animal that the inner planes become safely accessible.

Notes

1. Anglique Cook and G. A. Hawk, *Shamanism and the Esoteric Tradition* (St. Paul, Minnesota: Llewellyn Publications, 1992), 92-95.

2. G. M. Glaskin, Windows of the Mind (San Leandro, California: Prism, 1974), 178-180.

3. Jeremy Black and Anthony Green, *Gods, Demons, and Symbols of Ancient Mesopotamia* (Austin: University of Texas Press, 1993), 28-63.

4. Frater U.D., *Practical Sigil Magic* (St. Paul, Minnesota: Llewellyn, 1990).

5. E. Jean Matteson Langdon, "Dau: Shamanic Power in Siona Religion" in E. Jean Matteson Langdon and Gerhard Baer, eds., *Portals of Power: Shamanism in South America* (Albuquerque: University of New Mexico Press, 1992), 53-55.

About the Author

G. A. Hawk is the pen name of George A. Huaco, who teaches at a university in the Southwest. Together with Angelique Cook, G. A. Hawk is the coauthor of *Shamanism and the Esoteric Tradition*, published by Llewellyn in 1992.

The Geography of the Otherworld

by Angela Barker

> You will find to the left of the palace of Hades a well-spring, and beside it a white cypress. Drink not of the water thereof, but proceed to the Lake of Mnemosyne, from which chill waters flow. You will find Guardians before it. Say: "I am a child of Earth and of starry Heaven; I am dry with thirst and I perish. Give me, quickly, the cold water which flows from the Lake of Memory." They themselves will give you to drink from the holy well-spring. And then you can follow the Sacred Way, the glorious procession of the other *Mystai* and *Bacchoi*.
>
> —Orphic funerary inscription, first millennium B.C.E.

Occasionally, when in a meditative mood, I construct a mental image of a corporation boardroom and seat around the table those men and women of wisdom from ancient and more modern times who, I instinctively feel, have contributed to the present state of our metaphysical understanding. Not only humans assemble here. The company includes gods, animal forms, and nature spirits who, on that subtle plane of inspired imagery, are able to discourse with those mortals who have known and respected them since the inception of our race.

Such is the way of the eclectic, for he or she who follows that path will know that Truth is not be experienced from a single source but from the continual weighing and sifting of many traditions' fruits. As the refining process continues, times occur when the siftings, as they fall on the table of experience, will produce patterns triggering far memories that combine to produce the phenomena we call a "true initiation." On the physical plane, with goodwill and sanction from the boardroom, a person or group can achieve similar results, and it is with such a meeting of complementary personalities that I introduce this chapter.

For some time I had dreamt secretly of being present at a meeting between two cherished and long-standing friends. Both Murry Hope and Alan Richardson are well-known authors on esoteric matters, and I saw that should they meet on neutral ground with me, we might form a triune juxtaposition possessing something more than ordinary potential.

This unplanned meeting occurred seemingly by accident. As one who is inclined to treat sacred places with some reserve, it is with a little embarrassment that I have to relate that it took place in the Isle of Avalon itself, the English market town of Glastonbury. With little or no preamble, there we were: Murry—opera singer, healer, and very psychic; Alan—tireless worker on behalf of the physically and mentally handicapped, keen follower of football, and a devoted family man; and myself—retired jazz musician, teacher of comparative mythology and metaphysics, and as an acquaintance once said of me, "she is a catalyst," because he saw my presence as causing things to happen to others. Providing such events are meaningful or at least pleasant, then I have no objection to being a catalyst.

Murry had written to me informing me that she was to be the guest speaker at a function to which outsiders would be admitted for a nominal fee. Under these circumstances, she said, she would be delighted if some of her friends would care to attend. I arrived early, far too early as it happened, and after exploring the town, went to the assembly rooms and the small refectory–cum–anteroom that provided coffee to while away the last half hour before the event. I did not know that Alan had planned to attend until his cheery voice from behind my chair brought me to the realization that this was to be a special kind of day, the manifestation of a long yearned-for hope.

The meeting was well-attended, and Murry's lecture inspiring as she brought her audience into communion with the "Old Ones," those archetypes who have always formed the framework of our common heritage. Afterward we returned once more to the refectory where the speaker was, of course, in great demand. My thoughts were nevertheless concerned with that trinity that I felt so strongly at that time and place: an almost visible energy bond uniting three friends for some obscure purpose. It would be wrong for me to give the impression that we sat there with our refreshments discussing matters of high import; we did little more than exchange pleasantries. Nor would I wish to convey the impression that I thought some great pillar of power was rising above us. This was the only occasion that the three of us had been together, and, metaphysically speaking, three— or rather threefoldness—denotes potential. We must look to the number seven for kinetic events.

The time for farewells arrived all too soon. By this point, two other people were in our company: a charming Buddhist couple who, out of interest in the day's proceedings, had volunteered to drive me to and from Glastonbury. As it was their first visit to the town, I suggested that before leaving they might like to visit the Chalice Well Gardens, to which they readily agreed. I find Glastonbury rather ostentatious, I confess, but that description does not apply to the beautiful gardens on its periphery, the fabled repository of the Holy Grail. The place is immaculately maintained by the Companions of the Chalice Well, one of whom will accept a donation at the gate house and hand you an explanatory leaflet. Apart from a perfunctory reference to the alleged arrival of St. Joseph of Arimathea in 37 C.E. (almost certainly an invention), the leaflet describes the symbolism of the Grail in most scholarly terms. No ordinary tourist handout, this: it could have been written by Carl Jung.

So it was that we, mingling with the other visitors, seated ourselves in the small rock garden that surrounds the Well head. Within a hundred yards to our left, the ground swept abruptly upward, 520 feet, to form Glastonbury Tor, beneath which, as legend has it, is the entrance to the Otherworld.

My eyes followed the line of the Tor down to ground level and back to the Well, which, as customary, had its lid down. The ornate cover (an replica of earlier Victorian ironwork) features the ancient symbol of the *vesica piscis:* two interlocking circles, each with its circumference passing through the center of the other, said to be the basic figure of sacred geometry.[1] I compared it to the similar figure used in mathematical "set theory," where it is called a Venn diagram. At this point I experienced an almost unearthly sensation. It was as if my blood were being displaced by a strange and much subtler fluid. Could it really be the case, an inner voice was saying, that an American scientist had, without realizing it, discovered the meaning of the Grail?

As I sat in that magical garden contemplating the symbolism of the Well's cover, it was as though spectral figures were passing by, each imparting a seemingly incongruous piece of information with which I was already familiar, but in an order that made a meaningful pattern. Overwhelming as the experience was, I was obliged to return to some semblance of normality when my friends said it was time to depart. I mentally sealed all that had happened into a package and stored it carefully for later scrutiny.

Our journey was relatively short, just over thirty miles to a canal wharf close to the city of Bath, where I boarded the 35-foot motor cruiser that is my home. That night I slept and dreamt well, continuing the saga that had been initiated in Glastonbury.

A couple of days later, I was sitting on a bench beside the canal while the boat took on a fresh supply of drinking water. Suddenly I was aware of Alan, seated beside me. I was not surprised at this as he has a facility of appearing at opportune moments. Many have been the times, while out walking, that I have felt the need to ask Alan something or other and have seen him conveniently step out from behind a tree or appear from around a corner, a kind of serendipity on the human level.

Not surprisingly, our conversation turned to holy wells, particularly one or two in the immediate locality. Without warning, he leapt to his feet. I felt sure he had left the ground as he shouted, "That's it! That's it!" and with true Archimedean fervor, he made off toward his car. "I'll be in touch," he shouted as he slammed the door and was gone. A note duly arrived explaining that our conversation had provided him with the last piece of a jigsaw he needed for a new book. The result of this episode was his *Earth God Rising*, published in 1990; his side of the encounter is given on page 167.[2] Needless to say, there is much of the Otherworld in the text.

I, meanwhile, had already begun writing what was to become a long essay entitled "The Legomonism of the Fisher King." Legomonism is a word of Greek derivation which implies a cryptic message from the past, possibly left in symbolic form by our forebears for the enlightenment of later generations—assuming they can decode it, of course. (These days we indulge in similar practices when we bury time capsules under prominent buildings and even fire them into space, for instance, the Voyager space probes.) The Fisher King was the title given in legend to the guardian of the Holy Grail.

My essay followed the theme of something that had been lost, stolen, or withdrawn from human possession by divine edict—but with the difference that had that indeed happened, then there was a strong possibility that that something was in the process of being recovered. Along with the Grail story, I found it necessary to take a long, hard look at those ancient myths of magic cauldrons, cornucopias, golden fleeces, and all such items that were considered so important that select groups of people were inspired to go in search of them. I recalled the fascinating thesis of Julian Jaynes's book *The Origin of Consciousness in the Breakdown of the Bicameral Mind,* which makes a hypothesis that our distant ancestors were motivated mainly by mental processes emanating from the right hemisphere of the brain more than the verbal, logical left hemisphere.[3] Jaynes suggests that this faculty gradually faded away, disappearing completely around 1200 B.C.E., and we can assume that those old stories were formed around the same period. At the Chalice Well I had imagined an ancient sage preparing a message for future generations. He wanted to describe the bicameral (two-chambered) mind for future generations in the simplest way, and so he prepared a legomonism, a symbolic time capsule. He drew a *vesica piscis.* Our benevolent legomonist could scarcely have had greater success: not only was the floor plan of Glastonbury Abbey based on that geometric form, but throughout the town there is no souvenir shop or jewelry shop that does not flaunt it in the form of pendants, broaches, table mats, and similar paraphernalia. In Glastonbury, the vesica piscis is rarely out of sight.

It was Dr. Roger Sperry, a Californian, who received the Nobel Prize for physiology in 1981 for his work on split-brain techniques. He established that our logical thinking is primarily the product of the brain's left hemisphere whereas the right half is primary in matters artistic, creativity, dreams, and a number of other phenomena, largely conjectural, that we call paranormal. Among the last we can list the projection of poltergeist activity, psychokinesis, clairvoyance, extrasensory perception, and, it follows, familiarity with the Otherworld. If Jaynes is right, our ancestors did not need recourse to altered states of consciousness (ASCs). They were as familiar with the invisible as they were with the material, and they existed alongside their gods.

Now, I am well aware that many interpretations of the Grail story have been put forward, most of them highly conjectural. These range from seeing the Grail as a fertility symbol to a cup of blood. I make no apology, therefore, for adding my own: that the Grail, or the right-brain intuitive faculty—was lost to humanity around 3,200 years ago but rediscovered during the 1960s by Dr. Roger Sperry and his colleagues at the California Institute of Technology. (Here I would like to emphasize that any readers who are inclined to review my evidence in light of their own data and experience do me the greatest honor. Those who reject it out of hand—or who take everything without question—will have misconstrued my motives.)

I see the original Grail as that which ancient Egyptians showed on the head of their goddess Nephthys. An aspect of the triple goddess Isis, the other being Hathor, Nephthys was known as the "goddess of hidden dimensions."

In the Greek myths we have the cornucopia or horn of plenty, described as one of the horns of the goat Amalthea, a miraculous horn said to dispense unlimited quantities of whatever sustenance was called for. Most scholars, however, agree that the story refers to food of an ethereal kind, what esotericists refer to as *mana* or *prana*. Mythological references to the cornucopia are sparse, and we are not told whether the horn came from the right or left side. There is, nevertheless, some indication in the story of Deianeira where Herakles (Hercules) broke off the right horn of the bull-headed monster Achelous. We are told that this horn became one and the same as Amalthea's while in the hands of the Naiads.

Moving to early Celtic Ireland, another story tells how the Dagda, father-god of the mysterious Tuatha de Danaan (pronounced "Too-har-day-dahnahn"), the people of Dana, owned a cauldron with cornucopia-like qualities. Some people assume that this magic vessel later found its way to Wales, where it became the property of the Welsh giant god, Bran the Blessed, and was subsequently returned to Ireland in the possession of King Matholwych (pronounced "Matt-o-loo"). By this time the cauldron had taken on the added property of being able to resuscitate dead warriors who were boiled in it overnight, but the revived men remained mute.[4] Since the left brain controls the power of speech, perhaps they were reconstituted on a different level.

The most famous cauldron story of all is that of the Cauldron of Cerridwen, which I see as a gift to my thesis. The hag-goddess Cerridwen had concocted a noxious brew in her cauldron, the first three drops of which were to be given to her ugly son, Avagddu (pronounced "Avaghdoo") with the object of making him into an inspired poetic genius. The remainder of the contents were poisonous. The cauldron had to be stirred for a year and a day; for this purpose she employed a young lad, Gwion Bach, who duly carried out his task until, on the last day, three drops spat from the liquid and landed on the back of his hand. Sucking his hand to cool it, he realized that he had deprived Avagddu of his intended destiny and in so doing had incurred the wrath of Cerridwen, who pursued him as he fled for his life. Much shape-changing took place between the two until Gwion, in the form of a grain of wheat, was swallowed by Cerridwen, transformed into a black hen.

Now pregnant with Gwion, she gave birth to him after nine months, intending to kill him. But the boy was so beautiful that she changed her mind and cast him adrift in a coracle, from which he was later rescued by one Gwyddno, who brought him up as his own son. Gwyddno named the boy Taliesin, and he became the prime bard of Cymru (Wales). The three drops of liquor from the cauldron had given him supernatural insight.

The story is chock-full of symbolism: the three drops, being twice-born (as were also a number of Greek gods), and the acquisition of a superb right-brain faculty. I have had to leave out more symbolism in the interest of brevity.

I agree with those who hold the view that the mythologies of the Greeks and the Celts both originated in predynastic Egypt and, some would add, in Atlantis before that. The stories vary according to the people who tell them, but miraculously the basic themes and symbolism remain intact.

Chronology is difficult where mythology is concerned, but, as a yardstick, I usually place the arrival of the rather supernatural Tuatha de Danaan in Ireland at about 2000 B.C.E. and the very human Milesians, who followed them, at little over a millennium later. The latter, having been expelled from Crete, traveled to Ireland as the "People of Milèd" from Caria, in Asia Minor. The two races mixed like oil and water, but eventually a compromise was reached whereby the Milesians would live above the ground and the Danaans beneath it. The Danaans hated the Milesians for driving them from the surface and, being adept at shape-changing, turned up in various guises as tricksters throughout Irish mythology. They later became known as the Fairy Folk or Sidhe (pronounced "Shee"). Their main dwelling was said to be the very large tumulus, New Grange, by the side of the River Boyne.

There is some confusion here, for some other entities and deities have also been referred to as "fairy folk," including giant-gods like Gwyn Ap Nudd, the king of the underworld, later known as the king of the fairies. It was he also who was generally accepted as the Fisher King, the king who through an apparent misdemeanor lost the Grail. At that time he was struck by a magic spear that made him impotent: that same spear is represented in the ornate *vesica* on the Chalice Well cover, where it serves as the draw-bolt.

A nineteenth-century American collection of myths, *Bullfinch's Mythology*, in a chapter called "The Quest of the Sangreal," notes that after the loss of the Sangreal (Holy Grail), "...an iron age succeeded to the happiness which its presence had diffused among the tribes of Britain." This is the cup-of-blood idea that I mentioned before, a Christian distortion, and since I know of no "iron age" that began in the Sixth Century C.E., I tend to disregard "sang real" (holy blood) stories.[5] An iron age did, however, commence circa

1000 B.C.E.—not too far from the date suggested by Jaynes for the breakdown of the "bicameral mind."

My essay included much metaphysical data which would be inappropriate here, but one aspect of it is essential, and that concerns triads. Athanasius Kircher, in his *Iter Exaticum Coeleste* (1660), tells us that the entire universe is composed of triads, and with more than forty years of metaphysical studies behind me, I agree. Dualism exists only in the minds of politicians, priests, lawyers, and some deluded scientists like Descartes! Plato acknowledged the universality of the threefold law in his *Timaeus*, and mythology throws it at us from all directions. Why then the bicameral mind? It is because the mind, broadly speaking, is contained in two compartments, but the third-order component of the triad is the energy exchange between them. It is just this part of the system that has broken down as surely as if it had been pierced by a magic spear. We know we have a left brain that functions and a right brain that functions, but Sperry, along with other investigators like Marilyn Ferguson (*The Aquarian Conspiracy*)[6] and Marilee Zdensk (*The Right Brain Experience*)[7] have demonstrated conclusively that neither hemisphere is remotely aware of the other. To describe a condition wherein the two hemispheres do work together, I coined the term (with respect to Jaynes's terminology) "bicameral balance."

In most of us the balance is tilted to the left. The minority in whom it tilts to the right is described variously as "artsy-craftsy," "dreamers," "peculiar," "not to be taken seriously" and "not to be trusted." Communities such as the African Bushmen, Australian Aborigines, and American Indians that historically had a bias to the right are seen as primitive. This is a tragedy, for we could have learned much from these peoples had we been worthy of their respect.

Hugh Brody, in his *Maps and Dreams: Indians and the British Columbia Frontier,*[8] relates how the Beaver Indians of that area habitually dreamed of their future hunting expeditions and drew maps of the locations upon awakening. The future hunt, it seems, always accorded with the dreams. While under siege by missionaries they undertook to dream a map of heaven. This they did, but, alas, it is not reproduced in Brody's book.

The procedures adopted by the Beaver Indians raise an important question. Is the Otherworld the place where we sometimes find ourselves in our dreams and presume to go to permanently when we die? I strongly recommend keeping a dream diary, which I have done for many years. It will become apparent from analyzing the collected material that dreams occur on many levels, from purely personal feedback systems to mysterious, magical scenarios that could well represent another plane of existence. Using the as above, so below concept, I often employ a tree analogy that is my own but which closely corresponds to the *Gish Gana tree of Apsu* from early Sumerian myth, which symbolized the interaction between the conscious and the unconscious as did the *vesica piscis*. *Apsu* was the Sumerian Lower World.

Closely associated with the dream world are so-called "out-of-body experiences" (OOBEs), which I prefer to refer to as "remote viewing." In 1973 an American businessman, Robert Monroe, who apparently was unusually talented in this direction, published his book *Journeys Out of the Body*[9] in which he categorized three main zones encountered in his excursions. The first he called "Locale 1," which is terrestrial but nonphysical. It is followed by "Locale 2" and "Locale 3," which have fewer earthly counterparts. He emphasized that Locale 2's most striking feature was its timelessness. In Locale 3 the time dimension prevails once more, albeit differently from that on Earth.

These latter observations are significant in that a British dowser, T.C. Lethbridge (in *The Power of the Pendulum* and other books) came to similar conclusions through his art. Lethbridge was no ordinary dowser. He varied the pendulum's length using a miniature windless that he operated with the fingers of his right hand. He found that all those things with which we are familiar here on earth—not only material items but abstract ideas like emotions and time—respond to pendulum lengths up to 40 inches. When a given length indicates a number of different things, which is generally the case, then the number of times the pendulum gyrates specifies which it is. For example, a length of 40 inches indicated both sleep and death as well as cold, North, black, and falsehood. Between 40 and 80 inches the pendulum responded to all the same things, that is, 40 plus whatever it was before. But the response was weaker and there was no time. After 80 inches, a similar sequence again began in which time, of some sort, was restored, thus providing parallel evidence to Monroe's.

Lethbridge referred to his findings as "Zone 1" (0 to 40 inches), "Zone 2" or "static time" (40 to 80 inches), and "Zone 3" or "time again" (80 to 120 inches). These zones clearly correspond to Monroe's Locales 1, 2, and 3. Incidentally, T.C. Lethbridge died a year before Monroe's book was published.

Both my partner and I use the typical short pendulum successfully, but although I always carry one of the extendible type with me, I have to confess to having no success with it. Lethbridge, however, was often tested and found to be genuine. He was a genius of our time.

Robert Monroe was not a genius although gifted. By his own admission, his behavior on entering "Locale 3" fell short of exemplary. He tells how he entered the body of an inhabitant of that region, giving the poor fellow symptoms of what we might call "demonic possession" with Monroe, of course, being the demon! "Locale 3's" bizarre characteristics may make the authenticity of Monroe's book seem questionable, but he seems to have satisfied the examination of Charles Tart, psychologist and author of the seminal work on ASCs.

According to Monroe, entry to "Locale 3" is via a dark tunnel, an image that brings to mind the vast amount of data collected on near-death experiences, particularly by the International Association for Near-Death Studies (IANDS), founded by Professor Kenneth Ring of the University of Connecticut. Information provided by a large number of respondents to a questionnaire given to people reporting near-death experiences revealed the existence of a core experience. Its five characteristics included (1) a sensation of peace and well-being, (2) feeling separated from the physical body (this I would call "remote viewing"), (3) entering darkness, in other words, a tunnel, (4) seeing light, and (5) entering the light (another world?). Margot Grey, the British representative of IANDS, notes that the suspension of time has been reported in terms of stopped watches and so on.[10]

Timelessness is one of the Otherworld's most significant features. The Dreamtime of the Australian Aborigines is timeless, and so is the Celtic Fairyland that is variously known as The Underwave Land, The Yonder, and Tir-na-nOg (pronounced Tier-nahn-Ohg), the land of the young. No one ages in Tir-na-nOg since there is no passage of time. Oisin (pronounced Oshun), son of Finn MacCool, returned after a sojourn that lasted three hundred Earth years and met Saint Patrick before old age rapidly caught up with him. A similar story tells of the abduction of Thomas the Rhymer into Fairyland by the Queen of Elphame and another of a visit to Tir-na-nOg by Murragh (Murra), the son of the eleventh-century Irish king Brian Boru. This, incidentally, is another cauldron story and can be found in J. J. Campbell's *The Legends of Ireland*.[11]

My search for a story that might support the IANDS core experience, particularly its dark tunnel or black hole aspect, did not take long. I found it in the Fenian Cycle of Irish myths. It is called the *Gilla Deacar* (gheela day-car) or the *Hard Ghillie*, "ghillie" meaning servant.

The story tells of a long journey undertaken by Finn MacCool and his companions in search of a number of their friends who had been kidnapped by the Hard Ghillie. Their travels took them to the west coast of Ireland and then by boat across the sea to an island surrounded by high cliffs. Finn sent his second-in-command, Dermot, who was able to climb the cliffs, to survey the island. Dermot found himself in a forest, where he discovered a well from which he drank. He was challenged by its owner, and a fight followed that ended with both men plunging down the well shaft (the dark tunnel), the bottom of which proved to be the entrance to Fairyland.

Searching for Dermot, Finn and the rest of the party scaled the cliffs by means of ropes. In the forest they found a cave (the tunnel again) through which they arrived in Fairyland, finding not only Dermot being royally entertained but their kidnapped companions also. The Fairy King, who turned out to be the Hard Ghillie, had brought them there by a ruse in order to enlist their help in overcoming a powerful enemy. Finn and his companions agreed to help him and, following their victory, were magically returned to Ireland.

I see that story as symbolizing an excursion through all the ASCs, from what we assume is full consciousness to the threshold of death, where Fairyland serves as common ground for mortals and other evolutionary strains. I counted seven discrete states, of which the last five correspond reasonably well with the near-death experience. When—I feel sure it will come to pass—human beings achieve the state I have called bicameral balance then there will be no altered states because all those so called will fall within the area of "normal" consciousness. The techniques we now know as hypnosis, mediumship, and psychoanalysis will become obsolete. At the present time I see ever-increasing signs of what might be termed "bicameral effect." It is my earnest hope that this will be encouraged, especially in the young.

Finally, the most important question: Is the Otherworld that we dream about (and I have had many dreams that correspond to the near-death experience format) or experience at times when ill the same place we go when we die? (If, indeed, we go anywhere.) The NDE investigators are the first to recognize that their information comes from people who have never been really dead. They have, throughout their experience, been in possession of those organs of perception, however impaired, that can receive and process the kind of data they later record. What happens when all that apparatus has decomposed and returned to the Earth. Can we assume that we have a soul that lives on?

The esoteric teacher George Gurdjieff (1872?-1949) courted considerable unpopularity when he stated that Man does not have a soul. His first duty in the course of his life on Earth is to make one. A person who lives only for the gratification of the physical self, the unremitting hedonist, simply dies, is buried, decomposes, and that is that—*finito*! Regrettably, that process applies to most of us in this age, and there is nothing new about the concept. Most of the ancient mystery religions taught it in one form or another. Where people go wrong, it seems, is in using the energy received for the nourishment of the "spirit body" to feed a grossly distorted ego instead.

P. D. Ouspensky, Gurdjieff's wayward pupil, endorsed an old Hindu/Buddhist idea in his notion of eternal recurrence, which asserts that the time of death coincides with the time of birth, such that the lifespan is an ever-continuing cycle of the same events until some induced impetus can free the individual from this "wheel of lives." He was so taken with this concept that he wrote a novel based on it, called *The Strange Lives of Ivan Osokin*.[12] J. B. Priestley, an English writer, also used the theme as the basic plot of his play *I Have Been Here Before*.[13] He credited Ouspensky with the idea but disclaimed any personal belief in it.

Another Gurdjieff pupil, J. G. Bennett, advocated the theory of the "soul-stuff pool," a kind of reservoir of unevolved soul material from which portions are decanted for the newly born. A person who has properly developed his or her individuality while on the Earth-plane would bypass this process and continue along the evolutionary path. The same idea is presented allegorically in Henrik Ibsen's play *Peer Gynt*, where Peer, approaching death, meets a button-molder with a huge ladle at a crossroads. "Are you going to melt me down with Tom, Dick, and Harry?" asks Peer. "Why not?" replies the button-molder. "You didn't have any individuality in life, so why should you expect it after death?"

The Egyptian *Book of the Dead* undoubtedly covers the subject adequately. Approaching the Otherworld, led by the jackal-god, Anubis, the dead meet a monkey with a pair of scales who weighs their hearts against a feather. If they pass the test, they go on to meet the great god Osiris. Otherwise, there is a monstrous creature with crocodile jaws standing by called The Devourer—enough said!

I emphasize that it would be a great error to assume that those who, like me, are possessed by a compulsion to unravel the enigmas of life and death have some sort of advantage over others. It is almost certainly the contrary since to embark on such an exercise carries with it the obligation to resolve it satisfactorily.

The message seems to be quite clear: We should contrive to lead our lives according to the dictates of pure conscience or, as wise Confucius would have it, "The first duty of every [person] is diligently to carve [his or her] own destiny." If we manage to comply with that, then the light at the end of the tunnel might become ours by right.

Unlike the Beaver Indians, I have decided not to attempt a map of the Otherworld but to opt instead for a guided tour. What follows is a dream-sequence on what Jung would have described as the "collective" level. It may be used as a pathworking if you wish.

Crossing the Bridge:
A Study in Imagery

You are sitting in the foyer of a smart, rather Art Nouveau-styled hotel on the outskirts of a city. To your right is a glass-paneled entrance through which you can see a wide road extending away from the city, narrowing and becoming hazy as it reaches to the horizon. On the opposite side of the foyer where you sit is a small cocktail bar where the bartender is mixing a drink in a silver cocktail shaker. You hear the sound it makes, which reminds you of an instrument used in Latin-American music.

You are aware that the hotel is in a city called Consciousness, and, as you sit and wait, the sound of the cocktail shaker becomes softer and changes to a subdued, continuous sound like running water. The impassive expression on the bartender's face becomes inert, and finally his movements appear to cease although the sound continues.

You decide to go for a walk and explore that road, for it radiates a strange fascination. Passing through the door, you cross the small forecourt and begin your walk. The weather is fine, like a spring day, and the subdued sunlight enhances the colors of the foliage bordering the road. With the hotel now some distance behind you, you decide to turn off the main road into a small wood to take a short rest. Within this wood you suddenly find yourself in a clearing in which other people, traveling the same road, have also stopped to rest.

As you seat yourself on a fallen tree, one of the other resting travelers turns to you and says, "This wood that you have entered is called Light Repose, and this clearing where we sit is known as the Grove of Contemplation."

You are feeling rested, and after an exchange of pleasantries, the genial stranger indicates a wish to accompany you—a suggestion you find attractive—so you return to the road together and continue your walk. Farther along the road you find that the woods on either side are becoming more dense. The trees now arch across the road, reducing the amount of sunlight that is able to penetrate the foliage. People pass you in both directions as you pause to admire the majesty of the trees, and you notice that many small paths lead into the woods on both sides.

Choosing a path on your right, you leave the main road once again. The path narrows, and you and your companion must walk in single file.

"Had we continued along the main road," the stranger says, "we would have come to a bridge, but there are many indirect routes which will take us to that same place, this being one. On the other side of the main road is a wood called Negativity, but you have chosen well, and we are now approaching a pleasant place called the Vale of Trance."

A short distance farther the forest opens out into a large clearing in which are a great many temple-like buildings. You notice that some of them have names on their gates, like "Aesculapium" and "Oracularum." You discover that each temple has its own direct path to the bridge, all converging with the main road at that magical place.

"There are many side roads that lead to the bridge," says the pleasant stranger, who seems to have elected to become your guide. "We do not always choose to approach it by the direct route.

"Those who have problems with their health or domestic affairs come here first, whence they subsequently may be directed to specialists who can help them and who have their places of existence on the other side of the bridge. There are occasions, however, when correct protocol is observed, when those benevolent, illumined beings see fit to appear here in person."

Passing a particularly beautiful temple bearing the insignia of the Pythoness, you allow your guide to lead you to a side road at the end of which the bridge is clearly visible.

"By taking this road," says your mentor, "you have the opportunity to discover your best evolutionary path."

Both of you withdraw into your thoughts and walk for a while in silence. The bridge is approached via a semicircular plaza around which are number of bench seats upon which travelers may rest if they choose. On entering the plaza, you decide to take advantage of them, and once you are settled, your companion begins to speak.

"I would like you to know," your friend continues in measured tones, "since you have shown friendship and respect towards me, that the landscape on the other side of the bridge resembles in many ways that which we have left behind us, just as the branches of a tree resemble its roots. By that analogy, the bridge you see before us is represented by the trunk, and a tree with a rotten trunk cannot sustain its foliage nor can the foliage sustain the roots. Each person must build and strengthen his or her bridge just as a tree must grow a strong trunk.

"On the other side of the bridge the main road continues with many side roads branching off. The place of my own existence is to be found over there. It is known as Tir-na-nOg, the Land of the Ever-Young. Time does not exist there, as was explained by Oisin, son of Finn, and experienced by Murragh, the son of Brian Boru. Anyone can experience the wonders of 'The Yonder' who has the courage and the diligence to strengthen his or her bridge."

You pause to come to terms with the revelation that the benevolent stranger seated beside you is of a different evolutionary strain than yourself when you feel your friend take you gently by the arm, and you both float effortlessly over the bridge.

You find yourself on a broad plain, looking along that same straight road that disappears into the distance, apparently through a nearby range of hills via a tunnel-like structure formed from some kind of black, honeycombed material. There is not much color in that vista, but on each side the landscape brightens up, with lakes and rivers bathed in an incandescence which seems to emanate from the very land itself. Mist-like whorls of varying hues appear to be in constant motion, flowing over the hills and through the valleys of a countryside that seems to be ever-changing. Here and there you sense the existence of towns and cities nestling on the side of distant slopes. You feel you have seen this place before—that feeling is called *déjà vu*.

"The ideal situation," says your companion, "would be one in which you could be as aware of your existence in this world as in the one you have just left behind you. It was like that at one time, but due to certain aberrations that were allowed to creep into the human psyche, the ability was forfeited. Humanity became arrogant and neglected the reverence that was due to the Great Mother of Nature. This

posed a threat to those of other evolutions, of whose existence they became unaware.

"I would like you to realize," continues your guide,
"that the bridge we have just crossed may not only represent the transition from consciousness to sleep but also that
between what you call 'life' and 'death.' Those approaching
death sometimes find that there is no bridge, and they fall
into the abyss beneath. More often, though, those who have
experienced sudden damage to their physical bodies cross
the bridge at high speed, continue along the road, and
through that tunnel over there."

You venture to ask where the main road ultimately leads.

"Should you go to the very end," your guide replies,
"you might find yourself on the opposite side of the City of
Consciousness, but you would need a new body and to be
born again. Be warned, though, that you would find yourself with the same body, born to the same parents, and
would live the same life that you have experienced thus far.
Such is the cyclical nature of time, as the Buddhist priests
well know. Most people prefer, if they are able and they
know that their physical existence is ended, to turn off on a
side road marked 'Eternity.' How far you are able to proceed
in that direction depends on how you have utilized your
time on Earth."

We decide that the place where we stand would be more
pleasant if it were not for the all-too-frequent appearances of
shapeless phantoms speeding across our field of vision and
emitting insane noises. Some screech, some weep, while others laugh hysterically.

"They are the drug users," says your companion. "They
think they are visiting the spirit world, but we arrange special scenery for them to keep them happy."

You move a little farther along the road to where it is
quieter.

"This plain," says your friend, "is known as Hypnogog,
and the range of hills before us surrounds that zone of timelessness within which, as I have mentioned, is the place of

my existence. Within that dark tunnel ahead is the Great Library of Akasha. All the records are in there, not just the material for what you call prophetic dreams. All people have experienced this place, some more than others. Those who narrowly escape death see the whole of their lives pass before them here, in zero time, of course."

Floating forward, as though drawn by some magnetic force, you feel quite a severe jolt as you enter the tunnel. In spite of the darkness, visions appear on each side, quite brilliantly illuminated as in a picture gallery. Some seem familiar; others are quite unknown to you.

The end of the tunnel approaches with great speed. You pass through and find yourself in a beautiful landscape that is bathed in warmth and light. Shadowy figures observe your approach and appear to look upon you with affection mixed with compassion. Pleasant and congenial as this place seems to be, you find yourself overwhelmed by a feeling that now is not the time to remain too long. This feeling of itself initiates a reverse movement: you find yourself traveling backwards along the road by which you came.

You rapidly accelerate as the tranquil vista before you recedes. Through the tunnel...across the plain...and the bridge is quickly crossed. Suddenly you realize that your companion is no longer with you, but now hear the now familiar voice, clearly, but as from a distance: "Remember the words of the Goddess," your erstwhile companion is saying, "'If that which you seek you find not within you, then you will never find it without you.'"

The sound of a cocktail shaker reaches your ears. Through misty eyes you see that a clock above the bar does not seem to have moved.

The bartender smiles and asks, "Your usual?"

You pull yourself together quickly and reply, "Oh, yes—yes, please," adding, "I must have been far away."

• • •

The Lake of Memory is within all of us. I implore every-one to seek it out. And when you find it, which you surely will, look carefully and you may see in its center a castle wherein the Fisher King awaits. For you, in your essence-self, can withdraw the spear and thereby end his suffering.

Notes

1. The literal meaning is "fish bladder," probably a Christian term, since the middle part can be seen as a fish shape, but the symbol is pre-Christian.

2. Alan Richardson, *Earth God Rising* (St. Paul: Llewellyn Publications, 1990).

3. Julian Jaynes, *The Origin of Consciousness in the Breakdown of the Bicameral Mind* (Boston: Houghton Mifflin, 1976).

4. For the complete story, see T. W. Rolleston, *Myths and Legends of the Celtic Race* (London: Guild Publishing, 1985 [1911]).

5. In one interpretation, the "blood" is wine transformed in the eu-charist into the blood of Jesus. A more literal "holy blood" hy-pothesis, the idea that certain European royal families were descended from Jesus, was developed in Michael Baigent et al., *Holy Blood, Holy Grail* (London: Jonathan Cape, 1982). More re-cently Margaret Starbird in *The Woman with the Alabaster Jar* (Santa Fe: Bear and Co., 1993) also explored the possibility of Jesus marrying and having descendants.

6. Marilyn Ferguson, *The Aquarian Conspiracy* (Los Angeles: Jere-my Tarcher, 1980, 1987).

7. Marilee Zdenek, *The Right Brain Experience* (New York: McGraw-Hill, 1983, 1988).

8. Hugh Brody, *Maps and Dreams: Indians and the British Columbia Frontier* (New York: Pantheon, 1982).

9. Robert Monroe, *Journeys Out of the Body* (Garden City, New York: Anchor Press, 1973, 1977).

10. Margot Grey, *Return from Death* (London: Arkana, 1985), 39. The watch must have been on the "wrist" of the dreambody.

11. J. J. Campbell, *The Legends of Ireland* (London: Batsford, 1955).

12. P. D. Ouspensky, *The Strange Life of Ivan Osokin* (New York: Arkana/Methuen, 1988 [1947].

13. J. B. Priestly, *I Have Been Here Before* (London: French, 1939).

About the Author

Angela Barker was born in the Isle of Thanet in southeast England in 1932. Displaced by World War II, her family moved variously to London, Brighton, Devonshire, and West Wales. Mainly influenced by her Pagan father, who taught her mythology from an early age, she later studied music and physics. Traveling as a freelance musician in India, Southeast Asia, and the United States, she took every opportunity to study local myths, belief systems, and folklore. During the late 1950s and early 1960s she spent five years living in a community whose members were engaged in the intensive study of the teachings of G. I. Gurdjieff. Now retired, she lives on a boat on the River Thames with her partner, Richard, and two dogs, and teaches mythology, symbology, and metaphysics at Braziers Adult College in Oxfordshire.

© Malcolm Brenner / Eyes Open

Seeing the Sun at Midnight:

Ordinary and Nonordinary
States of Consciousness

by Kisma K. Stepanich

As the Wiccan and Pagan communities delve into the indigenous traditions of North and South America, Siberia,
Africa, Australia, and other countries, we discover more
about the prevalent practice of inducing spiritual/religious
vision/experience through the usage of psychoactive drugs
known as plant teachers and plant spirits.

Psychoactive drug use is not a form of shamanism encouraged in modern Western society because of the epic levels of drug abuse and, consequently, the drug hysteria
produced by the politicians' "drug wars." Yet psychoactive
drugs are not those drugs connected to the get-high mentality of street-drug users or the synthetic street-drugs manu-
factured as a form of big business. The psychoactive drugs
of shamanism are those plants, such as Carlos Castenada's
jimson weed (*Datura stramonium, L.*) and Terence McKen-
na's psilocybin mushroom.

In Peru the Matses Indians use an herbal powder called
nu-nu for divination and hunting (visions involving animal
imagery, shamanic "power animals"). Other indigenous

South American use secretions from a sacred frog to induce visions before hunting. In the Middle East there is the visionary *khat*.

Some American Indians hold *peyote* sacred and have developed a church around its sacred ceremonial usage: The Native American Church. In earlier times, Native American elders (often referred to as medicine people or witch doctors) created the elaborate paintings at the Pecos River that are believed related to the visions they received during a trance state induced by ingesting mescal beans, the fruit of the mountain laurel, a potentially fatal hallucinogen. Mescal bean cults are well known from the historic period when this hard shiny red seed with its magical qualities was traded as far north as Canada.[1]

But nonordinary states of consciousness can be achieved both mentally as well as chemically. Although the use of psychoactive drugs are common within traditional shamanic practices, the handling of such plant teachers are usually limited to individuals who are trained, who are the shamans of their culture's spiritual practices. At this point in our culture, however, such traditional paths and boundaries are largely missing.

In a traditional shamanic culture the future shaman often had a special mark placed upon her or his soul: the ability to naturally have profound vision at a young age. Such a child was designated as special, set apart from her or his community and closely observed by an elder shaman. In time, if the child continued to demonstrate special abilities, she or he would be apprenticed to the elder. Plant teachers could then be administered by the shaman for soul-searching, communing with spirit powers, and experiencing a unity of creation. Such plant teachers are used with full ceremony and specific ritual. In such rituals the vision seeker is carefully attended by the shaman. Such plant teachers are not ingested simply to get high, as is the emphasis of street-drug usage in Western society, but like any drug—psychoactive or not—their usage can be abused without proper guidance.

Of course, Western society does not celebrate the status of the shaman or witch; it has developed its intellectual capabilities and experienced the birth and growth of an technological age that far exceeded anyone's expectations. However, when any culture shifts away from the natural world and into that of machination spiritual practices take a back seat until the ancient spiritual practices are remembered and seekers of wisdom begin to bring such practices back into their society—which brings us to the reweaving of shamanic practices into Western society.

In the past decade Wicca has become the fastest growing religion in the United States, naturally so, since there are so many European descendants walking around this continent. With the environmental movement, the women's movement, the Goddess movement, the Native American Indian movements rising in society, European descendants who are frustrated with the sterility of the new mainstream religions have turned to their ancestral roots.

Many have discovered that Witchcraft, also referred to as Wicca, was the European shamanic nature tradition. A desire to reclaim that birthright and practice new forms of the ancestral tradition has played a major role in Wicca's growth. People have begun to compare Wicca to other shamanic traditions from around the world.

Within Wicca, the debate over whether religious experiences induced or enhanced by psychoactive drugs is purely a twentieth-century matter. If we reach back into the European roots of Paganism and Wicca, we find that the tradition is not without its own teacher herbs, described, for example, as "flying ointment" and "faery eye ointment." Such herbal concoctions were used for "seeing" (as in seership, which involves the Second Sight and powerful Underworld visions), working with an ally of the Otherworld, talking to ancestors, communing with the Old Gods, experiencing unity with creation, and eventually seeing the Sun at midnight.

WARNING: Many of the psychoactive herbs used in the following historical recipes are known to be poisonous.

Formula One: equal parts of poplar leaf, *fleur-de-luce*, cinquefoil; add a thickening of soot and oil or fresh lard.

Formula Two: equal parts of abortificent parsley, aconite, belladonna, hemlock, and cowbane; cinquefoil and the elusive four-leaf shamrock; bat's blood to assist nocturnal flight.

Formula Three: the fat of a newly-born lamb; *eleoselinum* (smallage) will help the cramps; *skiwet* (wild parsnip) used for poulticing; soot; bat's blood to be obtained at the wake of the new crescent; *pentaphyllon* (cinquefoil); popular leaves.

Formula Four: equal parts of mugwort, wormwood, and cinquefoil mixed with winter ashes from the Yule fire; one shamrock that has four leaves and was harvested between *La Baal Tine* (1 May) and Midsummer (21 June); yarrow for the heart's ease; with these herbs mix aloe and lard; breath three times upon the mixture in a black jar; let set from dark moon to dark moon; anoint the eyes and say this three times with eyes shut: *"Docuitim bolad an eireannait binn breutait faoi mfoldin ducait,"* and you will see what you will see!

Obviously, these formulas are offered as a study only rather for ingestion. All four recipes present inadequate measures of the herbs and other ingredients. Several of the ingredients are quite ridiculous. After all, who is going to kill a bat or lamb? Finding a four-leaf shamrock is rare, let alone between the month of May and June.

Many of the herbs listed are obscure, while others cause disorientation, nausea, headaches, and dehydration. The amount of the concoction to be applied to the body is not provided, therefore, quantity usage is guesswork at most, which basically communicates the knowledge that such recipes necessitate trial and error.

When I began weaving the shamanic tradition of Europe with the shamanic tradition of North America, it was experiential; there were no guidelines as how one should go about the process. Naturally, I focused on the herbology of the two traditions, since I was a healer-in-training. Peyote, mushroom, mugwort, datura, wormwood and belladonna usage—or at the least the investigation of such plants—was a natural component of my journey.

I regularly traveled miles into the wilderness to commune with the plant spirits and receive vision. Forging through local wilderness areas in search of plant teachers consumed a steady three-year apprenticeship in my life. Learning the properties of each plant involved hours of research. My kitchen was turned into an apothecary, while my dining room became my laboratory. I became the guinea pig.

In search of greater truth and deeper wisdom, I opened myself to the plant spirits. Sometimes the results were empty, leaving me with slight trembling or nausea, while other times I transcended linear reality. In the beginning the vision sometimes came the following morning after utilizing a plant spirit. The first time this happened I woke to find myself in the Dreamtime flying over land, through corridors, down streets, past buildings. I did not try to control anything: my speed, the scenes, the subtlety of color. Going with the experience, I suddenly found myself in the middle of destruction. Erupting power of golden light. Women bound in chains, wearing black blindfolds. Men were fighting, killing one another.

At first when I saw these scenes I worried why I was in the middle of such destruction, such horrors. Why was I experiencing the Spirit world in such a hostile manner? In that moment I became aware of someone holding my hand. I was being led through this world, past buildings raging with fire, children frightened and crying, the Earth screaming and exploding.

Then, through the self-realization we all hope to undergo in times such as these, I understood. I was witnessing the wars of my internal reality. I was witnessing the manifestation of the dreamtime of the mind, the journey which dealt with the realizing of self-bondage, the breaking apart of the blockages of the mind.

I had to pass through these areas that were my closed gateways to the realm of realities and nonrealities. I had to pass through this destruction to witness the drama which I created internally. By passing through, I would break apart, opening the doorway, the access which led to the greater truth and deeper wisdom I sought. It was this experience that led to my "shaman's death" of the nonreality—my shaman's death of this reality having taken place a few years earlier.[2]

Several years later I began to move deeper. I had made contact with several spirit allies and co-walkers of the Dreamtime and Underworld, respectively. As if my mind had been set free, I began to also have vivid experiences without the usage of plant teachers. One such occurrence took place during the Harmonic Convergence in 1987.

I traveled to Baja California, Mexico, with a friend to undergo the new wave of light-energy hitting the Earth-plane while at a remote locale. On the final day of the Convergence, she and I went down to the shoreline where we'd been performing our early-morning ceremonies, and as we sat on the sand, watching the playful waves, we dreamed of future days and ceremonies that could be performed as an intensive study of the element of water.

In our musing we became undines and adorned ourselves with the kelp, clothing of the sea. Seaweed became our jewelry, algae and seagrass became ornaments for our hair, and shells our tokens.

We rose out of the water, sister undines, dancing the water dance, the haunting call of a conch shell announcing our arrival. We kneeled at the edge of the shore-break, the place where the white foam from Poseidon's sea-horses lay bubbling as the air consumes it.

We lamented for the polluted state the waters were in and the dying relatives that swam therein. We offered our tokens to the rising waves and watched each shell disappear from sight. Then quiet, at the water's edge, we opened to the ebbing flow of life and witnessed the sparkling energy come to life (the dance between fire and water), and deep inside—in that place of woman power—I felt my own shifting tide and rose, as Venus would, out of the clutching foam.

Spreading my arms open wide, I turned with laughter, allowing the whole world to feel my Otherworldly presence.

Out of the waters Venus did rise. "Love will begin," whispered the breezy voices of the ocean undines as they danced closer and closer to shore, to the place where the presence of Goddess on Earth stood.

Columns of spinning white light appeared over the ocean, gold and silver beams of light shooting out from them, piercing my solar plexus, cementing in my belly button—the umbilical cord of life. "The new way will be through the light of the heart," thundered a clear blue sky. My head tilted back; laughter exploded from my belly.

I fell to my knees and honored reality—the reality that we take for granted. I wanted to reach out and touch all life, everything, and nothing. In that moment of exalted awareness the physical became too much. My body longed to simply be the water, allowing my consciousness to be fully expanded and connected with the inner core of knowingness, flowing with the life current that constantly runs through all things physical, which hides behind all things unknown, to have no limitations or boundaries of mind.

The water of my body mixed with the seawater. Water mingling with water. Current of life. No boundaries. Vibrating out. Ripples of awareness. Rising and falling. Rushing and crashing. Pouring over. Stillness. Reflecting...

I learned that day to visualize my sense of touch as being as expansive as water. That by doing so I could feel everything and send my "feelers" to distances never thought possible. I learned that the essence of water is the antenna of awareness to feeling, the teacher of feeling, togetherness, one vibration.[3]

I have continued to work with plant teachers, moving deeper and deeper beyond time and space into worlds vastly different than ours. I feel honored to partake of the soulstuff of Mother Earth, connecting with her energy, being admitted into her inner sanctum. Yet if asked whether the Wiccan shamanic movement should incorporate psychoactive drugs, I would admit that I have had just as powerful spiritual visions without them.

Spiritual vision or religious experience is also gained through a form of discipline, connecting the bodymind and merging these with Spirit, which allows the participant to enter non-ordinary states of consciousness at will—meaning to contact and utilize an ordinarily hidden reality in order to acquire knowledge, power, and to help other persons. For many, undergoing a disciplined training program is too much work, which (in my opinion) is why plant teachers have become so appealing today in attaining vision.

Visions! This single word conjures more in the imagination then most words in the English language. Why? It is a word that speaks to the deepest core of our desire to truly receive a great message, a great teaching from the Spirit Realm or from Goddess or God. Visions are seen as an indication that an altered state of reality has been achieved.

Mind-altering herbs, if abused, can have serious side effects, possible addiction at the very least and potentially death. Therefore, let us turn to altered states of consciousness that can be achieved through the disciplined practice of meditation and guided visualizations, which are far safer forms to practice, and although such methods require diligent practice, nonordinary states of consciousness are achieved. This happens when the creative intelligence (imagination) is allowed to work.

In today's society we have been taught to deny creative imagination, or spiritual intelligence. We have been conditioned not to allow our spiritual intelligence to live. Such intelligence can raise too many questions, questions that challenge enforced religious doctrines, political structures, economic guidelines, gender-specific roles, and more.

Spiritual intelligence transforms abstract thoughts and ideas into overt, audible, knowable, and tangible realities. Using spiritual intelligence, using our creative imagination, allows us to examine numerable aspects of life through pictures or images.

Creative imagination allows us to shapeshift any aspect of life through visualizing. Through visualizing, we are able to get in touch with deeper understanding or ways of knowing that were not considered before.

Guided visualization is used to attempt to begin to spark the creative imagination, to awaken spiritual intelligence through images. Images are three-dimensional, and whether they are images visually seen before us or within our mind's eye, our unconscious will respond to them.

R. J. Stewart describes using images through the technique of visualization as working upon various levels of consciousness to produce a variety of effects. He tells us that "Empowered visualization is something very specific; it involves a range of images and works through underlying patterns with the connecting sequence of the images. While sets of images or single images are relatively static, even when they are potentially powerful, it is often the pattern or combination of images that brings a response from within ourselves, and generates inner changes associated with such response. The art of defining and selecting these changes, through intent and rhythmic repetition, was well established in pre-materialistic cultures."[4]

Stewart goes on to say that it is not necessary for the images to be accurate or real, merely that they connect various levels or states of consciousness and energy.

Through learning to work with the creative imagination, one begins to enter altered states of consciousness, while at the same time developing the art of Second Sight. One of the primary keys to developing Second Sight through guided visualization is the ability to surrender and allow the mediator, or group guide to "talk" one through the experience. For many, surrendering is quite difficult because they want to "roam" on their own.

Roaming on one's own is classified as a form of meditation, and meditation is quite a different practice then guided visualization. The late Dion Fortune said, "It is well known to mystics that if a man meditates upon a symbol around which certain ideas have been associated by past meditation he will obtain access to those ideas, even if the glyph has never been elucidated to him by those who have received the oral tradition 'by mouth to ear.'"[5]

Psychoactive drugs bypass mind-body-spirit connection and affect only the mind. This explains why drug-induced visions can often be "mind-blowing." Meditation and guided visualization is an psycho-active discipline; yet once achieved, such a discipline can, and often will, produce vivid visions.

I began working with meditation in the early 1980s as part of my spiritual training. For several years I met with a group of four like-minded individuals once a week. We actually focused on the Egyptian tradition; astral traveling as a group to certain temples, succeeding in unlocking a forgotten chant of which each of us had remembered a fragment.

One night, as we sat under a pyramid in meditation, I journeyed back into the crevice of my memory. I went back to a world, or dimension called *Iixlanda,* and was shown a miraculous—and unbelievable—transmigration from *Iixlanda* to Earth. This meditation reawakened the journey of my soul into this dimension: the experience of my original (meaning first) birth in life on this planet.

I know, I can hear you saying, "Ridiculous!" But is it really? Modern medicine, specifically through the specialized studies of endocrinology and neurology, says that such a ghost of memory can and does exist.

Research and theory is indicating that at any point in the bodymind, two things come together—a bit of information and a bit of matter. Of the two, the information has a longer life span than the solid matter it is matched with. As the atoms of carbon, oxygen, hydrogen, and nitrogen swirl through our DNA, like birds of passage that alight only to migrate on, the bit of matter changes, yet there is always a structure waiting for the next atoms.

Dr. Deepak Chopra tells us that "DNA never budges so much as a thousandth of a millimeter in its precise structure, because the genomes —the bits of information in DNA—remember where everything goes, all 3 billion of them. This fact makes us realize that memory must be more permanent than matter. What is a cell, then? It is a memory that has built some matter around itself, forming a specific pattern. Your body is just the place your memory calls home."[6]

In esoteric teachings we know that the universe is in essence our soul. Why then, with such research findings, would it be so hard to believe that I reexperienced the origin of my life on this planet? If cells are simply houses for our memory, is our memory only limited to one incarnation, one dimension of existence? If it is true that we exist within a multi-dimensional universe, where past-present-future co-exists, an existence in which all realms, all time-periods, simply overlap the other, then accessing such a deep-memory is indeed possible, albeit hard for our rather limited and puny egos to handle.

This memory awakening—this vision—came at a time in my life that was a threshold, a portal—so to speak—into my Soul-Monad (awakened spiritual intelligence). At the time of the experience, the impact of this knowledge was so great I had to be coached back in to my physical body. I could not speak, I could barely move. Rather, I sat there stunned, tears spilling down my face, unable to share the experience with my fellow travelers.

This experience helped me realize that I could successfully alter my state of consciousness at will. But you see, all my experiences, whether drug-induced or produced through mind-altering techniques such as meditation, have been woven in a deepening of my spirituality, my life-path, which is that of being a healer, a vision finder for the individuals who come to me. As a child I saw things that were unexplainable, and so, naturally for me, as I got older I began a journey in search of an explanation.

Esoteric teachings from any culture sparked a desire in me to understand the invisible worlds, or non-realities. Being born in California with a matrilineage of Irish ancestry and a patralineage of Rumanian Gypsy, it only seemed natural for me to get in touch with the traditions of all three. In my journey to date, I have successfully woven my Irish Faery Wicca with my Native American Indian tradition, while still studying the Gypsy tradition.

Expanding my mind through both mental and chemical techniques has served a balanced purpose in my spiritual quest. Although I honor the plant teachers I much rather prefer having the ability to enter a nonreality at will. To me, and many of the Elders I've had the blessing to work with, this is the true sign of a spiritual person. Such a sign shows the disciplined character.

The ancient art of meditation is a discipline all serious spiritual students will, at one time or another, encounter. However, to successfully arrive at, or dwell in a true meditative state depends on attitude.

In one of my earlier books the first area of focus I discuss in relationship to working with magick and Spirit is "attitude."

> As with most beginnings, the pace from the starting point determines the outcome. Likewise, the starting point of Spring will determine the rest of the year. If we begin to pay attention to Spring and work with the new energy of this season, we set into motion events we desire to unfold throughout the year. And so checking our attitude becomes important at this time because it is this mind-set that will become the year's foundation...If our attitude is positive, then goals will be easier to obtain and less expenditure of energy will be required to obtain them. The possibilities for growth become infinite.[7]

Although I discuss attitude in relationship to the Wheel of the Year, and the energy of spring, this theory can be applied to the art of meditation.

When one's attitude is positive and supportive toward a discipline, then the ingredient of desire is birthed. Desire is what leads one forward into deeper realms of spiritual understanding, relationships, searching for knowledge, etc.

Pamela Eakins, in her study of Tarot, says, "In our spirits, and most likely our bodies, desire takes us closer and closer toward that which is desired. It is desire that propels the mover upon the spiritual path. Through desire, our perception is awakened...The seeker is driven by emotion. The seeker is driven by feeling. The way of the seeker is the Way of Desire. The Way of Desire is focused attention. Focused attention is synonymous with deep meditation."[8]

For desire to develop, the attitude must first be present. Without both desire and attitude, a student will not take the first step toward spiritual development. Likewise, such an attitude of desire must exist toward the discipline of meditation or that of numerous systems of discipline, in order for the student to achieve a true altered state of consciousness through continual practice.

The true function of obtaining an alteration of mind is not necessarily to receive messages from self or Deity for that matter, but rather to be able to develop the ability to translate certain key images or intuitions of the spiritual realms into words and, more importantly, to be able to act as a channel for a specific power to flow out into the world. This is the true function of the shaman, seer, witch, cunning one—whatever term we use. Through the achievement of this state, one will come to know the meaning of the term "seeing the sun at midnight"—for this is the true state of enlightenment.

This obscure statement entices and excites one with the desire to know the mystery of its proclamation. But like many teachings found within our esoteric systems, there is no mystery at all, but basic fact. The mystery of seeing the sun at midnight is to be able to find the light in the darkness; it is a state of enlightenment that comes when we have successfully accomplished the art of seership or are able to alter our state of consciousness at will. For when we can successfully perform such a feat then we have arrived at a deeper level of awareness and the more obscure becomes reality, becomes natural, common.

But how many will give themselves over to a disciplined practice toward altering consciousness without the use of psychoactive drugs? Hopefully, many. For here is the secret: seeing the sun at midnight can be as easily accomplished through such disciplines as turning your face up to the full moon shining bright in a midnight blackened sky. All it takes is desire, dedication and discipline.

Notes

1. Sovieg A. Turpin and Jim Zintgraff, "Shamanic Motifs in Pecos River Rock Art." *Shaman's Drum* 30 (Winter 1993), 32-39.
2. I tell more of his experience in my book *The Gaia Tradition: Celebrating the Earth in Her Seasons* (St. Paul: Llewellyn, 1992), 286-290.
3. Stepanich, *The Gaia Tradition,* 145-150.
4. R. J. Stewart, *Earth Light* (London: Element, 1992) 62.
5. Dion Fortune, *The Mystical Qabalah* (York Beach, Maine: Samuel Weiser, 1984), 5.
6. Deepak Chopra, *Quantum Healing* (New York: Bantam Books), 77-94.
7. Stepanich, 39-40.
8. Pamela Eakens, *Tarot of the Spirit* (York Beach, Maine: Samuel Weiser, 1992), 52.

About the Author

Kisma K. Stepanich was born July 4, 1958, in Santa Anna, California, and continues to live in the coastal region of southern California. She is of Irish and Romanian gypsy ancestry, from which she proudly draws her spirituality. Grounding into the roots of her heritage, Kisma became an initiated High Priestess of Celtic and Faery Wiccan Traditions. She also holds a ministerial credential with the Covenant of the Goddess, has studied and undergone initiation with several shamans of native traditions from around the world, and founded Women Spirit Rising of Costa Mesa. Presently she directs Moon Circle Lodge Network in collaboration with Brooke Medicine Eagle, and travels throughout the southland providing ceremonial workshops of Goddess spirituality. Kisma is also the author of *An Act of Woman Power*, *The Gaia Tradition*, and *Sister Moon Lodge*.

Communication with Spirit Guides

by Oz

"I had resisted. After college, I was a suburban mom with kids and a house and all of that. I had had inklings as a child. I would have thoughts, and then these things would happen. That made me feel frightened, and sometimes guilty. There was a definite psychic awareness going on, but my family was against it. There was fear of reprisal, so the whole thing was squashed in me. Then, when I was grown, I was driving one day with one of my children and another car drove right into us, broadsided us. I saw glass coming in from everywhere. I looked over at my son, and I just said, 'I surrender.' The next day, in the hospital, I told my family that I had to be initiated. I didn't know what that meant. 'It' had called to me when my life was in danger. I was the only one who was hurt in the accident, and it was at the moment that my arm exploded that I knew. So when I got out of the hospital, I got on an airplane to go to Haiti. That was thirty years ago, and I didn't know anyone there. Two men were waiting for me at the airport. They said, 'Now you're ready.' They took me and initiated me, and I was panicked…At first I worked on the lower levels with spirit entities. It was years before I got to the big-gun entities, only after I had shown my level of commitment and my ability to keep the secrecy…"

As I sat listening to Shakmah Winddrum, an initiate in Voodoo and a teacher of the African Solomonic Tradition, I reflected back on my own first experiences in communicating with spirits as guides and teachers. I had asked Shakmah to explain to me how she had first come into contact with the entities she works with. I was trying to find out what differences there are, and what similarities, between the way Witches communicate with spirit entities and the ways of those from other cultural backgrounds.

A few days later, I called a friend of mine named E'Star who is a hereditary Wiccan and whom I knew had been working through spirit guidance for over fifty years. I asked her the same question: How did these spirits first come to you? She described to me her childhood growing up in nature around many animals, both wild and domesticated. As young as the age of five she was allowed to take only her horse, donkey, and dogs and go off into the wilderness. There spirit, man and animal were not separated. There she began her awareness of and communication with spirits, skills that were later honed by participation in her mother's Wiccan circles and by other human teachers.

I remembered when I was a teenager sitting in a class in a metaphysical church learning psychic skills. Wicca was still in the closet then. For years voices had been coming in my head, but at first I found no support for my experiences in the culture in which I lived. After I managed to escape being institutionalized and accepted that these voices were not insanity, I slowly began to find others who could teach me how to develop and use this skill. I also remembered the day a voice had told me to follow whatever came in the mail that day. The letter in the mail led me to a college in Florida where I and a handful of others began our first Wiccan circles and developed a tradition based on communication with spirit guides. The spirits were our first teachers, giving us direct guidance in how to find others, how to work our circles, how to lead our lives so that we could grow and do our spiritual work. Indeed, it was the spirits themselves who told us about Wicca and led us to begin our work as Witches again in this life.

Wakeyatu-ta-shoka-ee-hambalay calls himself an "intercessor" and a visionary, although those who introduced me to him describe him as an exceptional medicine man. He said that when he was seven years old the spirits came to him in a way that is traditional to Native American peoples. He described his first encounter as the receiving of an offer to take on a responsibility, saying that he had to choose whether to accept the duty or not. Following the initial contact, he says, there is a testing period both for the human communicator and of the spirit beings. "Not all those that come are good. They can fool or trick you. You have to use a lot of discernment, and ask—will they guide you or help you?"

In the first decade of my regular communications with spirit entities, I had learned this the hard way. The School of Spirit Hard Knocks, I often call it. Most of the entities who came were beneficial, supportive, and informative. But there were also times when I and others around me were deceived by certain spirits. I came to learn that sometimes the beings who could talk in my head or through a medium in one of our circles might be subject to such mortal shortcomings as envy, jealousy, and possessiveness, or might seem to be intentionally misleading. Sometimes it almost seemed the spirits were testing our degree of gullibility. I also learned how easy it is for even those of us with the best and highest intentions to color the information as it comes through our own human minds. It was many years before I learned the proper protections and methods to help avoid these often painful and confusing experiences.

Another Witch was recently being initiated into our tradition. This was one of those not uncommon cases where the person had been practicing and living his life completely in accord with Wicca for many years, but had just discovered this actual path. Aobo said that it was his spirit guides who led him to both magick and Witchcraft. His first encounter with spirits was in a therapy situation. He was playing a drum, and the spirits began to use his voice to speak aloud. He described the experience as like a sudden vision. Since then, the four spirits who originally spoke with him have constantly continued to do so for years.

Elena Avila is a *curandera*, the Spanish word for healing woman. She is first-generation Chicana and also a professional nurse. She described to me a process of gradual development in which she became aware of the spirits who now help her perform her healing work. She began to notice that she would "know" things, but not where the information came from. "How did I know that?" she would ask herself over and over again until she became more comfortable with receiving information. She journeyed into Mexico to seek out teachers who taught her how to evoke the spirits and speak to them. Through practice, she eventually developed her own unique way of working both from what she was taught and what she experienced on her own.

I had many times attempted to teach Wiccan initiates how to communicate with beings of spirit. Some times it worked, but many times it did not. As I thought about the stories of those who had made this their life work, I began to see that in every case it was the spirits who chose the humans, not the other way around. Wakeyatu-ta had cautioned very strongly that many people, both Native and those of European descent, often created problems by believing that they were "hearing" grandfathers or spirits guide them when in many cases it was simply their own egos or some spirit-like delusions speaking to them. We both agreed that the phenomenon of channeling had opened many vulnerable people to the deceptions, allures, and illusions of the spirit planes. I also noted that each of the persons I had talked to about their spirit-guided experiences had found human teachers to give them guidance in how to handle the spirit connection once it was made. The teaching seemed to be a necessary part of both refining the process, learning how to protect oneself, and learning how to put the skill to the best use. I knew that I had not been originally able to find teachers within the Craft, but had searched both in mystical Christianity and in traditions as diverse as Sufism and the Native American to continue and develop my path of working with these spirits.

Today the Craft is growing widely and continually. The teachings that we have lost are being revived, and this aspect of our spiritual work must be addressed. The ins and outs of being a communicator with spirit is apparently one aspect of our role in this world, at least for some Witches. There is a need to provide our own teachers, within our own traditions. Those who are called to follow this work need to be able to go to others within the Craft for training. There are many factors that must be addressed, including the need for protection, ability to discern who and what to listen to, the uses of the skill, and sharing this work with those of other traditions.

To the outside world, Witches have always had the reputation of associating with spirits, but the images are often macabre: dancing with the dead, flying with ghosts, conjuring up demons. Unfortunately, most of the world believes that the way Witches work is totally unlike the work of shamanic practitioners, healers, and teachers from Native backgrounds. A Native practitioner who has come from a culture which supports such work will often insist that there is no similarity between what her or his people do and what Witches do. Their teachings say that spirits are not to be commanded, for it is assumed by others that Witches control their spirits. They believe that their spirits are benevolent divine forces working through them, and yet often mistakenly believe that Witches choose to work with harmful or demonic entities.

The work of the Native shamanic practitioner has become more and more understood and accepted. The spiritu-

al revolution occurring today has led many to seek out
teachers who regularly work with and teach about spirit
guidance. Anthropologists and psychotherapists no longer
try to deny, rationalize, or explain away the transformative,
healing powers of such work, but in fact are studying the
phenomena with increasing respect. While working with
spirits is still not a completely accepted practice in the Western societies, it is now relatively easy to find a counselor or
therapist who may integrate such concepts as "power animals," spirit teachers, or angelic guides into their work.
Many more people are coming to have not only respect but
even awe for such a connection with the unseen worlds.
Those who have been traditionally trained in such work
find themselves caught between a strong adherence to their
own ways and the force of the giant wave of hungry seekers
wanting to experience and even usurp these ways for their
own purposes, whatever they may be. This has brought a
rash of books, workshops, retreats and spirit-speaking advi-
sors out into the world. The non-native peoples are coming
in droves to the spirit realms, with a horde of novices claiming to speak with or for the spirits in just about any manner
or upon any subject imaginable. Unfortunately, in many
cases, there is very little discretion employed regarding
what spirit or what type of spiritual entity may be freely
giving out its advice. The spirits, whomever they may be,
are finding plenty of willing if inexperienced and uninitiat-
ed voices to speak for them.

Communication with spirits among Witches is even
today a form of an ancient and venerated transference of information from the higher planes of consciousness into the
mundane or earthly world. Once Wiccans may have shared
this in their circles much as happens in the shamanic-type
rites of other cultures today. The peoples whose traditions
have survived have learned how to adapt their ageless
methods, more or less, to the modern world. "Medicine"
women and men may live in cities and fly on airplanes as
well as in the spirit realms. Yet they retain their training

within their traditions as well as strong links to spirit allies. Witches, however, suffer from the handicap of having their hereditary lineage broken during the years of persecution. As well, Witches suffer from years of calculated slander designed to destroy us, our worship, and our work with spirit. Like the traditions of other people who once lived very close to the land, our ways have been all but wiped out. The main difference seems to be that while teachers and elders still exist for those of many other cultures, we are having to rebuild our traditions after centuries of being hidden, and of being nearly lost. Most Witches today will never know another Witch who could go to her grandmother and ask for guidance. The fact that there is still a great deal of difference in both the reputations and resources of "shamanic" practitioners and that of Witches only complicates the confusing position of a young Witch who might find himself suddenly contacted by entities who have messages for him.

In most Wiccan covens today, the leaders are trained by peers rather than elders, if indeed they have received any training at all. Many Witches feel that they have been initiated by spirit itself and thus they are called to this path with a prior connection to Spirit or to spirits. Those Witches who have come from hereditary traditions often still guard the secrets of this training perhaps even more closely than the shamanic practitioners of the Native people. Many well-trained Witches have never worked with direct spirit communication and have neither experience nor training in this field. Witches who do communicate with spirits often come to this work first outside the Craft, as was the case for me and for many Witches I know. When I first joined the Neo-pagan movement after years of isolated working within my own group, I was quite surprised to find that direct and consistent communication with entities was not that common. A few years later I visited with Alex Sanders, the founder of Alexandrian Wicca, in England. In the last years of his life I found him spending long hours recording communications from spirit entities. He acknowledged, however, that in Europe as well as in the United States, relatively few Witches actually practiced or were trained in this type of work. I and one of my sister Witches led a workshop about spirit guidance at a large Neopagan gathering in the early 1980s and found that among several hundred attending, perhaps barely over a dozen were experienced in spirit communication.

Yet the fact remains, the spirits are choosing to talk to Witches, and Witches are receiving more and more from the spirit realms as our religion returns, grows, expands, and redeveloped. Communication with spirits is certainly not a path or skill for everyone, even among Witches. It seems to be a particular gift that some possess and others do not, like healing or prophecy. Nevertheless, nowadays Witches commonly speak of profound experiences of the reception of information into them or through another. This happens in private circles, at gatherings, and in individual work. I have met dozens more Witches in the last few years who include regular work with spirit entities in their lives and magick. Much is being learned already from these entities, but much more needs to be learned in order for us to redevelop our knowledge of these realms and beings. It is helpful if we can know whether the way Witches are experiencing this really is similar or comparable to how others are interacting with the hidden worlds. In comparing the spirit experiences of Witches to those of other cultural backgrounds, a great many similarities can be found. In my limited survey, it seems apparent that there are far fewer differences than parallels.

Elena, the *curandera*, says that her personal spirit guides are aligned to the five directions. In the North are the spirits of the ancestors. To the East she attributes rebirth. The South is the place of the student and of innocence, while the West is associated with death. A fifth element is also included and relates to community. Elena calls herself a "sensate," and says she has no images generally of these beings but senses their presence. Sometimes the images do come to her in dreams. Some are human-like; others are animals. Some seem to have lived mortal lives before; others are definitely angelic. To her, their forms are not important although she says that once an old woman saw one of her guides as an ancient Aztec Indian. She knows her guides are with her when she experiences a certain sense of knowing. She may be performing a healing, and she will be guided in what to say. She will feel her hands being directed where to move over someone's body. The sensation is effortless and automatic. She explains that it is difficult to describe the experience well, because she never tries to analyze it. In fact, she seems to struggle for words as I ask her to explain these things to me. She says she has no concrete conception of where the beings come from or reside, indicating again she does not really question this work in a rational way. She also describes an interaction and restimulation between guidance she receives for herself and the work she and the spirits do for others. Thus, the work she does upon herself, she is doing for others. And the work she does for others is also for herself. She works with and is able to call upon many different entities, often depending on who is needed in each instance. Like other communicators, she has one group that is more constantly with her. Not all of the spirits she has worked with are still with her, but sometimes new ones come. Once a spirit came to her in the form of an owl, which spoke to her.

"There is danger in writing these things in books," Wakeyatu-ta cautions me. "The danger is for those who know little, but who believe they have power. We have no power: we are only vessels."

His guides will show themselves when people are telling the truth, he says. They can manifest as human-like, part-human and animal, or as animal spirits. He says there are two types, both good and bad, and prayer is needed to keep the distinction clear.

"The greatest danger is in a person's own mind. They can conjure images that don't exist."

Wakeyatu-ta hears his guides speak to him most often in literal voices and occasionally through telepathy, or what he calls thought-images in the mind. Their information comes either as direct communications or through symbolism that may relate to or take place during a ceremony. The beings come to him when he is performing a ceremony or a healing. He says that many spirit beings have been with him since he was a child, but that at different times in his walk different beings have come into his awareness. At first there was only one, and later others came, because for a human this needs to happen in stages that can be handled. He does not speak with beings who were formerly mortal.

I asked him to tell me where he believes these spirits come from. "Between earth and Him, there is nothing," he says, gesturing with one hand flat before him and the other just above, "so they are of the Creator."

"They are never wrong," emphasizes Shakmah, explaining her experiences with her guides. Four guides come to her frequently, and other entities must get permission from her main guides to come through. They come in ceremony, using her voice to speak aloud. At other times, there is a sensory perception, like a knowing or realizing, but not as a voice in the head. She describes how in the beginning she would completely leave her body when an entity was speaking through her, but nowadays she is able to stay present during the communication. This form of mediumship is called mediation. She says she does not see these beings, but rather that they see through her.

"When they see through you, they see everything. You cannot be false. If there are others trying to be with me, they will only be able to stay through 'their' permission."

Most of her spirit guides are human-like although more recently animal spirits have come to her, including that of a lion who seems to be especially important. I notice that each of her earlobes is adorned with a small golden lion head. When I ask her about the home or source of these spirits, she says that she was taught that it is not important to know, and that such information would only add to the ego.

To contact her guides, she goes into a special circle, prepares, and sets up protections at the four quarters. She then "sends up a petition," and they answer either yes or no; they either come or they don't.

"There absolutely has to be a purpose to call them. They are not toys. You do not disrespect them."

Witches I have known have a variety of ways in which to communicate with their spirit guides. Some will always set up a circle first before calling them. Others seem to have the presence with them constantly. Dolores Ashcroft-Nowicki, a respected British teacher of Western esotericism and a Wiccan priestess, teaches about spirit guidance in very informative workshops all around the world. She can often be seen looking over her own shoulder and responding in a half-whisper to some voice from the unseen.

In my own original circle, each of us called our guides regularly most often in a fully cast and protected circle. After years of experience, some of us became more comfortable receiving guidance in any setting. Today my guides come to me if I merely give a mental signal and will occasionally "knock" at the base of my brain to get my attention. I find that the relationship with them is much like a good relationship with a respected human elder. Simple politeness is of great importance, as is sincerity, graciousness, and appreciation.

Aobo's primary guides are also four, one for each of the four directions. He calls them the Grandfathers of the North, West, South, and East. Their images change, although they mainly appear in humanoid character. Usually they are like old Indian medicine men, but they have also appeared as young Black men and once as Arabs. They seem to transmute their appearance easily, and once appeared just as sticks. He does not hear them in his head; they speak aloud using his voice, and they speak in this way both to him and to others who may come seeking guidance. They also take him on imaginative journeys. Two other spirit teachers have come to him since he first was contacted about ten years ago. Each time his guides come, he writes down what they say. He has recorded over two hundred communications. I ask where they come from.

"I imagine they live southwest of here, at a place I fly to. It's across the mountains, out to the plains. I don't know where. It's another reality."

The source and nature of the spirits is part of the mystery. "I hate calling it a spirit. Whatever it is can be any kind of form," says E'Star. They come to her as animals, as entities, and also as formless energies that have life and can communicate. Some of them are definitely beings that have lived on the earth plane before. She tries to get to know each one on a personal level. They communicate with her through physical and mental feelings, an ESP-like "knowing," and sometimes with audible sounds, depending upon the circumstances. There is a team of spirits that is with her always, and other entities are called to her at important times such as when a particular life-accomplishment is needed. She said that three entities helped her raise her children. She came to depend greatly upon them, but they are no longer with her. She also describes an entity who came to her once as a spirit teacher whom she resented because he seemed quite young and too new. She had to make an effort to work out a relationship with him, but once this was achieved he left her.

Her contacts with spirit are constant and daily. "I don't go into their world. Mostly they're in my world." The few times she has had occasion to go to where they are, just to observe, she says the experience was like delirium. "Their world is not comparable to what we have here."

Aside from individual differences from person to person, I find that the experiences I have had with spirits and those of the many other Witches I have worked with over the years reflect the experiences of every spirit communicator I have spoken with, no matter their background. In looking for big differences, I have found questions being answered again and again in virtually the same way. Wakeyuta-ta had said to me that the differences between one tribe and another reflect the culture of that tribe. For example, a Hopi's spirits might appear as *kachinas* whereas in other tribes the spirits may appear as animals indigenous to the region. I know that many Witches' spirit guides can appear to them as entities from the Western mythologies: Egyptian, Celtic, Babylonian, as well as East Indian, Native American, or even Polynesian. This reflects our diversity as a group. But even this is not unknown in the shamanic world, for a *kahuna* I have worked with in Hawaii communicates with both Mesoamerican and European spirits as well as those from his own native land.

Witches who speak with spirits tend to have one or a few close personal guides, which are sometimes called "familiar spirits." Most will also call upon other beings, especially deities—goddesses and gods—sometimes for guidance and often in ceremony. Similarly, I am told that this is common for other practitioners. While a particular rite or healing may require certain, specific entities being called, the individual practitioner usually has his or her own regular spirit team. The way in which the communication is received seems to be a matter of personal talent or style, both for Witches and others. Some Wiccans are "clairaudient" (literally "clear hearing"), and others rely heavily on divination or sensing. Some others act as mediums or mediators as the spirits use their voices to speak aloud. From Dolores's teachings I have learned that there are very many levels and types of both mediumship and mediation, and I have since found that the entire range exists both within the Craft and in other traditions.

Witches frequently use the divinatory arts in connection with spirit guidance. Virtually every Wiccan I have spoken to over the years believes that sometimes the cards or runes are the message-bringers of spirit voices. Many other cultures do not contain these practices, and hence the question of divination through spirit guidance often elicits a blank look from a Native practitioner. However, while only a few Wiccans I know commonly practice the reading of omens as part of their spirit guidance, this symbolic relationship with the worlds seems to be more alive in the Native traditions.

The perceptions and images of spirit also include a gamut of possibilities both within and outside Wicca. Animal spirits, ancestors, angelic-forms, human-like teachers and beings of myth seem to appear in every culture. Like the different ways in which the messages are perceived, the images likewise can be quite visual, mainly sensed, or may manifest in a number of other ways. Only in the highly philosophic studies have I found attempts to categorize or explain the source or realm of these beings. Those who speak with them seem to be more concerned with the relationship and the work than with defining their benefactors. I once asked my own familiar spirit to explain to me the world in which she lives, and she said only that it would be almost like me trying to explain my world to an ant. This work is often quite humbling.

The relationships of communicators to their guides is remarkably similar among both Witches and the other intermediaries I have known. Most were contacted relatively early in life, gradually getting to know first one and then a few more entities. As time went on and the communicator grew in ability, stronger and more significant guides made contact. In virtually every case, the original guides remain with the communicator throughout life. Occasionally spirits will come into the human's life temporarily, and usually this is connected to a specific need of that time. The regular contact with personal guides seems also to lead to an enhanced ability to invoke and evoke spirits in general, including angels and deities, for special occasions such as in ceremony or for healings.

I have asked Witches, Natives, and healers and teachers wherever I have gone about the concepts of devotion, adoration and offerings. In some ancient traditions, it was believed that certain spirit beings required gifts and sacrifices to maintain both a positive outlook and good mood in relation to the humans. Some of the current schools of modern shamanism maintain that guides require regular attention or certain actions to keep the connection strong. The general feeling of those I have discussed this with is that spirits will choose to be with a person, and although any person has the right to decline this connection at any time, that there is very little in the way of expectation from the invisible entities. Most persons who have developed a good relationship with entities feel that ceremonial work and honoring of the beings is a much appreciated form of both give-and-take and of expression of gratitude. Wiccans, who often model their practices upon the ancient European and Mediterranean cultures, seem to enjoy the practices of building altars and giving gifts such as energy, flowers, beverages and incense. Both Elena and Wakeyatu-ta say that within their traditional ceremonies they give honor to their spirits, with adorations or prayers, and by giving of themselves in service to the work. No one I have spoken with has indicated that they feel their guides would leave them or become unduly angered, and certainly not because of inattention or lack of gifts or offerings. Shakmah admits that she has been reprimanded by her guides for not doing what was needed for others. But she says that by nature her guides are nurturing and healing, and very kind. She also emphasizes that these relationships do not take away your free will.

I have found that it is very common in Native cultures to find that the gift of spirit communication leads one into a full-time career as a healer or ritual leader of the community. Many Witches are not devoted in this way, but receive spirit guidance directed primarily towards personal evolution. It is possible that this is related to a phase of training or re-learning. Witches have every right to envy those who come from cultures where express teaching in these and other spiritual works is available. My own experiences and the words of many others indicate that while spirit guidance may first come either in an initial transformative experience or in a gradual awakening, that it is best, most wisely, and most safely used if instruction and guidance is available from other humans who have had greater experience. This, and community support, are what is lacking for most Wiccans today. This may be why our primary lessons for now seem to be about evolving ourselves rather than healing others. Perhaps we need first to remember how to be keepers of this work in the most beneficial way before we will have our own teachers within our own groups. By simply being open to such guidance, we are learning and being guided.

Yet the generations of information available to traditional people indicate that openness and willingness are not enough. The spirit realms contain real dangers. Many people who learn of this work and who wish so much to have it for themselves can easily open themselves to being misguided. Others can find their lives disrupted by chaos or can become so dependent upon the guidance as to mistakenly lose their own will and life direction. The balance of interaction between our world and the spirit world is one that needs to be carefully maintained. People do end up in mental institutions. Jim Joneses and David Koreshes do exist, and many are today leading followers in less dramatic but nevertheless destructive paths.

It seems wise for us to begin to gather the skills to train our own. We can help the younger and newer communicators to avoid many pitfalls and to put their skills to great use. There are many places we of the Craft can look for guidance. Those who have established positive and healthy relationships with spirit guides find that the spirits themselves can be some of our best teachers. It usually happens that a credible spirit teacher will guide a human to other human teachers that will be of benefit, as well. Although there are mixed feelings often on both sides of the fence, many Native and traditional practitioners are beginning to understand that the work of Witches is not so different than theirs, and they are beginning to offer their teachings to us. Some feel we are trying to steal their ways, but others recognize that the spirit is all one and that we are only seeking to resurrect our own right spirituality with the help of those who still have theirs. Many other Witches are beginning to look into the Western esoteric systems, such as Hermetic, Gnostic, and Kabbalistic

Magick. In these systems are precise trainings both for better understanding of the realms of spirit and for personal discipline and protection, two skills that are often underrated in eclectic Pagandom. The Witch who chooses to walk between the worlds, however, will eventually find that both are absolutely necessary.

I asked Wakeyatu-ta to tell me what was required of him to keep his connections to spirit alive and in the right way.

"Truth. Honesty. Compassion. Respect. Those four. In that order," he answered.

When asked the same question, Elena responded, "Being in nature consistently. Working with my own shadow. Being impeccable. And to die all the time."

Shakmah replied, "To serve, lovingly and gladly. Nothing else matters. All the beautiful costumes, words, and temples don't mean a hill of beans if you aren't kind. It's about love, it's not new. I didn't discover it, I'm just carrying a torch of understanding."

Everyone I have ever spoken with who has carried this work successfully for very long says it has totally changed her or his life. While there is talk of hardship, obligation, sacrifice and painful realizations, there is even more talk of the joy and the discovery. It is credited with teaching humility and love, bringing ecstasy, bringing purpose and sense to life. Many say they are no longer afraid of death, or of life, because of their communications.

"I have a feeling of connection with the planet, the galaxy and all life," says Elena.

"The message," says Shakmah, "is that everybody is necessary. Everybody is necessary for this planet to work. Everybody can learn something from everybody, everybody has something to teach. We are just their tools."

If the spirits are truly speaking to all of us despite our diverse backgrounds, then may this be a message we all hear.

About the Author

Oz grew up in New Mexico and was educated at a radical college in Florida, where she studied mysticism, Tarot, dreamwork, and altered states of consciousness. At the age of 19 she was part of a group that began work in Wicca and spirit communication. Ten years later, she began to teach and organize a ceremonial community in her home state. Over the next decade, her work included organizing Neo-pagan events, facilitating ceremonies, presenting work-shops, public speaking and media outreach for the Craft, and training individual students. During this time she also studied the Golden Dawn system of magick.

She now lives on an urban sanctuary dedicated to the goddess Hekate, the home of an organization devoted to work with the dying. (For more information, see "Pagan Rites of Dying" in Book Two of this series, *Modern Rites of Passage*.) She continues to pursue broad magickal studies and ongoing spiritual work, interspersed with priestess duties and teaching. She is often blessed by opportunities to share the ways of spirit and ceremony with Native practitioners and others from diverse cultural backgrounds. In recent years she has contributed to several books on Wicca and ceremonial magick. Her own works in process include a handbook for ritual and a description of her personal odyssey with the Hawaiian goddess Pele.

Appendix:

A Word About Feathers

Demon or bird! (said the boy's soul.)
Is it indeed toward your mate you sing?
or is it really to me?

—Walt Whitman,
  Out of the Cradle Endlessly Rocking

Birds and shamans have been associated since ancient times: the freed soul is often experienced as a bird, and birds appear as messengers from the Upper World in numerous traditions. In one of the most famous Paleolithic cave paintings, from the Lascaux Cave in the Dordogne region of France, a naked man lies on his back. (See page 28.) He is seen by some as an entranced shaman and by others as an injured or dead hunter—an aurochs, the extinct wild ox, is nearby. Some viewers claim to see a bird mask on his head, but there is no doubt of the bird-figure on the staff beside him—which lends credence to the view that he is an ecstatic shaman.

It is a short step from trance visions of birds or magickal happenings involving birds to wanting to create physical reminders of these experiences, keys to reopening or recreating them. Students of shamanism often become fascinated with animal parts: antlers, skulls, bones, and feathers. Through our work with totems or power animals, we exhibit a natural human biophilia[1]—we like to have such things around us as symbols, reminders, things of wild beauty.

"What but the wolf's tooth whittled so fine/the fleet limbs of the antelope?" wrote the poet Robinson Jeffers in his poém "The Bloody Sire."[2] But in their enthusiasm, some people risk bringing down the unwanted attention of law-enforcement agencies.

The problem is not interference with freedom of religion but rather the chance of breaking laws set up to stop the multi-million dollar trade in animal parts. Consider an advertisement that appeared in a magically oriented American magazine in 1992 offering "prayer arrows" and "painted hawk and eagle feathers." This advertisement (withdrawn after one insertion, I might add) crossed the line into illegal activity. I wonder if the mail-order merchant might not have received a polite letter from the U.S. Fish and Wildlife Service, the agency whose duties include policing illegal interstate and international trade in wildlife parts.

For it is "trade" that so often turns otherwise innocent people into criminals. Obviously, if someone finds a red-tailed hawk feather on the ground under a nest, takes it home, and ties it to a rattle handle, Fish and Wildlife Service agents are unlikely to come after him, even though that action is technically against the federal law that prohibits the killing of raptors (hawks, eagles, owls) or possession of parts. The only exceptions are for government agencies, educational institutions, and Indian tribes, which are allowed to possess eagle feathers for traditional rituals. Through some bureaucratic procedure, the Indians are allowed to draw on the stocks of seized or otherwise collected eagle carcasses stored at the Fish and Wildlife Service's forensic laboratory in Ashland, Oregon.

The Fish and Wildlife Service is particularly sensitive about eagles, because hundreds have been killed for the artifact-collector market.

"For the last six or seven years, there has been a cowboy-and-Indian craze in western Europe that's more than we can handle," said Terry Grosz, the Fish and Wildlife Service's deputy regional director for law enforcement in the

Rocky Mountains, in a 1989 interview. "Germans and British [buyers] make circuits, buying eagle feathers, eagle war bonnets, single and double-train dance bustles, medicine wheels, eagle-feather fans—'Indian arti-fakes.'"

The creation of "Indian arti-fakes" using protected species such as hawks and eagles is just part of the billion-dollar business in illegal wildlife parts. Obviously, no Earth-respecting Pagan would wish to participate in that trade, but the temptation is always there, and, as the old saying goes, "ignorance of the law is no excuse."

In the United States, protection is also extended to other migratory birds with only a few exceptions. The move for protection began in the nineteenth-century and grew with the fashion of decorating women's hats with birds. A turn-of-the-century naturalist counted feathers or wings of forty species ranging from warblers to woodpeckers on a walk down Fifth Avenue in New York City.[3] Despite organized protest from the milliners' lobby, "migratory and insectivorous birds" were given federal protection by the Migratory Bird Act of 1913. Exceptions include species that under some circumstances may be considered pests, for example starlings, crows, and "English" sparrows (*Passer domesticus*). Another exception was granted for the feathers of wild ducks and geese gathered legally by hunters and used for tying fishing flies. Otherwise, trading in songbird feathers and skins is also banned except by museums, schools, and so forth.

Some traditions of modern Wicca have maintained for decades that no money should be taken in return for magickal work. Others are not so strict, while almost everyone agrees that money must be spent for such expenses as renting festival sites. I think, therefore, that a parallel rule could be proposed: if it is important for you to have that hawk feather, do not take money for it. And to be completely safe, leave it under the tree.

This caution applies only to feathers; when dealing with other animals, state laws usually apply. For example, I know

of no law in my region against picking up antlers shed by
deer in late winter or against selling something made with
them nor against selling antlers, skins, or bones of animals
taken legally by hunters. If in doubt, check with your state
or provincial wildlife agency.

—Chas S. Clifton

Notes

1. A word coined by the biologist Edward O. Wilson, who used it
   as a book title: *Biophilia* (Cambridge, Mass: Harvard University
   Press, 1984).

2. Robinson Jeffers, *Selected Poems* (New York: Vintage Books,
   1963).

3. Joseph Kastner, *A World of Watchers* (San Francisco: Sierra Club
   Books, 1986), 74.

Stay in Touch

On the following pages you will find some of the books now available on related subjects. Your book dealer stocks most of these and will stock new titles in the Llewellyn series as they become available. We urge your patronage.

To obtain our full catalog, to keep informed about new titles as they are released and to benefit from informative articles and helpful news, you are invited to write for our bimonthly news magazine/catalog, *Llewellyn's New Worlds of Mind and Spirit*. A sample copy is free, and it will continue coming to you at no cost as long as you are an active mail customer. Or you may subscribe for just $10.00 in the U.S.A. and Canada ($20.00 overseas, first class mail). Many bookstores also have *New Worlds* available to their customers. Ask for it.

Llewellyn's New Worlds of Mind and Spirit
P.O. Box 64383-378, St. Paul, MN 55164-0383, U.S.A.

To Order Books and Tapes

If your book dealer does not have the books described, you may order them directly from the publisher by sending full price in U.S. funds, plus $3.00 for postage and handling for orders *under* $10.00; $4.00 for orders *over* $10.00. There are no postage and handling charges for orders over $50.00. Postage and handling rates are subject to change. We ship UPS whenever possible. Delivery guaranteed. Provide your street address as UPS does not deliver to P.O. Boxes. UPS to Canada requires a $50.00 minimum order. Allow 4-6 weeks for delivery. Orders outside the U.S.A. and Canada: Airmail— add retail price of book; add $5.00 for each non-book item (tapes, etc.); add $1.00 per item for surface mail.

For Group Study and Purchase

Because there is a great deal of interest in group discussion and study of the subject matter of this book, we offer a special quantity price to group leaders or agents. Our Special Quantity Price for a minimum order of five copies of *Witchcraft Today, Book Three* is $29.85 cash-with-order. This price includes postage and handling within the United States. Minnesota residents must add 6.5% sales tax. For additional quantities, please order in multiples of five. For Canadian and foreign orders, add postage and handling charges as above. Credit card (VISA, MasterCard, American Express) orders are accepted. Charge card orders only ($15.00 minimum order) may be phoned in free within the U.S.A. or Canada by dialing 1-800-THE-MOON. For customer service, call 1-612-291-1970. Mail orders to:
LLEWELLYN PUBLICATIONS
P.O. Box 64383-150, St. Paul, MN 55164-0383, U.S.A.

WITCHCRAFT TODAY, BOOK ONE
The Modern Craft Movement
edited by Chas S. Clifton

For those already in the Craft, and for those who stand outside the ritual circle wondering if it is the place for them, *Witchcraft Today, Book One* brings together the writings of nine well-known Neopagans who give a cross-section of the beliefs and practices of this diverse and fascinating religion.

The contributors live in cities, small towns, and rural areas, from California to Ireland, and they have all claimed a magical birthright—that lies open to any committed person—of healing, divination, counseling, and working with the world's cycles. Written specifically for this volume, the articles include:

- *A Quick History of Witchcraft's Revival* by Chas S. Clifton

- *An Insider's Look at Pagan Festivals* by Oz

- *Seasonal Rites and Magical Rites* by Pauline Campanelli

- *Witchcraft and Healing* by Morwyn

- *Sex Magic* by Valerie Voigt

- *Men and Women in Witchcraft* by Janet and Stewart Farrar

- *Witches and the Earth* by Chas S. Clifton

- *The Solo Witch* by Heather O'Dell

- *Witchcraft and the Law* by Pete Pathfinder Davis

- *Witchcraft and Shamanism* by Grey Cat

- *Being a Pagan in a 9-to-5 World* by Valerie Voigt

Also included are additional resources for Wiccans including publications, mail order suppliers, pagan organizations, computer bulletin boards, and special-interest resources. The Principles of Wiccan Belief are also restated here.

0-87542-377-9, 208 pgs., 5 ¼ x 8, softcover   **$9.95**

WITCHCRAFT TODAY, BOOK TWO
Rites of Passage
edited by Chas S. Clifton

This book is about the ritual glue that binds Pagan culture. In contrast, much writing on modern Paganism, whether it be Witchcraft or some other form, seems to assume that the reader is a young, single adult—a seeker. The reader is seen as a member of a coven or other group made up of adults. This collection of writings takes a wider view with the long-term goal of presenting a living Pagan culture. If modern Pagan traditions are to persist and have any effect on the world community in an overt way, they must encompass people of all ages, not just young adults. *Witchcraft Today, Book Two: Rites of Passage*, therefore, is organized according to some of life's significant markers: birth, puberty, adulthood, partnership, parenthood, Wicca conversion, maturity or eldership, and finally death.

- *Childbirth and Wiccaning* by Patricia Telesco

- *Raising a Pagan Child* by Karen Charboneau-Harrison

- *Between the Worlds: Late Adolescence and Early Adulthood in Modern Paganism* by Anodea Judith

- *Working with the Underaged Seeker* by Judy Harrow

- *Reflections on Conversion to Wicca* by Darcie

- *Initiation by Ordeal: Military Service as a Passage into Adulthood* by Judy Harrow

- *Handfasting: Marriage and the Modern Pagan* by Jeff Charboneau-Harrison

- *Puberty Rites for Adult Women* by Oz

- *Pagan Approaches to Illness, Grief and Loss* by Paul Suliin

- *Witches after 40* by Grey Cat

- *Pagan Rites of Dying* by Oz

0-87542-378-7, 288 pgs., 5 ¼ x 8, softcover   **$9.95**

SHAMANISM AND THE ESOTERIC TRADITION
by Angelique S. Cook & G.A. Hawk

Recharge and enhance your magical practice by returning to the *source* of the entire esoteric tradition—the shamanism of the ancient hunters and gatherers. Whether you're involved in yoga, divination, or ritual magic, *Shamanism and the Esoteric Tradition* introduces you to the fundamental neoshamanic techniques that produce immediate results. Shamanic practice is a tremendous aid in self-healing and personal growth. It also produces euphoria by releasing beta-endorphins, an effective antidote against depression.

The enormously powerful techniques presented here include inner journeys to find a power animal and teacher, past-life regression, healing methods, and journeys to help the dead. Properly used, shamanic power helps you generate positive synchronicities that can alter so-called chance life events, and enhance personal satisfaction, freedom, and wholeness.

0-87542-325-6, 224 pgs., 6 x 9, illus., index, softcover $12.95

SHAMANISM AND THE MYSTERY LINES
Ley Lines, Spirit Paths, Shape-Shifting & Out-of-Body Travel
by Paul Devereux

This book will take you across archaic landscapes, into contact with spiritual traditions as old as the human central nervous system and into the deepest recesses of the human psyche. Explore the mystery surrounding ley lines: stone rows, prehistoric linear earthwork, and straight tracks in archaic landscapes around the world. Why would the ancients, without the wheel or horse, want such broad and exact roads? Why the apparent obsession with straightness? Why the parallel sections? The theory put forth in *Shamanism and the Mystery Lines* is startling: all ancient landscape lines, whether physical manifestations as created by the Amerindians or conceptual as in the case of Feng shui, are in essence *spirit lines*. And underlying the concept of spirit and straightness is a deep, universal experience yielded by the human central nervous system: that of shamanic magical flight—the out-of-body experience.

0-87542-189-X, 240 pgs., 6 x 9, illus., softcover $12.95

SISTER MOON LODGE
The Power & Mystery of Menstruation
by Kisma K. Stepanich

Modern women have been deeply conditioned to believe that menstruation is an inconvenience, something to be ashamed of and hidden. Many women still view this most natural and sacred aspect of their biology as "the curse" inflicted upon them by the mythology of patriarchal religions.

Sister Moon Lodge is a woman's guide to reclaiming and recreating the honor and dignity of the menstrual cycle through celebration. It provides the knowledge that shamanic powers lie dormant in a part of a woman's physiology. Getting in touch with their cycle puts women in touch with their lost sense of power. Through prayers, poetry, rituals, and journaling, women of all ages can get in touch with the Goddess within and heal the deep wounds that continue to foster weakness in their ideas, creativity, and attitudes about being a woman. Contains four pages of color photographs.

0-87542-767-7, 272 pgs., 6 x 9, illus., softcover $14.95

DANCE OF POWER
A Shamanic Journey
by Dr. Susan Gregg

Join Dr. Susan Gregg on her fascinating, real-life journey to find her soul. This is the story of her shamanic apprenticeship with Miguel, a Mexican-Indian Shaman, or *Nagual*. As you live the author's personal experiences, you have the opportunity to take a quantum leap along the path toward personal freedom, toward finding your true self, and grasping the ultimate personal freedom—the freedom to choose moment by moment what you want to experience.

Dr. Gregg details her studies with Miguel, her travel to other realms, and her initiations into the life of a "warrior." Learn how you create your own reality and how you may be wasting energy by resisting change or trying to understand the unknowable. Practical exercises at the end of each chapter give you the tools to embark upon your own spiritual quest.

0-87542-247-0, 5 ¼ x 8, illus., photos, softbound $12.00

BUCKLAND'S COMPLETE BOOK OF WITCHCRAFT
by Raymond Buckland

Here is the most complete resource to the study and practice of modern, nondenominational Wicca. This is a lavishly illustrated, self-study course for the solitary or group. Included are rituals; exercises for developing psychic talents; information on all major "sects" of the Craft; sections on tools, beliefs, dreams, meditations, divination, herbal lore, healing, ritual clothing, and much, much more. This book unites theory and practice into a comprehensive course designed to help you develop into a practicing Witch, one of the "Wise Ones." It is written by Ray Buckland, a respected authority on Witchcraft who first came public with the Old Religion in the United States. Large format with workbook-type exercises, profusely illustrated and full of music and chants. Takes you from A to Z in the study of Witchcraft. Never before has so much information on the Craft of the Wise been collected in one place.

0-87542-050-8, 272 pgs., 8 ½ x 11, illus., softcover $14.95

THE FAMILY WICCA BOOK
The Craft for Parents & Children
by Ashleen O'Gaea

Enjoy the first book written for Pagan parents! The number of Witches raising children to the Craft is growing. The need for mutual support is rising—yet until now, there have been no books that speak to a Wiccan family's needs and experience. Finally, here is *The Family Wicca Book,* full of rituals, projects, encouragement, and practical discussion of real-life challenges. Is magic safe for children? Why do some people think Wiccans are Satanists? How do you make friends with spirits and little people in the local woods?

When you want to ground your family in Wicca without ugly "bashing"; explain life, sex, and death without embarrassment; and add to your Sabbats without much trouble or expense, *The Family Wicca Book* is required reading. You'll refer to it again and again as your traditions grow with your family.

0-87542-591-7, 240 pgs., 5 ¼ x 8, illus., softcover $9.95

ANCIENT WAYS
Reclaiming the Pagan Tradition
by Pauline Campanelli, illus. by Dan Campanelli

Ancient Ways is filled with magick and ritual that you can perform every day to capture the spirit of the seasons. It focuses on the celebration of the Sabbats of the Old Religion by giving you practical things to do while anticipating the sabbat rites, and helping you harness the magical energy for weeks afterward. The wealth of seasonal rituals and charms are drawn from ancient sources but are easily performed with materials readily available.

Learn how to look into your previous lives at Yule...at Beltane, discover the places where you are most likely to see faeries...make special jewelry to wear for your Lammas Celebrations...for the special animals in your life, paint a charm of protection at Midsummer.

0-87542-090-7, 256 pgs., 7 x 10, illus., softcover $12.95

THE URBAN PAGAN
Magical Living in a 9-to-5 World
by Patricia Telesco

Finally, a book that takes into account the problems of city-dwelling magicians! When preparing to do ritual, today's magician is often faced with busy city streets and a vast shortage of private natural space in which to worship. This leaves even experienced spiritual seekers trying desperately to carry a positive magical lifestyle into the 21st century.

The Urban Pagan is a transformational book of spells, rituals, invocations, and meditations that will help the reader build inner confidence, create a magical living environment, and form an urban wheel of the year. It updates interpretations of symbolism for use in sympathetic magic and visualization, shows how to make magical tools inexpensively, provides daily magical exercises that can aid in seasonal observances, shows practical ways to help heal the earth, and explains the art of cultivating and using herbs, plus much more.

0-87542-785-5, 336 pgs., 6 x 9, illus., softcover $13.00

WICCA
A Guide for the Solitary Practitioner
by Scott Cunningham
Wicca is a book of life, and how to live magically, spiritually, and wholly attuned with Nature. It is a book of sense and common sense, not only about Magick, but about religion and one of the most critical issues of today: how to achieve the much needed and wholesome relationship with out Earth. Cunningham presents Wicca as it is today: a gentle, Earth-oriented religion dedicated to the Goddess and God. This book fulfills a need for a practical guide to solitary Wicca—a need which no previous book has fulfilled. This book, based on the author's nearly two decades of Wiccan practice, presents an eclectic picture of various aspects of this religion. Exercises designed to develop magical proficiency, a self-dedication ritual, herb, crystal and rune magic, recipes for Sabbat feasts, are included in this excellent book.
0-87542-118-0, 240 pgs., 6 x 9, illus., softcover $9.95

LIVING WICCA
A Further Guide for the Solitary Practitioner
Scott Cunningham
Living Wicca is the long-awaited sequel to Scott Cunningham's wildly successful *Wicca: a Guide for the Solitary Practitioner*. It provides solitary practitioners with the tools and added insights that will enable them to blaze their own spiritual paths. *Living Wicca* takes a philosophical look at the questions, practices, and differences within Witchcraft. It covers the various tools of learning available to the practitioner, the importance of secrecy in one's practice, guidelines to performing ritual when ill, magical names, initiation, and the Mysteries. It discusses the benefits of daily prayer and meditation, making offerings to the gods, how to develop a prayerful attitude, and how to perform Wiccan rites when away from home or in emergency situations. *Living Wicca* is a step-by-step guide to creating your own personal vision of the gods, designing personal ritual and symbols, and developing your own book of shadows.
0-87542-184-9, 208 pgs., 6 x 9, illus., softcover $10.00